Human Security for All

Pt. Lookout, L.I.
4/21/12

For Rachel
Celebrating your first
day in this beach town,
your appointment to
Bob Orr's team, your
americana
- preparing
"debate"
PGA

INTERNATIONAL HUMANITARIAN AFFAIRS SERIES
Kevin M. Cahill, M.D., series editor

1. Kevin M. Cahill, M.D., ed., *Basics of International Humanitarian Missions.*
2. Kevin M. Cahill, M.D., ed., *Emergency Relief Operations.*
3. Kevin M. Cahill, M.D., ed., *Traditions, Values, and Humanitarian Action.*
4. Kevin M. Cahill, M.D., ed., *Technology for Humanitarian Action.*

Human Security for All

A Tribute to Sergio Vieira de Mello

Edited by
KEVIN M. CAHILL, M.D.

A Joint Publication of
FORDHAM UNIVERSITY PRESS
and
THE CENTER FOR INTERNATIONAL
HEALTH AND COOPERATION
New York • 2004

International Humanitarian Affairs Series, No. 5
ISSN 1541-7409

Library of Congress Cataloging-in-Publication Data

Human security for all : a tribute to Sergio Vieira de Mello / edited by Kevin M. Cahill.-- 1st ed.
    p. cm. -- (International humanitarian affairs series, ISSN 1541-7409 ; no.5)
  Includes bibliographical references and index.
  ISBN 0-8232-2398-1 (hardcover) -- ISBN 0-8232-2399-X (pbk.)
  1. Humanitarian assistance. 2. War relief. 3. Peace-building. 4. Human rights. 5. Refugees. 6. Mello, Sérgio Vieira de, 1948-2003. III. Title. IV. Series: International humanitarian affairs ; no. 5.

  HV639.H84 2004
  361.2'6--dc22

2004020440

Printed in the United States of America
07 06   05 04   5 4 3 2 1
First edition

This book is dedicated to the memory of a dear friend and colleague, Sergio Vieira de Mello, and to those who were killed with him while on a humanitarian mission in Iraq, and to all humanitarians who carry on their important work in the face of danger.

CONTENTS

ACKNOWLEDGMENTS

This book is a token of love and respect for a fallen colleague. All the contributors had worked with Sergio Vieira de Mello at one time or another during his long and illustrious career as an international humanitarian. Despite their own busy schedules, they accepted the challenge of writing a chapter distilling their own experiences because they shared my belief that a lasting tribute to Sergio should be one to help guide future generations.

The symposium and book were supported by generous grants from the Institute of International Humanitarian Affairs of Fordham University and the office of the Coordinator for Humanitarian Affairs (OCHA) of the United Nations. Ed Tsui, and many of his colleagues in OCHA, including Marina Skuric-Prodanovic, graciously offered ideas and contacts during the planning stage of the symposium that led to this book. Special thanks are due to Father Joseph McShane, S.J., the President of Fordham University, for hosting the symposium at the Lincoln Center campus, and for conferring the first posthumous honorary doctorate in the 162-year history of the University. Sergio's widow, Mrs. Annie de Mello, and their son, Laurent de Mello, accepted the honorary degree. Thanks are also due to Denis Cahill and Renee Cahill who worked as editorial assistants and to Mr. Robert Oppedisano and the staff at the Fordham University Press for their interest and help throughout the publication process.

ACRONYMS

ANC	African National Congress
ASEAN	Association of South East Asian Nations
AU	African Union
CHA	Consortium of Humanitarian Agencies
CIHC	Center for International Health and Cooperation
COE	Council of Europe
CPP	Cambodian People's Party
CSSDCA	Conference on Security, Stability, Development and Cooperation in Africa
DDR	Disarmament, Demobilization and Reintegration
DRC	Democratic Republic of Congo
ECOWAS	Economic Community of West African States
ERC	Emergency Relief Coordinator
ESCE	Economic and Security Cooperation in Europe
EU	European Union
IASC	Inter-Agency Standing Committee
ICC	International Criminal Court
ICFY	International Conference on the Former Yugoslavia
ICRC	International Committee of the Red Cross
ICTY	International Criminal Tribunal for the Former Yugoslavia
IDHA	International Diploma in Humanitarian Assistance
IDP	Internally Displaced Person
IGAD	Inter-governmental Authority on Development
IHL	International Humanitarian Law
IIHA	Institute for International Humanitarian Assistance
JIM	Jakarta Informal Meetings
LICUS	Low Income Countries Under Stress
MCDA	Military of Civil Defence Assets

MOU	Memorandum of Understanding
NATO	North Atlantic Treaty Organization
NGO	Non-governmental Organization
OAS	Organization of American States
OCHA	Office for the Coordination of Human Rights
OHCHR	Office of the High Commissioner for Human Rights
OPT	Occupied Palestinian Territory
OSCE	Organization for Security and Cooperation in Europe
OSO	Operations Support Officer
RAO	Refugee Affairs Officer
RSG	Representative of the UN Secretary-General
SNC	Supreme National Council of Cambodia
TRC	Truth and Reconciliation Commission
UNAMIC	UN Advanced Mission to Cambodia
UNDP	United Nations Development Programme
UNHCR	UN High Commission for Refugees
UNRWA	UN Relief and Works Agency for Palestine Refugees in the Near East
UNTAC	United Nations Transitional Authority of Cambodia

THE CONFERRAL OF THE DEGREE OF DOCTOR OF HUMANE LETTERS ON SERGIO VIEIRA DE MELLO (1948–2003)

On 11 November 2002, two months after being named United Nations High Commissioner for Human Rights, Sergio Vieira de Mello described the task of an international community committed to the promotion of human dignity:

> "To guide us to the greatest truth, to help us transcend the repetitions and the contradictions of our earthly experience and—perhaps even more important—to discover the unity of the world."

Less than one year later, while striving to realize these goals, Mr. Vieira de Mello and several other senior United Nations. officials were killed in a terrorist attack on the United Nations Mission in Baghdad.

A native of Rio de Janeiro, Mr. Vieira de Mello joined the United Nations High Commission for Refugees in 1969 while still a philosophy student at the University of Paris. For the next three decades his compassion and courage took him to countries on the brink of independence—Bangladesh, Mozambique, and East Timor—as well as to Sudan, Lebanon, and other places where people suffered under the yoke of oppression. The new millennium ushered in even more ruthless disregard for human life, calling him to service in Rwanda, Kosovo, and, ultimately, Iraq.

During his 33-year career with the United Nations, Sergio Vieira de Mello worked to advance the cause of peace and mutual understanding. Recalling the words of the *Universal Declaration of Human Rights*, he proclaimed "freedom from fear and want . . . as the highest aspiration of the common people."

Sergio Vieira de Mello's memory is best honored by recalling that life is a gift of immeasurable value, and that human dignity is to be both advanced and protected against all that would abridge or debase it. With gratitude and admiration, Fordham University posthumously bestows on Sergio Vieira de Mello, the degree of Doctor of Humane Letters, *honoris causa.*

8 December 2003
Rev. Joseph McShane, S.J.
President
Fordham University

A MESSAGE FROM THE UNITED NATIONS SECRETARY-GENERAL, H.E. KOFI ANNAN

I am delighted to join all the friends and colleagues of Sergio Vieira de Mello and pay tribute to him by considering a topic that was dear to his heart and central to his professional life—human security for all.

Sergio would have been glad that this book addresses this simple but powerful theme: the notion that every man, woman, and child must have clean water, enough food to eat, adequate shelter, basic health care, a decent education, protection from violence, and a popularly elected government.

He would have been equally glad to see that experienced professionals carefully consider the real complexities that arise when trying to turn this simple principle from words into action.

Sergio knew, as a staff member of UNHCR for many years, the challenges of ensuring the rights of refugees. He was acutely aware, particularly from his time as the Emergency Relief Coordinator and Under-Secretary-General for Humanitarian Affairs, of how difficult yet important it is to protect humanitarian space in conflict zones. And as the head of United Nations (UN) efforts in Kosovo, East Timor, and Iraq, he understood how central promoting justice and the rule of law is to post-conflict transition.

In everything he did, Sergio reached out to local communities, empowering them to take up leadership roles. He sought to ensure that the United Nations was not simply implementing projects, but helping to build the basis for good governance and long-term peace. If anyone had the diplomatic skill, insight, compassion, and commitment to make local communities true partners in the work of the United Nations on the ground, it was Sergio.

Sergio, and many other outstanding people, gave their lives as they sought to empower Iraqis to build their own future. Their deaths were a shock to us all—and a terrible illustration of the new dangers we face in seeking to bring relief to suffering populations.

Sergio set a standard for all humanitarians, peacekeepers, peacemakers, and peace-builders. I hope his legacy will inspire those who will read and reflect on this book in the years ahead.

INTRODUCTION

Kevin M. Cahill, M.D.

Human security is increasingly recognized as a basic right for all people. It is an essential for the development of a healthy society as well as for the protection of the individual from the arbitrary power of the state or the threat of harm from criminals and terrorists. Human security transcends national borders and restrictive laws, viewing every person as deserving of fundamental freedoms and universal rights.

For humanitarian workers personal security is a *sine qua non*. Professional humanitarians know that danger is an almost inevitable part of most complex emergency situations in which they struggle to offer assistance and help bring order out of chaos. The experienced humanitarian learns how to predict and prepare for trouble and minimize risks. Nevertheless, even the best-organized humanitarian programs may be thwarted or aborted by a climate of violence and insecurity. Unarmed humanitarian workers are particularly vulnerable in such situations.

In fact, today more innocent civilians and humanitarians are lost in the crossfires of conflicts than are the armed combatants. On rare occasions the tragic death of one humanitarian can help re-focus the determination of the entire world to find better ways to preserve and even expand our precious human security.

When Sergio Vieira de Mello was killed in the line of duty in Baghdad on 19 August 2003, his death was mourned in numerous memorial services in many parts of the world. Memorial services are appropriate at a time when the impact of sudden death seems overwhelming, and, in this case, they allowed those who knew, admired, and loved Sergio to struggle with their own grief and loss and pain and anger. Such services provide a necessary catharsis for those who survive death in this lonely, yet still lovely, world. Emotions and decorum do not encourage careful scholarly analysis at memorial services. But with the healing of time we can move beyond mourning and create, from the ashes of those who go before us, new and better programs to protect the innocent, and alleviate the pains of those who are ill and oppressed.

For example, physicians are accustomed to performing an autopsy on the deceased, not merely to confirm the cause of an individual death but to find clues to prevent further tragedies, to learn from the finite past that the living, and future generations, might enjoy a safer existence. Viewed in this way an autopsy is a final gift. This volume on *Human Security for All* is, I think, one that Sergio would have wanted to offer his family, friends, and co-workers as a final part of his rich legacy.

In this book the contributors discuss some of the major themes to which Sergio devoted, and for which he ultimately sacrificed, his life. It is most fitting that this tribute takes place in a university. The admirable purpose of institutions of higher learning is—and has always been—the evolving and endless search for meaning and vision and, maybe, truth, including the attempt to understand the emotions and passions and thoughts—or distortion thereof—that lead to wars and famines, conflicts and disasters. Academia tries to translate the tragedies of humanity into knowledge and to help create the traditions and values that sustain our civilization. In fact, Sergio had often participated in the teaching efforts of the Center for International Health and Cooperation and its academic arm, the Institute of International Humanitarian Affairs at Fordham University. He shared his wisdom and experience with a new generation training for international humanitarian and relief work.

He knew that, in the harsh reality of his work, in the midst of conflict and chaos, there was rarely "neutral space," even for humanitarians. He recognized that "neither dignity nor equality could take root in the absence of basic security." The safety of humanitarian workers is an absolute fundamental if they are to be able to contribute to healing and rebuilding war-torn societies. This was his life's task, his noble goal. Shortly before going to Iraq he wrote, "we are, once again, at a crossroads: we will make the most of it and regret nothing. Unless we aim for the seemingly unattainable, we risk settling for mediocrity."

This book, based on Sergio's vision, considers some of the most difficult topics facing humankind today, and we clearly cannot afford mediocrity.

Human Rights and the Rights of the Displaced

There has been a striking evolution—maybe revolution—in the last two decades in international humanitarian law. The absolute sovereignty of states has been gradually eroded in favor of recognition of certain inalienable rights of individuals. This new appreciation has led to the legal justification for humanitarian interventions in oppressive and failed states. Mrs. Sadako Ogata, the former UN High Commissioner for Refugees, notes that "to tackle the threats of the 21st Century, shifting attention to the security of the individual people, as complement to state security, has become a requirement." Irene Khan, currently Secretary General of Amnesty International, writes that human rights are not incompatible with global security; in fact, she argues forcefully that diluting human rights as part of a "war on terrorism" will make the world less—not more—safe. Francis Deng, the UN Special Representative for Internally Displaced Persons, finds reasons for optimism despite the horrendous plight of those he represents. He sees the "crisis as offering opportunities for addressing the root causes" and notes that the reassessment of international law regarding the internally displaced may result in new legal standards where "in due course, what ought to be becomes recognized as what is." David Rieff, a critical observer of international humanitarian operations, cautions against substituting emotion and rhetoric for reality: "In retrospect, this approach begged at least as many questions as it answered. There was the uncomfortable question of why, if the norms were so terrific, the reality of the world was so dire?"

Human Security as Framework for Post-Conflict Nation-Building: Lessons from Iraq and Afghanistan

Sadako Ogata

CHANGING NATURE OF CONFLICTS

UNTIL only about a decade ago, the Office of the United Nations High Commissioner for Refugees and humanitarian aid workers faced challenges mainly in protecting refugees who fled across the borders for safety from individual persecution or war between nations. But since the dissolution of the cold-war structures at the turn of the twentieth century, there emerged changes in the nature of conflicts from wars between states to conflicts within a state as well as to violence that impacted globally by transcending boundaries and borders as in the terrorist attacks on 11 September 2001, and the military engagements that followed.

How do we protect people from the evolving nature of conflicts and violence? Is redefining refugees necessary and sufficient? How do we protect internally displaced persons who are in a refugee-like situation, but nevertheless do not fall under the protection of any international instrument? How do we begin to address the indiscriminate violence of terrorism?

With the changing nature of violence that affected people, situations also emerged where humanitarian aid efforts found themselves entangled in the field of military operations, posing a dilemma for the United Nations and other aid workers who strive to remain neutral while delivering aid to the people in need. More often, humanitarian activities became a fig leaf to cover up the international community's inability to come up with political solutions. Increasingly, the humanitarian actors, such as the UN High Commissioner for Refugees, became frustrated over having to repeatedly deal with the devastating consequences of conflicts, while no constructive actions were taken by political actors to tackle the root causes of the displacement of people. The concept of human security was born partly through the experiences of humanitarian workers on the ground, who recognized the heavy toll that conflicts exacted on the poorest parts of the population all over the world.

The concept of human security provides a framework and direction to apply to international efforts that seek to protect people caught up in rapidly developing and incredibly complex threats and challenges. Paying more attention to human security, as a complement to ensure state security, can also begin to directly protect and empower people who suffer from various forms of repression and poverty, particularly in post-conflict situations, where state institutions are not yet strong. The international community's current efforts to assist in the peace-building and reconstruction of Afghanistan, for example, may become a model of how human security, if addressed through international, inter-agency, and inter-ethnic cooperation, can contribute to nation-building efforts and the prevention of future conflicts.

The state-building challenges in Iraq are perhaps far more complex than those in Afghanistan, but human security perspective may still serve to guide the international community in dealing with the current challenging issues of helping Iraqi people and the country of Iraq recover from the years of repression and the recent war. But how does the international community gain the trust of the people of Iraq to effectively help them in the aftermath of the recent war, ongoing conflict, and a history of political repression and a highly politicized war? This was the near-impossible challenge that UN Secretary General's Special Representative for Iraq, Sergio Vieira de Mello, grappled with until his last breath under the rubble of the UN building in Baghdad. Sergio was one of the leading promoters and enactors of human security. He must have thought that even amid the fiercest political and military debates, human security could guide the way forward in addressing the fundamental requirement to protect the people. Those of us left behind must solve the questions that survive him.

SERGIO IN IRAQ

In a personal correspondence sent shortly before he was fatefully murdered, Sergio Vieira de Mello wrote of the experience in Iraq as "undoubtedly a very peculiar, bizarre and disconcerting situation the Iraqis, the Coalition and indeed ourselves [the United Nations] find ourselves in."

Since he was assigned for four months as Special Representative of the UN Secretary General for Iraq, taking a brief break from his full-time assignment as United Nations High Commissioner for Human Rights (UNHCR), Sergio's concerns were first and foremost to find out what the people of Iraq wanted for themselves. His long years of experience working for refugees during his assignments with the UNHCR and his subsequent appointment to help in the nation-building of East Timor had taught him to pay particular attention to the needs of the people when attempting to help states solve their problems.

Even with all of his experience, including his accomplishments in East Timor, his new assignment in Iraq was a daunting task that bothered him immensely. His immediate task was to map out what the United Nations could do in Iraq. He asked himself, "What makes the discussion of the UN intervention in Iraq particularly difficult, compared to previous post-conflict UN involvements in Cambodia, Kosovo, East Timor, or Afghanistan?" His list of answers may have been long, but at its base was the almost virulent split in the international community over the legitimacy of the war on Iraq. As a result of this divide remaining unresolved on the eve of the military strikes on Iraq, the United Nations had lost its function as a multi-lateral forum in pursuit for world peace.

After the fall of the Iraqi regime, it was clear that the Iraqi people needed enormous assistance in recovering from the past injustice and violence and in rebuilding the country. But how could the United Nations reassert its role to effectively help the people of Iraq? This was the question to which Sergio had to find answers. For the UN to have a meaningful role in the peace-building phase of Iraq, first and foremost, they must gain the trust of the Iraqi people, ensuring that they knew that the UN was indeed there to support their interest and not that of particular governments. Likewise, as a world organization, the UN must clear whatever perception that might exist among its non-aligned constituencies that the UN had somehow been a stooge of particular governments, while at the same time working with the occupying powers defined as "the Authority," under the UN Security Resolution 1483. Indeed, it was imperative not to antagonize these powers that had the necessary will and means to contribute to the peaceful reconstruction of Iraq. Sergio's thoughts centered on a riddle of *real-politic,* which seemed to be hopelessly void of an answer at the time.

SERGIO'S SPEECH AT THE SECURITY COUNCIL

On 22 July 2003, as Special Representative of the Secretary General for Iraq, de Mello made an impressive speech before the UN Security Council, responding to Resolution 1483, paragraph 8 in particular, which requested an active role of the United Nations in post-conflict processes in Iraq. He emphasized two important points before presenting the way forward for the UN involvement.

First, he stressed the importance of respecting the Iraqi people and the long history of Iraq, from which much of the world's civilization originated. He reminded the audience that Iraq became a victim only in a recent history of unfortunate political and ideological developments. The tragedy of the Iraqi people, who suffered much pain and injustice in the recent past, should not be ignored as a problem just for the people of Iraq; they deserved better. The tragedy of the people of Iraq affected the entire world, he said.

Second, Sergio emphasized that whatever role the United Nations would have in the reconstruction of Iraq, it must be for the benefit of the Iraqi people and the country of Iraq. To do this, he insisted that the people of Iraq must be consulted and placed at the center stage. The UN's role should be to help empower the Iraqis and support their quick restoration of sovereignty and have them rejoin the international community as soon as possible.

De Mello knew that these two principles must be at the core of the UN mission in Iraq, in order to form a basis of international assistance in the areas of establishing a political process, law and order, humanitarian assistance, reconstruction, human rights and the media. His opening statement summarized simply and powerfully UN Secretary General Kofi Annan's earlier statement to the Security Council on the same day, which underlined five fundamental principles as the basis for the United Nations activities in Iraq: 1) the need to respect the independence and territorial integrity of Iraq, 2) the need to restore sovereignty to the people of Iraq as soon as possible, 3) the need to respect the Iraqi people's right to determine their political future 4) the need to respect Iraq's sovereignty over its territory and natural resources, 5) and the need for Iraq to be restored to the position of a full and responsible partner in the international community, at ease with its neighbors.

What Went Wrong in Iraq?

As difficult as the situation in Iraq was, Sergio remained realistic and optimistic till the end. Those who continue to engage themselves in work for the United Nations must also have these two qualities to be able to find ways to forge ahead in difficult situations. Sergio did, however, hint to the Security Council that he recognized the near impossible tasks that he and the United Nations had been assigned by the member states. The issue of UN staff security on which he also reported became a sad omen as to what was awaiting him and his precious colleagues in Baghdad less than a month after his New York presentation.

He clearly stated in his speech that the United Nations was vulnerable. UN staff security solely depended on the reputation of the United Nations and the Iraqi people's trust that the UN was working to help them. The crucial need for the UN to achieve such trust relied on the UN's ability to demonstrate its neutrality and independence from world politics. What Sergio told world governments was that for the UN to be effective in the reconstruction of Iraq, offering all its expertise and experience from the past involvement in nation-building, support must be given by governments to the United Nations, particularly by the powerful actors in the Security Council.

Not only the United Nations, but all those who truly strive for world peace must learn from Sergio's experience, insights, and courage. But what are the lessons to be learned so as not to repeat? How can we avoid the painful tragedy of Baghdad, which shook the core of the

United Nations and the world? Although the world has yet to understand fully the human drive toward terrorism, one answer to this ominous question must be the crucial need to attain human security—to
listen to the voice of the people and address their needs to put an end
to the cycle of suffering and violence, as Sergio had proposed. How can
this be achieved in practice? Every situation is necessarily different, but
de Mello's human security principles could begin to provide answers
to the riddle and offer a guiding framework for future actions in nation-
and peace-building processes.

WHY HUMAN SECURITY NOW?

The idea of the Independent Commission on Human Security was
launched at the 2000 UN Millennium Summit where Secretary General Kofi Annan advocated the building of a world that embodied the
twin ideals of "freedom from fear" and "freedom from want." To do
this, there was a need first to find a new understanding of the concept
of security, which served to protect the people. The military action in
Iraq and its tragic consequences were yet another challenge on our
traditional approach to security, serving to fuel this urgency to redefine security.

What are the threats confronting us in the twenty-first century?
Threats to national and international security seem to come much more
from internal sources than external aggression. Even prior to the war in
Iraq, there were ongoing conflicts in Palestine, criminal networks and
international terrorism, the HIV/AIDS pandemic, growing economic
inequalities and the apparent diminishing relevance of multilateralism.
In fact, today's threat to security emanates more often from the very
states which should be protecting those people who are forced to flee
from insecurity and poverty and weak states that are unable to protect
their citizens. What is notable also is that these threats transcend borders
and boundaries with the inevitable proliferation of globalization.

State security is essential, but it would not necessarily ensure the safety
of individuals and communities. Moreover, addressing state or national
security can no longer be limited to protecting borders, institutions, values, and people from external aggression. To tackle the threats of the

twenty-first century, shifting attention to the security of individual people, as complement to state security, has become a requirement.

THE HUMAN SECURITY COMMISSION

As a step toward realizing the UN's Millennium goals, the Commission on Human Security, co-chaired by Professor Amartya Sen—Master of Trinity College, Cambridge, Nobel Laureate in Economics—and the author, published the human security report in May 2003. The report addressed the need to protect people from appalling situations affecting their daily lives.

The Commission's work focused on six broad interrelated areas of conflict and poverty: 1–3) the protection of people in violent conflicts, on the move, and in post-conflict situations; 4–6) and measures to overcome or to improve economic insecurity, deprivation in health and education. The Commission formulated ten policy recommendations to address human security priorities as follows: 1) protecting people in violent conflict, 2) protecting people from the proliferation of arms, 3) supporting the human security of people on the move, 4) establishing human security transition funds for post-conflict situations, 5) encouraging fair trade and markets to benefit the extreme poor, 6) providing minimum living standards everywhere, 7) according high priority to universal access to basic health care, 8) developing an efficient and equitable global system for patent rights, 9) empowering all people with universal basic education, and 10) clarifying the need for a global human identity while respecting the freedom of individuals to have diverse identities and affiliations.

The Commission viewed human security as "protecting the vital core of all human lives in ways that enhance human freedoms and human fulfillment." The goal was then to empower people who, with their increased sense of self-reliance, can proceed to fulfill their potentials and aspirations. Focus on empowerment, the commission proposed, could help strengthen people and prepare them against severe and pervasive threats, be it natural or societal, that may arise in the future.

The Commission also defined people as communities that bind individuals along ethnicity, religion, social links, and values. The goal was to empower individuals and communities and develop their capabilities for making informed choices with increased self-reliance. As seen among many civil society organizations, often linked in informal networks across borders and regions, empowered communities can play an increasingly important role in the prevention and mitigation of violent conflicts as well as the eradication of poverty.

THE HUMAN SECURITY AGENDA

To attain the goals of human security, the Commission proposed a framework based upon the protection and empowerment of people. It argued that neither of these can be dealt with in isolation as they are mutually reinforcing.

Protection refers to the norms, processes, and institutions required to shield people from critical and pervasive threats. It implies a "top-down" approach, such as establishing the rule of law, institutional accountability and transparency, and democratic governance structures. States have the primary responsibility to implement such a protective infrastructure.

Meanwhile, the concept of empowerment emphasizes people as actors and participants in defining and implementing their vital freedoms. This implies a "bottom-up" approach. People protected can exercise choices, and people empowered can make better choices and actively prevent or mitigate the impact of threats and insecurities.

Human security seeks also to build upon and combine insights from various other perspectives. In addition to complementing the state security perspective, human security also reinforces human rights and human development concepts.

Respecting human rights is at the core of protecting and empowering people. Human rights identify basic rights and obligations that are to be upheld as legally binding responsibilities among nations as well as moral imperatives. Human security, through the protection-empowerment framework gives better means to realize human rights. It gives equal importance to civil and political as well as to economic, cultural and social rights, thereby providing more power in addressing violations in integrated and comprehensive ways.

The human development approach born in the last decade broadened the concept of development beyond mere economic growth to incorporate human lives and well being. In the words of Amartya Sen, human development carries a positive quality, of progress toward "growth with equity." In common with human security, human development is about widening the range of people's choices, but the former accounts for unforeseen downfalls, or reversals of development. The concept of human security protects people against downward risks and reminds state authorities of its responsibilities to assure security in sudden and unforeseen downturns, including political instability that, if left unattended, may lead to violent conflicts.

To implement the human security agenda, networking and cooperation between actors is essential. In addition to vertical strategies—with the ideas and policies flowing from international agreements and sovereign states to people—more attention must be given to horizontal approaches at the community, state, and international levels. Strengthening civil society organizations, therefore, is vital to the implementation of human security.

PRACTICING HUMAN SECURITY: THE AFGHAN EXPERIENCE

Even if the concept of human security were to be accepted by all, practicing its principles remains a constant challenge. The military action in Iraq offered the starkest example of the tension between the rhetorical commitment to human security and the imperatives of state security. How can the international community recover from the bitter experience of Iraq? How can we help the people of Iraq to regain security, not only physically, but also about their future? How can we protect human security while the authorities are still weak or non-existent in efforts to protect its people? Taking a closer look at the nation-building strategy for Afghanistan may offer some ideas.

The protection-empowerment framework is embodied in the functioning of any well-governed state. It is the framework for nation-building, and provides crucial insights into the reconstruction endeavors of war-torn societies. From the human security perspective, nation-building in Afghanistan is a case in practice, although many actors involved in supporting the reconstruction of Afghanistan may not be entirely aware that their activities are closely linked to human security principles. Assistance to Afghanistan may have begun as a military strategy to squeeze out terrorists, but the collaborative international efforts that followed are in fact proceeding toward fulfilling the human security agenda.

Once a forgotten country, left to suffer appalling human misery, Afghanistan emerged to the center stage prior to the military action in Iraq. Instinctively, perhaps, the international community became aware that helping a failed state like Afghanistan was the only way to avoid another human tragedy like the September 11 attacks on the World Trade Center and the Pentagon.

The international community's efforts to support nation-building in Afghanistan were broadly divided into three parts: 1) political institution building, 2) security, and 3) humanitarian aid and reconstruction. These are the three core areas that form the basis of human security, from which people's rights and freedoms can be protected. Much is still to be done in all three areas, particularly to strengthen institutional governing capacity and security, but overall, significant progress has been made in a relatively short period of time.

What is remarkable in Afghanistan is that the Afghans themselves are in the driving seat in the state-building efforts. Unlike many other situations, such as in Cambodia, Kosovo, and East Timor, where the UN became the transitional authority, the UN and the international community are working to support the Afghan authorities to set up political institutions, rules of law, basic education, and health and other services that protect the citizens. This approach, arguably, is the first step toward achieving human security.

Human security implies that to increase physical and psychological security, people need to be protected from weapons and other destructive instruments. In the Afghan context, police training and DDR (disarmament, demobilization, and reintegration) programs have been launched in an attempt to eliminate unlawful use of weapons that threaten people.

On the need to protect people on the move, the impressive scale of assistance for Afghanistan began with helping millions of Afghan refugees who were rushing back to participate in the long-awaited reconstruction of the country toward peace. UNHCR has been tasked to help assist and protect millions of refugees and internally displaced people who have returned to a war-torn country. The current challenge is to help them reintegrate into Afghan society and to include them in development schemes so that they can begin to participate in rebuilding their country.

Moreover, UNHCR has been working to protect Afghans who may still remain abroad when its large repatriation program eventually comes to an end. Through talks with host countries, efforts are being made to search for possibilities that enable Afghans to obtain legitimate status to remain in foreign countries and become productive citizens living abroad. With continued support by the international community, this initiative may become a building block toward setting up an international migration regime, which is sorely lacking in today's world—a world where borders are easily transcended.

One area that needs to be strengthened further in Afghanistan is the bottom-up approach to empower the communities. Throughout the devastating years of conflict and drought, people have been exposed to physical, economic, and psychological insecurity and as a result have paid an enormous price. Typical in post-conflict situations, many Afghans have stopped trusting each other, weakening the social fabric. Much creativity and courage is necessary to assist the Afghans to come together in national solidarity and to promote the spirit of co-existence so that that they may eventually overcome memories of brutal violence and begin to live constructively toward peace.

IRAQ AND BEYOND

Recent experiences in Afghanistan may provide hints to peace-building in Iraq. The progress made in Afghanistan was perhaps what Sergio had in mind while struggling to find ways to benefit and protect the security of the Iraqi people. But the events in Iraq have taught us, again, that for the international community, aid agencies, and donors to start putting human security into practice, minimum stability must be achieved first in the country of concern. The tragedy of Sergio in Iraq was that there was not yet sufficient space or security for humanitarian and development aid activities. It clearly showed that the UN member states' support to the United Nations is crucial if the UN is expected to succeed in efforts toward nation- and peace-building.

Still, it bears repeating that the need to address human security does not end with the termination of conflict. The end of military conflict, as in both Afghanistan and Iraq, marks the beginning of a peace-building process, which requires long-term international commitment and assistance. In today's world, humankind needs to enlarge its global capacity to address inevitable interdependence. In the twenty-first century, threat is no longer an isolated national security matter. Global security cannot be addressed without addressing people's needs for freedom from insecurity and poverty.

As the world witnessed on 11 September 2001, people left to suffer a desperate situation of conflict and poverty can strike back at the core of the developed world. The concept of human security offers a framework for humanitarian and state policies to begin moving forward and avoid the repeat of the Iraq tragedy, which took from us the lives of some of the few truly courageous and imaginative warriors who fought for the cause of humanity.

A Human Rights Agenda for Global Security

Irene Khan

"Where . . . do universal human rights begin? In small places, close to home—so close and so small that they cannot be seen on any maps of the world. Such are the places where every man, woman and child seeks equal justice, equal opportunity, equal dignity without discrimination. Unless these rights have meaning there, they have little meaning anywhere."

—Eleanor Roosevelt

ON 19 August 2003 the United Nations High Commissioner for Human Rights, Sergio Vieira de Mello, was killed in a bomb attack on the United Nations (UN) building in Baghdad. As the world's most prominent defender of human rights lay dead in the rubble, the world had good cause to ponder how the legitimacy and credibility of the UN could have been eroded to such a fatal degree that it could no longer protect those who served it. Discredited by its perceived vulnerability to pressure from powerful states, bypassed in the Iraq war and marginalized in its aftermath, the UN seemed powerless in the face of attack.

It was easy at that moment to wonder whether the events of 2003 had also dealt a mortal blow to the vision of global justice and universal human rights that first inspired the creation of the UN. International human rights are grounded in international law, which in turn is embedded in international institutions. If the UN is undermined, the protection of human rights becomes an even more difficult task.

Human rights are often used by governments as a cloak to put on or cast off according to political expediency, and the UN is often powerless to render states accountable for their adherence to international law and human rights performance. In the words of Michael Ignatieff:

> "Human rights treaties, agencies, and instruments multiply and yet the volume and scale of human rights abuses keep pace. In part, this is a problem of success—abuses are now more visible—but it is also a sign of failure. No era has ever been so conscious of the gap between what it practices and what it preaches."

That gap was accentuated in the aftermath of the September 11 attacks as governments geared up to fight "the war against terrorism." It deepened with the military attacks on Iraq. The drive for global security appeared to be trumping human rights with impunity.

Sergio Vieira de Mello was a victim of that security agenda. This chapter identifies the key challenges posed to human rights by the global security agenda. Recognizing that a narrowly focused security agenda has failed to make the world either safe or free, it argues for a paradigm shift in the concept of security. At the center are not the concerns of states but the human rights of people in the quest for a safer, more just world.

By virtue of his position as the UN High Commissioner for Human Rights, Sergio was the preeminent advocate for human rights. This chapter concludes by looking at the role of human rights defenders and their role to press on with the struggle for human rights when the international community fails to deliver.

SECURITY FOR WHOM?

In September 2002 I led an Amnesty International delegation to Burundi, just days after a massacre in which some 174 civilians had been killed by the army in a remote village. There were only four survivors. My colleagues and I went to the local hospital to meet them. One of them was a girl of six, called Claudine. She could not remember her family name, but she recalled in vivid detail the way in which her grandfather, father, stepmother, and two sisters were killed and her baby brother bayoneted to death by soldiers. She had somehow managed to crawl between the legs of the soldiers and escape in the commotion without being noticed. A neighbor found her wounded, naked, and unconscious in the forest, and had brought her to the hospital, but neither the neighbor nor the hospital had the means to buy her any clothes. That is why Claudine, the youngest of the four survivors of a bloody massacre, was still wrapped in a blanket ten days later when we saw her.

The next morning in my meeting with President Buyoya, I asked him what action he would take to protect civilians in the conflict. He replied, "Madam, you do not understand—we are fighting a war to protect our national security."

There was an unfortunate familiar ring to his response. How often have those words—"national security"—been used by governments to justify the killing of civilians, the torture of dissidents, the persecution of minorities, or the attack on political opponents?

BACKLASH AGAINST HUMAN RIGHTS

The erosion of human rights by governments in the name of security is not new. What is new is the zeal with which governments have launched a frontal attack on the very framework of human rights in recent times.

In the days, weeks, and months that followed the attacks of September 11, almost every country in the world—from Australia to Zimbabwe—expanded its powers, lawfully or unlawfully, to investigate, arrest, detain, and to restrict people's rights of assembly, free speech, and fair trials.

The United Kingdom had adopted a tough anti-terrorist law in 2000 that had already led to the banning of twenty organizations, including al Qaeda. Yet, within weeks of September 11, the British Parliament rushed through another piece of legislation permitting the government to detain, on the basis of secret evidence and without charge or trial, foreigners suspected of involvement in terrorism but who could not be deported. The United Kingdom is the only country in Europe to seek derogation from the European Convention on Human Rights to allow introduction of such a measure. Seventeen men have been imprisoned under the Act in high security institutions, and only one of them has been able to gain release following a judicial review. The hearings held to challenge the detentions uses secret evidence not available to the detainees or their lawyers. The Special Immigration Appeals Commission which hears the detention hearings has denied the people presumption of innocence, and has ruled that evidence extracted from a third party through torture is not only admissible but can be relied on by the Commission to rule on the detentions.

Many repressive regimes have used the so-called "war against terrorism" as a license to clamp down on political dissidents or minority groups. Others have escaped international scrutiny and censure of their appalling human rights records by professing to join "the global coalition against terrorism."

The enthusiasm of governments to fight "terrorism" has not been dampened by the absence of a common international definition of the term. On the contrary, governments have chosen to define it as broadly or as narrowly as their national, strategic, or political interests call for, making it a shifting concept that is tied to political and ideological interests and, therefore, open to abuse and misinterpretation.

At the international level, for many governments, terrorism signifies an act of violence for what they do not consider to be a good cause. At the domestic level, anti-terrorist laws often cover acts that are already criminalized, and so the focus is not on the act or its impact but on the motive. The propensity for abuse is aggravated by the fact that anti-terrorist laws are notoriously vague.

Notwithstanding the failure to agree on what constitutes terrorism, the UN Security Council adopted resolution 1373, imposing binding obligations on all UN member states to take counter-terrorism measures in a broad range of areas, including border control, information exchange, asylum and refugee policies, and extradition, but failed to remind States of their obligation to do so without undermining human rights obligations. Even the UN has deferred to security over human rights.

LEADING THE PACK

It is interesting to note the use of the term "war on terror" by the United States administration. By speaking of "war," it has sought to deny the applicability of human rights. By speaking of "terror," it has tried to avoid the application of international humanitarian law. By combining the two into a war without geographic or temporal limits, it has tried to create a zone of action that is a legal black hole. By taking it one step further to the doctrine of pre-emptive attack, it has made the world a potentially more dangerous and uncertain place.

The United States arbitrarily detained hundreds of its Arab and Muslim residents. It designated two of its own citizens as enemy combatants, depriving them of legal counsel and *habeas corpus*. It did both without even resorting to the draconian provisions of the Patriot Act, which was rushed through the US Congress in the wake of the September 11 attacks in 2001.

Doublespeak brings disrepute to human rights but is a common phenomenon among governments, and the US has been no exception. While professing to promote justice, the US administration has actively tried to undermine international justice and the International Criminal Court through bilateral agreements granting impunity to its own nationals. The message that there is one set of laws for the powerful and another for the rest of the world not only promotes impunity for abuse but also undermines the universality of human rights.

While professing to make the world more secure, the current US administration has undermined the collective security that international law and international institutions offer. It has detained hundreds of prisoners, including minors, at Guantanamo Bay, in defiance of the provisions of the Geneva Conventions. Detainees have been threatened with military trials that would violate US as well as international standards of justice, leading one commentator to describe the violations as "the Pentagon's Kafkaesque justice system." In Britain, Lord Justice Steyn, a judicial member of the House of Lords, described the US military commissions as kangaroo courts, a concept derived, as he put it, "from the jumps of the kangaroo . . . the idea of pre-ordained arbitrary rush to judgment by an irregular tribunal which makes a mockery of justice."

The US government has ignored allegations of torture and ill treatment by its officials at Bagram in Afghanistan. It has refused to investigate mass murder by its allies in Afghanistan or ill treatment of civilians by its soldiers in Iraq. Some of its actions in Iraq have been reminiscent of the violations of international humanitarian law committed by the Israeli Army in the Occupied Territories: house demolitions, humiliating restrictions on movement of civilians, and failure to investigate civilian killings.

Some governments have seen the actions of the United States as a message to jettison human rights in times of crisis. Others have used it to vindicate their own practices. For instance the Israeli government has quoted the missile attack by the US on al Qaeda suspects in Yemen as justifying its own targeted executions of Palestinians in the Occupied Territories.

COLLATERAL DAMAGE

In a climate of fear where even the most powerful and the protected feel vulnerable, people are easily persuaded that the price for safety is the erosion of liberty. Yet there is no empirical evidence to show that restraining freedom strengthens security on a sustainable, durable basis. On the contrary, the drive for security, far from making the world a safer place, has made it more dangerous by encouraging secrecy, shielding governments from scrutiny, promoting double standards, undermining international institutions and the rule of international law. To those consequences of the backlash against human rights must be added others. The war on terror and the war in Iraq have created a deep sense of injustice and alienation that has permeated and deeply divided societies and communities in a way not seen since the end of the Cold War. There is also growing cynicism about the universal value of human rights. Discriminatory anti-terrorist laws in some countries, including the US and the UK, have targeted only foreigners or foreign-born citizens. This kind of stigmatizing is a source of danger, encouraging a climate in which xenophobia and racism flourishes. Muslims, Arabs, and Asians are easy targets of Islamophobia. On the other side, anti-Semitism has also re-emerged, particularly with the worsening of the conflict in the Middle East. Political rhetoric about "good and evil,"—"you are with us or against us," "the forces of evil," "them and us,"—has accentuated this gulf.

New seeds of social discord and insecurity are sprouting between citizens and non-citizens. Racism and xenophobia are latent in all societies, but in some European countries they feature blatantly, with some politicians exploiting people's fears and prejudices for short-term electoral gains. Some aspects of the media have played into this strategy, dehumanizing and demonizing foreigners, foreign-born citizens, refugees, and asylum seekers. They are stigmatized as a source of danger, encouraging a climate in which xenophobia and racism can flourish. Those who need their rights protected the most have become the ones most targeted for attacks.

The increasing polarization between communities has strengthened the hands of those who have always feared the powerful appeal of human rights and who, in turn, are using arguments based on cultural and religious norms to undermine human rights in the Islamic world and in Islamic communities in the western world. Cultural relativism is being used as a ground to de-legitimise the universality of human rights, not only by some fundamentalist and extremist groups but also by some governments in non-western countries.

Whether at the hands of Christian, Islamic, or Hindu fundamentalists, a common casualty of the "war on terror" has been women's human rights, a hidden price that is being paid by women on the sidelines. Western countries manipulated the global security agenda in the name of women's human rights but did little to protect them in Afghanistan or Iraq. The backlash against human rights and the growth of fundamentalism have combined to tighten restrictions on the rights of women, and have reinforced the excuses for violence against women in the name of religion, custom, culture, and tradition.

Heightened security concerns have also increased pressure on human rights defenders. In many countries, governments have clamped down on activism as a security threat in itself. Activists and particularly small local groups have found that their space for action has shrunk, and that they are viewed with suspicion and even hostility.

In some countries, it has become more difficult to garner public support for human rights work. Human-rights advocates work through the pressure of public opinion. The basic premise of their work is that human rights violations anywhere are the concern of people everywhere. It is difficult to mobilize public opinion in affluent societies in favour of human rights when people fear that their own safety might be at stake. It is difficult to promote international solidarity for human rights among ethnic minorities, among the poor and the vulnerable when they see themselves as the targets, rather than the beneficiaries, of the international security agenda.

AN AGENDA FOR CHANGE

Restrictions on liberty have not paid dividends in greater security. The backlash against human rights indicates that the world today is less free. But the growing insurgency in Iraq, the increasing anarchy in Afghanistan, the unending spiral of violence in the Middle East, and the spate of suicide bombs and attacks in crowded cities also show that the world today is less safe.

Building a safer world requires a paradigm shift in the approach to security. Real security comes through respect of human rights and the rule of law. Insecurity and violence are best tackled by effective, accountable states which uphold, not violate, human rights. A trade-off between human rights and security is both unprincipled and shortsighted.

Security and human rights are not incompatible. Governments have the right, indeed the duty, to protect people from attacks by armed groups or individuals but they are obliged to do so within the rule of law and the framework of international human rights. It is possible to carry out both obligations within the human rights system. Human rights treaties are drafted by governments that are acutely aware of security concerns that range from internal subversion to international armed conflict. The treaties therefore grant governments the power to protect legitimate security interests without unduly restricting fundamental freedoms.

Governments are not entitled to respond to terror with terror. Just as criminal violence is best addressed through better—not brutal—policing, so too insecurity and violence are best tackled by effective accountable states that ensure the security of their people by upholding, not violating their rights.

There is now—slowly but surely—a better understanding of the balance between security and liberty, at least among some parts of the judiciary. The US Supreme Court has decided to examine the legality of detention of some of the people held at Guantanamo. A US Circuit Court of Appeals panel issued a ruling barring the President from declaring a US citizen an "enemy combatant" without Congressional authorization. A German court upheld the right to fair trial of a man suspected of terrorist activities and dismissed the charges against him. Legislatures in the UK and the US have been less ready to expand anti-terrorist powers of the executive. European governments have refused to extradite to the US any suspected terrorists without a guarantee against the application of the death penalty. A number of countries including Brazil have refused to sign bilateral impunity agreements with the US.

Human rights groups are often accused of double standards: of failing to condemn armed groups and "terrorists," while criticizing governments who respond to them. The truth is that most armed groups are not as susceptible to public campaigning as governments. "Naming and shaming" is hardly likely to have any impact on al Qaeda! Undoubtedly, human rights need to do more to find the levers of pressure on armed groups—for instance, through pressure on allies and supporters, or through exposing the sources providing arms and funding. But there should be no doubt that attacks on civilians by armed groups are a clear violation of international human rights and humanitarian law and can sometimes amount to crimes against humanity and war crimes. Those who commit such crimes must be brought to trial in accordance with international standards. Those who support them, whether governmental or private, are complicit in the crime and also liable under international law.

ADDRESSING REAL SOURCES OF INSECURITY

Building a safer world also means looking at the real sources of insecurity from which millions of people suffer. Promoting security is not just about fighting a war against terrorism. It is about looking at threats more broadly and understanding them in the context not of state but people's security.

For many people the threat to personal security does not lie in terrorist attacks but in the failure to eradicate extreme poverty and preventable diseases, to arrest and treat the spread of HIV/AIDS, or to halt the flow of small arms. For many women, life will continue to be insecure as long as they are unprotected from violence in their homes and communities. For many people, real security will remain illusory as long as police, courts, and state institutions in their country remain inept or corrupt.

A war was fought to rid the world of weapons of mass destruction. Yet the real weapons of mass destruction are small arms and conventional weapons which kill half a million people every year. Light weapons make it possible to recruit children to fight wars. The world is awash with weapons: there is one weapon for every ten people and two bullets produced each year for every man, woman and child on this planet. Developing ccountries spend about $22 billion a year on weapons. For $10 billion, they would achieve universal primary education. In the name of combating the so-called "war on terror," many governments, led by the US, have relaxed controls on exports to governments that are known to have appalling human rights records, among them Colombia, Indonesia, Pakistan, and Israel.

The uncontrolled trade in arms puts the world at risk. A global problem needs a global solution. A number of organizations and individuals, including Amnesty International, Oxfam, and Nobel Peace Laureates have launched a call for an Arms Trade Treaty to be adopted at the UN Conference on Disarmament in 2006. The proposal is to control the sales of arms in situations where they are likely to lead to human rights abuse. To date, some nine governments have agreed to sponsor the treaty. However, the permanent members of the UN Security Council are the main producers and traders of weapons. The success of the proposed treaty will depend on their willingness to address this problem. Their failure to do so will call into question not only their commitment to human rights but also their responsibility as guardians of international security.

Directly as well as indirectly, women's rights have suffered under a narrow security agenda. Not enough attention is being given to violence against women, which, whether in times of war or peace, remains an enormous scandal, with one in three women in the world suffering serious abuse, according to the World Health Organization. In many countries there are no laws to protect women. Even where there are laws, police and the judiciary fail to apply it properly. In some countries discrimination against women is severe, creating an environment in which women are routinely suppressed and attacked. Poor women are more exposed to violence, less able to escape it than women of wealthier means.

All women have the right to be free from violence by state or private actors. Governments need to introduce legislative and judicial changes to protect women's human rights. More support must be given to women's groups to organize themselves against violence. More investment must be made in education for girls and employment for women.

Extreme poverty is a major of source of insecurity for millions of people. In a world where globalization has brought unbelievable affluence and wealth to many, the number of people suffering from absolute poverty has continued to grow. More than a billion people out of a global population of 6 billion live on less than $1 a day, while Europe spends $2 a day to maintain a cow. More than 800 million people are chronically hungry today, a million more than last year.

More than 3,000 African children die of malaria every day, over 3 times the number of people killed as a direct result of armed conflict. Over half the population of Africa do not have access to life-saving drugs, while the five largest pharmaceutical companies in the world have twice the GDP of sub-Saharan Africa. Only 50,000 of the 26 million people infected with HIV/AIDS in Africa have access to the health care and medicines they need.

The UN Millennium Development Goals were adopted by governments as targets to be achieved by 2015. They include measurable, achievable goals such as reduction of child and maternal mortality, universal enrollment of children in primary schools, halving the number of people with no access to clean water. It is likely that these goals will not be achieved because, as some experts fear, the agenda on security has been shifting attention and resources away from issues of social development.

The *Universal Declaration of Human Rights* proclaims that people have the right not only to liberty and freedom of expression but also to a standard of living adequate for their health and well-being, including food, housing and medical care. Reorienting the security agenda in favour of human security and human rights will require enormous commitment and investment by governments and the international community, financial institutions and business leaders, and civil society. It will require a new approach to aid and trade. New funds must be found to meet the social needs of poor and marginalized communities. New money must be found to help countries build fair and effective justice and policing systems, so that legal justice can go hand in hand with social and economic justice.

GLOBALIZING HUMAN RIGHTS

Shortly after taking up his office as the UN High Commissioner for Human Rights, Sergio Vieira de Mello spoke about the globalizing power of human rights:

> We should seize the potential of globalization to become an inclusive force: a globalization that places the promotion and protection of human rights at the heart of its objectives and strategies. For human rights do indeed have a critical role to play today. In short, their indivisibility and universality are perhaps the closest concepts we have to being the foundations of a civilized world.

Global insecurity, far from diminishing the value of human rights, has actually heightened the need to respect them. The failure of the international community to effectively uphold those rights only underlines the importance of human rights defenders and activists in bringing about change.

Local human rights groups, social movements, and activists are the real lifeblood for change around the world, opening up societies, and fighting for international standards of human rights and good governance. They are also an important antidote to attacks on human rights by governments, armed groups, or others. Together with international human rights organizations they form a global civil society that, by exposing abuse, challenging injustice, and striving for change, can bring about change.

The challenges facing human rights activists today are stark: to confront the threat posed by callous, cruel, and criminal acts of armed groups and individuals; to resist the backlash against human rights created by the single-minded pursuit of a global security doctrine that has deeply divided the world; and to redress the failure of governments and the international community to deliver on social and economic justice.

The power of human rights in the hands of the people should not be underestimated. In the same week that the UN office in Baghdad was bombed, a group of women in Mexico won the first step towards justice for their murdered daughters. Marginalized and poor, they had fought for 10 years to get that far but, finally, they compelled Mexican

President Vicente Fox and federal authorities to intervene. A worldwide web of international solidarity globalized their struggle, showing that much can be achieved by globally-coordinated action for human rights—not just through the well-worn institutions of global governance, but through the dynamic virtual space of global civil society.

Human rights provide a tool to human rights defenders. They give voice to the powerless: the prisoner of conscience, the prisoner of violence, the prisoner of poverty. They bring hope to millions. Human rights are a banner to mobilize people globally in the cause of justice and truth. They provide a fractured world with a glue to bind people in favor of equality, freedom, and justice, and against violence and abuse. They offer a powerful and compelling vision of a better and fairer world for all men, women, and children, and provide a concrete plan of how to get there. That is why a sustainable agenda for global security is an agenda for human rights.

Trapped Within Hostile Borders: The Plight of Internally Displaced Persons

Francis M. Deng

TRIBUTE

SINCE the conference from which this volume emanated was a tribute to Sergio Vieira de Mello, I would like to begin with the effect of the news from Baghdad on 19 August 2003. Once the tragedy was announced, and, especially when Sergio's name was mentioned by CNN, I remained glued to the television, following the developments by the minute. The world waited with a mix of anxiety and hope; but then the tragedy hit—he was gone. Although we know that sooner or later we will all follow the same destiny, when death comes so prematurely and at a time when one is so desperately needed in this world, such news is simply devastating.

It is extremely rare to find an individual who achieved the level of excellence in virtually all aspects of his work as Sergio did. He was outstanding intellectually, charismatic, witty, charming, diplomatic but forthright, courageous, and firm. His service to humanity through the United Nations, which took him to trouble spots around the world—Sudan, Cyprus, Mozambique, Peru, Lebanon, Cambodia, Bosnia, Rwanda, Congo, Kosovo, East Timor and tragically, Iraq—attest to his dedication to the ideals of this world organization: the UN's search for peace, security, and the dignity of the human family.

I got to know Sergio in connection with our mutual interest in the UN's work on behalf of the internally displaced of the world, the topic on which I now want to focus.

The Problem

Some 25 million persons in over 50 countries are uprooted and forced to flee from their homes or areas of habitual residence as a result of internal conflicts, communal violence, or egregious violations of human rights, but remain within their national borders.[1] As a consequence of their forced displacement, they are deprived of such essentials of life as shelter, food, medicine, education, community, and a resource base for a self-sustaining livelihood. Worse, internally displaced persons, known by the acronym of IDPs, remain within the borders of a country at war with itself, and even when they move to safer areas, are viewed as strangers, discriminated against, and often harassed. Although entire communities where the causes of displacement prevail are generally affected, those persons who are uprooted from their homes have been shown to be especially vulnerable to physical attack, sexual assault, abduction, disease, and deprivation of basic life necessities. They have been documented to suffer higher rates of mortality than the general population, sometimes as much as fifty times greater.[2]

While the crisis is truly global, some regions of the world are more affected than others. Africa, with 12.7 million internally displaced persons in 20 countries is the worst hit; Asia-Pacific hosts 3.6 million in 11 countries; the Americas 3.3 million in four countries; Europe 3 million in 12 countries; and the Middle East 2 million in 5 countries.

What is particularly ominous about the situation is that the conflicts, the generalized violence, and the human rights violations that cause internal displacement are often characterized by acute crises of national identity. As both a cause of and exacerbator of conflict, a crisis of national identity hinders official responses to resulting humanitarian tragedies. Countries in which ethnic factors are key to national identity crises include Burundi, Indonesia, Myanmar, the Russian Federation, Sri Lanka, Sudan, Turkey, and the former Yugoslavia. In Latin American countries, such as Colombia, Guatemala, Mexico, and Peru, the problem tends to be viewed largely in class terms, with race and ethnicity as aggravating and confounding factors.

Although the concept of state responsibility to guarantee the protection and general welfare of citizens and all those under state jurisdiction is becoming increasingly accepted in international law, it poses practical problems in countries experiencing cleavages among various groups who differentiate themselves based on race, ethnicity, religion, language, or culture. Often, the most affected are minority or marginalized groups who are peripheral to the dominant identity group. In most cases, elements of these peripheral or marginalized groups are in conflict with the dominant group. Either because they support rebels or dissidents, are sympathetic, or are victims of mere association, marginal groups tend to be identified as part of the enemy, if not the enemy itself. Rather than be protected and assisted as citizens, they tend to be neglected and even persecuted. Under these circumstances, citizenship becomes only of paper value, without the enjoyment of the rights normally associated with the dignity of being a citizen. As argued elsewhere, marginalization becomes tantamount to statelessness. [3]

The irony is that if these victims of conflict or persecution had crossed international borders, they would be classified as refugees. The international community has a well-established legal and institutional framework of protection and assistance for refugees through the 1951 Refugee Convention, its 1967 Protocol, and the UN Office of the High Commissioner for Refugees (UNHCR). The internally displaced are paradoxically assumed to be under the care of their own government, despite the fact that their displacement is often caused by the same state authorities, which, in any case, often neglect or even persecute them. Refugees number about half of internally displaced populations, but by virtue of having fled across international borders are outside the danger zone, they are the subject of international concern, while IDPs fall into the vacuum of contested or divided sovereignty.

Findings from my country missions around the world in my capacity as Representative of the UN Secretary-General on Internally Displaced Persons underscore the degree to which the expectation of internal protection by states is for the most part a myth. During these missions, I meet and dialog with national authorities at all levels as well as local authorities, visit the internally displaced for an on-site assessment of their conditions and needs, and then return to brief the authorities on my findings and offer preliminary conclusions and recommendations. This usually includes asking the displaced persons what messages they want me to take back to their leaders. In one Latin American country, the response I got was: "Those are not our leaders. In fact, to them, we are criminals, not citizens, and our only crime is that we are poor." In a Central-Asian country, the response was: "We have no leaders there. None of our people is in that government." In an African country, a senior UN official explained to the Prime Minister who had complained of inadequate support for refugees in his country that UN resource capacity to assist refugees in the country was constrained by the need to assist "your people," the internally displaced and other war-affected communities. The Prime Minister's response was, "Those are not my people. In fact, the food you give those people is killing my soldiers." These anecdotes highlight the cleavages of identity, which often characterize the conflicts that generate internal displacement and the resulting vacuums of responsibility in which IDPs fall.

Where there is an external dimension to the conflict, as is the case with the conflicts over Nagorno-Karabakh, between Azerbaijan and Armenia, or over Abkhazia and South Ossetia in Georgia, governments tend to identify with their displaced ethnic group members. But even here, the displaced populations tend to be held hostage to the political agendas of the governments and used as pawns to pressure the international community to resolve the conflicts involved, rather than have their current needs addressed. In the case of Azerbaijan, I was told by all the authorities and by the displaced themselves, that finding solutions to the problems of the displaced would undermine urgency of the need to resolve the conflict over Nagorno-Karabakh so that the displaced could return to their original homes. I eventually raised the issue with President Aliev. He surprisingly agreed with me that while the search for peace was an urgent objective and the eventual return of the IDPs a right that could not be denied, no one could tell when the conflict would, in fact, be resolved. It was unacceptable to leave the IDPs in their present situation of pressing need for decent housing, employment, and other essentials of life. We agreed that Azerbaijan, with the cooperation of the international community, should attend to those needs as a matter of urgency. That would indeed enhance the capacity of the displaced populations to play a more constructive role in the future. This became the foundation of what Georgia subsequently adopted under the label of "The New Approach" to address the IDP crisis in the country.

Whether a crisis of identity is involved or the authorities are unwilling to address the needs of their displaced populations, far too often these populations are not only dispossessed by their own governments but are outside the reach of the international community because of the negative approach to sovereignty. We live in a world in which the principle of national sovereignty is still the cornerstone of international relations, despite significant modifications and moderation in the application of the principle. While international humanitarian and human rights instruments offer legally binding bases for international protection and assistance to needy populations within their national borders, those people are for the most part at the mercy of their national authorities for their security and general welfare. International access to the internally displaced can be tragically constrained and even blocked by states in the name of sovereignty. Factors include the collapse of states and rampant insecurity, as has been the case in countries like Angola, Colombia, the Democratic Republic of the Congo, Indonesia, Liberia, Sierra Leone, and the Sudan to mention but a few. Diplomacy and the art of persuasion can help to tear down the barriers but, in extreme circumstances, more assertive intervention may be imperative, as was the case in Bosnia-Herzegovina, the Democratic Republic of the Congo, Kosovo, East Timor, Liberia, and Sierra Leone.

Formulating a pragmatic basis for a diplomatic dialog that would moderate the negative implications of a narrowly conceived application of sovereignty involves postulating it positively, not as a barrier against international involvement and cooperation but as a concept of state responsibility that seeks to protect and assist its citizens in need. Where lack or inadequacy of resources and operational capacities necessitate, invite or at least welcome international assistance to complement national efforts. While this is largely a persuasive argument, there is an implicit assumption of accountability behind responsibility. This means that where the needs of sizeable populations are unmet under the exercise of sovereignty and large numbers suffer extreme deprivation and are threatened with death, the international community, obligated by humanitarian and human rights normative standards, cannot be expected to watch passively. Humanitarian intervention then becomes the last resort. The best guarantee for sovereignty is, therefore, to discharge minimum standards of responsibility, if need be with international cooperation.

Nonetheless, the prevailing vacuum of responsibility for the internally displaced and the need for international involvement pose a series of critical and practical questions. What principles of international law provide a basis for their protection and assistance? What institutional arrangements are in place or should be developed to provide them with adequate protection and assistance? What durable solutions are open to them? What standards and strategies should be applied to address the root causes of displacement? More specifically, what principles should govern the management of identity differences based on ethnicity, religion, language, and culture within a state? Should the overriding norm be to assimilate, integrate, or co-exist separately, or forge independent entities where that is feasible? As the arbiter and guarantor of global peace and security, the UN is called upon to address these issues, credibly, effectively, and comprehensively.

THE RESPONSE

The emergence of the crisis of internal displacement on the international scene with the end of the Cold War in the late 1980s made some response on the part of the international community necessary. During the Cold War, most domestic and regional conflicts around the world were in one way or another perceived as part of the proxy confrontation of the super powers. Similarly, internal or regional crises and their humanitarian consequences used to be managed through the bipolar control mechanisms of the super powers, who offered effective support to their less capable ideological allies. The outcome of this was that such domestic crises as internal displacement were not visible to the outside world as the exclusionary interpretation of sovereignty was rigidly applied.

With the end of the Cold War, and the withdrawal of the strategic interests of the super powers, these conflicts began to be seen in their proper national or regional contexts. The support of the major powers also disappeared, leaving former allies of the super powers with significantly reduced capacity for managing conflicts and responding to their humanitarian consequences. Worse, the post-Cold War era witnessed the proliferation of internal conflicts, which have tended to target women, children, and the elderly. Indeed, the overwhelming majority of the internally displaced are women and children. Without external support, both in the management of conflicts or in addressing their humanitarian consequences, and with complex emergencies and their tragic impact on the increase, governments were confronted with mounting crises they could hardly manage. In 1982, there were 1.2 million internally displaced persons recorded worldwide. Today, as noted earlier, that figure is estimated at 25 million.

Concomitantly, human rights and humanitarian concerns began to replace strategic national interest as driving norms in international politics and the development of standards. By the same token, human rights, humanitarian, and developmental organizations began to intensify their activities as the watch-dogs of the degree to which these universal standards were being adhered to or violated within national borders. To reinforce their capacities for their new responsibilities, NGOs began to receive increased support from the donor community, which saw them as more transparent and credible than governments in meeting the humanitarian needs of the affected populations. With these new developments, the rigid observances of sovereignty as a barricade against international monitoring and scrutiny began to fall under pressure. In the name of human rights and humanitarian concerns, media spotlights began to focus attention on the human tragedies within state borders. The narrow view of sovereignty became increasingly challenged as the media and non-governmental organizations (NGOs) exposed the plight of millions who fell victim to the new types of wars that were fought internally, with devastating loss of lives, egregious violations of human rights, and dehumanization of the civilian populations. It was under these emerging circumstances that the crisis of internal displacement began to surface on the international scene. In 1992, in response to this growing phenomenon and as the issue began to garner international attention, the Commission on Human Rights decided to place the issue on its agenda and requested the United Nations Secretary-General to appoint a Representative on Internally Displaced Persons.

A fundamental guiding principle in my approach with governments has been to recognize that the problem of internal displacement is inherently internal and sensitive because it touches on matters of national sovereignty. Because of this sensitivity, it requires a special approach that is significantly different from the usual human rights mechanisms of the UN system. My view is that it does not help IDPs to confront their governments in an adversarial promotion of human rights. Whether one is denied access or ignored, the protection and assistance of the affected population suffers in consequence. This is not to say that there is no room for the adversarial role on human rights issues; it is to say that while making use of the information available from various monitoring sources, including NGOs and human rights advocates, creating a constructive and cooperative dialog with the authorities promises better results.

Another guiding principle in the struggle to achieve human rights for displaced persons is to recognize that the problem cuts across the entire UN system and the international community at large, linking human rights, humanitarian, development, and security issues. Therefore, although the mandate on IDPs was created by the Commission on Human Rights under the Special Procedures Mechanism, we have operated across all UN agencies and the wider international community in collaboration with humanitarian, human rights and development organizations, both governmental and non-governmental. Sometimes, the mandate is even more clearly identified with the Office for the Coordination of Humanitarian Affairs (OCHA) and other humanitarian agencies than with the Office of the High Commissioner for Human Rights (OHCHR). This suits me well because, since the mandate was created by the Commission on Human Rights, being identified with other organs of the system means broadening the scope of inter-agency cooperation. In addition, I have, from the start, found it appropriate not to limit my scope of operations to the UN system. We, therefore, have developed an approach that keeps one foot within the UN system and another outside. This approach has been carried out through the Brookings Institution-SAIS Project on Internal Displacement, which I co-direct with Roberta Cohen, a Senior Fellow at the Brookings Institution.

This arrangement gives us the opportunity, in a sense, to divide roles. There are certain things one can do more effectively within the

UN system; and there are things better done outside the system. I try to make use of my multiple identities. When I have to be diplomatic or sensitive to my UN role, I put on that hat. When I feel I need to be more assertive, and I fear being inhibited by the constraints of my UN status, I put on the hat of the Co-Director of the Brookings-SAIS Project. And, of course, we commission scholars to carry out independent studies, which are published by the Project.

MANDATE ACTIVITIES

Our work has, of course, been defined by the various resolutions of the Commission on Human Rights and the General Assembly. We have worked closely with the drafters of the resolutions, so that over the years, the pillars of the mandate have tended to increase with the kind of work we do and our reports to the Commission and the General Assembly. Initially, work focused on four pillars: 1) developing and promoting a normative framework, 2) developing improved institutional arrangements, 3) undertaking country missions, and 4) conducting research on the causes and consequences of internal displacement. Since then, the reports of the Mandate and the Project have tended to specify raising awareness of the plight of IDPs, in fact, placing it ahead of our initial focus on the four pillars listed above. In addition, cooperation with regional, national, and local partners, particularly civil society, has been added to the list of pillars. The pillars have, therefore, grown from four to six.

Awareness Raising

The primary pillar of our strategy has been raising awareness of the struggles of internally displaced persons. This is a function of generating and sharing information, as part of an advocacy strategy that can be pursued through a wide variety of approaches, including reports to UN bodies, scholarly and popular publications, speeches, seminars, workshops and conferences, and direct dialogue with governments, non-state actors, and all those concerned with the problems of internal displacement.

Much progress has been made in raising awareness. When we started some twelve years ago, if one spoke of IDPs, almost certainly the question would have been "What is that?" In fact, I recall at a reception in Addis Ababa, interacting with the Ambassador of a country that had a significant IDP problem, but that was considered to be one of the countries in denial. When I was introduced to him as the Representative of the Secretary-General on IDPs, he asked, "What's that?" When it was explained to him that IDPs meant Internally Displaced Persons, he remarked: "We don't have that problem." But sure enough, they did have the problem. Indeed, theirs was one of the countries that a Brookings project labeled "tough nuts to crack," precisely because they were in denial.

Today, not only do most people in the international community recognize the dilemma of IDPs, but virtually all governments, having gone from being initially very sensitive about the problem, would now recognize it as a legitimate area for international concern. The credit for this is widely shared, being a cause that has captured the commitment and dedication of all UN agencies and many outside the UN system, all of whom are in one way or another involved with internal displacement.

Developing a Normative Framework

Another aspect of our work has been to develop what was defined by the Commission and the General Assembly as "an appropriate framework." Initially, it was meant to be a legal framework because people recognized that, unlike refugees, IDPs did not have a legal instrument providing for their protection and assistance. And yet, it was obvious that the international system was not ready to welcome the development of a legal instrument on IDPs. So, when we were requested to develop a framework, members of the Commission rejected reference to a "legal framework" and preferred to call it a "normative framework." Some also thought that "normative" implied legal and so that too was opposed. In the end, what was agreed upon was the concept of an "appropriate framework." Indeed, the *Guiding Principles on Internal Displacement* are based on existing standards in human rights law, humanitarian law, and analogous refugee law. [4] We decided, however, that instead of considering it a legal document, and giving it a binding status, we would simply restate the fundamental principles of those sources of law in the form of guiding principles that would be persuasive rather than binding and therefore potentially threatening and controversial. In a sense then, the framework we adopted was in conformity with the persuasive approach behind constructive dialogue with governments and all pertinent actors.

The *Guiding Principles* address all "phases" of displacement, including a) prohibition of arbitrary displacement in the first instance, as well as provisions for the humane treatment of persons who are legitimately displaced, b) rights to assistance and protection while displaced, and c) rights to assistance and protection in voluntary return, resettlement or reintegration, and corollary rights to recuperate or be compensated for lost property. They also affirm the rights and duties of humanitarian assistance providers. The overarching rationale and foundation of the *Principles* is a positive interpretation of the notion of sovereignty as entailing responsibility, as stated in Principle 3: "[n]ational authorities have the primary duty and responsibility to provide protection and humanitarian assistance to internally displaced persons within their jurisdiction." At the same time, they call upon all relevant actors—including "non-state actors" (i.e. rebel armies)—to respect the rights of the internally displaced.

Although based on existing law, the *Guiding Principles* were considered to be very sensitive when first presented to the Commission in 1998. For this reason, we did not ask that they be "adopted" by that body, but rather that it "take note" of them, and also that it take note of my plans to use them in dialogues with states and other actors. Even before their formal submission to the Commission, the Inter-Agency Standing Committee (IASC) endorsed the *Guiding Principles* and decided to bring them to the attention of their governing bodies and field staff to guide them in their work. As the Emergency Relief Coordinator, Sergio Vieira de Mello chaired the Committee, which consisted of the heads of the operational agencies of the UN system, the International Committee of the Red Cross (ICRC), the International Organization of Migration, and representatives of NGOs. The Commission also took note of the action taken by the IASC. In subsequent years, the Commission and the General Assembly have grown gradually more supportive in their descriptions of the *Principles*. In their 2003 resolutions, both bodies "express[ed] [their] appreciation of the *Guiding Principles on Internal Displacement* as an important tool for dealing with situations of internal displacement" and "encourage[d] all relevant actors to make use of the *Guiding Principles* when dealing with situations of internal displacement."

These resolutions also "welcome[d] the fact that an increasing number of states, UN agencies, and regional and NGOs are applying them as a standard." Indeed, the growth in acceptance of the *Guiding Principles* at all of these levels in the last five years has been remarkable. Supportive resolutions and decisions have been adopted by the Organization of African Unity's Commission on Refugees (OAU), now the African Union (AU), the Commonwealth, the Economic Community of West African States (ECOWAS), the Inter-Governmental Authority on Development (IGAD), the Inter-American Commission on Human Rights, the Organization for Security and Cooperation in Europe (OSCE), and the Council of Europe Parliamentary Assembly. A number of state governments, including Angola, Burundi, Colombia, Liberia, and Sri Lanka have adopted policies and/or laws based at least in part upon the *Guiding Principles,* and several other states, such as Uganda and Mexico, are currently considering plans to follow suit. Even some non-state actors have begun to make active use of them. During my mission to Georgia in 2000, the *de facto* Abkhas authorities acknowledged the importance of the *Guiding Principles* and called for them to be translated into their language. Sudan's Peoples Liberation Movement/Army has referred to *Guiding Principles* in its consideration of its own internal rule making in dealing with the internally displaced. Indeed, the Movement has gone so far as to draft a policy on internal displacement based on the *Principles,* although it has not yet been endorsed by the leadership council. UN agencies, NGOs, local civil society representatives, and internally displaced persons themselves around the world are making increasing use of the *Guiding Principles* in their own programs and in advocacy with governments for better conditions for the internally displaced.

To facilitate their use by global and local actors, including the internally displaced themselves, the *Principles* have been translated into all six UN languages and twenty-six national and local languages around the world. It is particularly significant that the *Principles* have been a source of empowerment to the internally displaced, who are able to demand their rights rather than see themselves as recipients of humanitarian favors.

The success of the *Guiding Principles* provoked a mild backlash from some governments, while not contesting the authenticity of their legal sources, who questioned the manner in which they were developed and the fact that they had not been formally adopted by the appropriate UN bodies. Whatever their motivation, these governments would prefer that the *Principles* be tabled for discussion and adoption. Our response has been to explain that the development of the *Guiding Principles* was mandated by appropriate UN bodies, notably the Commission on Human Rights and the General Assembly, which were kept informed of our progress at various stages of the process. Through a dialogue, differences with these governments have been considerably narrowed, thanks to the then Swiss Observer, now Permanent Representative, who organized a series of dialogues with the concerned governments. In addition, OCHA has been a very strong partner in facilitating these dialogues with governments. As a result, an even broader consensus on the *Principles* is emerging.

I am often asked whether the *Guiding Principles* can be considered "law," given that they have not been formally adopted by states. To the extent that they restate and/or correctly interpret existing binding instruments, the rules expressed by the *Guiding Principles* are undoubtedly binding on states party to the underlying instruments. More broadly, however, the gradual acceptance of the *Guiding Principles* is helping them to grow into an international norm, whether strictly "legal" or not, that courts, policy makers, and advocates are using more and more "as a standard," as the Commission and the General Assembly rightly put it. Thus, for example, the Colombian Constitutional Court decided in opinions issued in 2000 and 2001 that although "the *Principles* have not been formalized by means of an international treaty," they "should be taken as parameters for the creation of new rules and interpretation of existing rules in the area of regulation of forced displacement by the state," and "all relevant government personnel . . . must conform their conduct not only to constitutional requirements but also to those of the *[Guiding] Principles.*"

It is important to recognize that law is not an abstract "neutral" concept above the realities of dynamic and authoritative decision-making in which the perspectives, demands, and expectations of various participants and interests at all levels influence the outcome. What is, therefore, important is not so much the prevailing letter of the law—what "is"—but the growing sense of how to meet the compelling need for normative response to the crisis of internal displacement—what "ought to be." In due course, what ought to be becomes recognized as what is.

Developing Institutional Arrangements

In parallel with the development and promotion of a normative framework for internal displacement, the international community has become more active and coherent in its own operational or institutional response to internal displacement over the last decade. However, much progress remains to be made.

Early in the work of the mandate, I identified three options for solving this "mandate gap" for internally displaced persons: 1) creation of a new agency focused on internally displaced persons, 2) designation of an existing agency (such as UNHCR) to assume responsibility for them, and 3) collaboration among all the various relevant agencies. The third option has been preferred over the last decade and institutions and policies have been put in place to enhance its potential.

In 1990, the General Assembly assigned to United Nations "Resident Coordinators" (who are UN officials otherwise charged with coordination of development activities) the responsibility for coordinating assistance to internally displaced persons in the field by the operational agencies. In 1991, the Assembly created the post of Emergency Relief Coordinator (ERC) at the level of Under-Secretary-General to coordinate the system-wide response to emergency situations. The following year the Assembly established the Inter-Agency Standing Committee (IASC) in which all the major humanitarian and development agencies and organizations and NGO umbrella groups participate. As part of the Secretary-General's reform program in 1997, the ERC was formally entrusted with overall responsibility for the coordination of assistance and protection to internally displaced persons. Also, the post of "Humanitarian Coordinator" was created (and frequently delegated as a second "hat" to Resident Coordinators) and assigned the task of ensuring coordination for IDPs at the country level.

At the headquarters level, a Senior Inter-Agency Standing Committee on Internal Displacement was formed with the support of a Working Group to facilitate inter-agency cooperation on the issue and, in 2002, a dedicated "IDP Unit" was formed within the Office for the Coordination of Humanitarian Affairs (OCHA) to assist the ERC in his duties with regard to IDPs. The IASC also remained engaged, generating policy and guidance for field collaboration, such as the 2000 *Policy Paper on Protection of Internally Displaced Persons,* which carefully laid out the responsibilities of agencies and their partners in the field.[5] Moreover, other human rights organs of the United Nations, including the bodies that interpret the major human rights treaties and a number of human rights *rapporteurs,* experts and working groups have increasingly attempted to address issues of internally displaced persons as appropriate to their various mandates.

Frequently, questions are asked about the difference between the OCHA IDP Unit and the mandate of the Representative. The answer is that there are significant differences in the mandate of the Unit and of the RSG, but the mandates are also meant to be complementary. Generally, the dividing line is that the RSG is expected to engage in general advocacy and dialogue with governments from the highest levels down the hierarchy of authority, as well as with all other pertinent actors, including UN agencies, donors, and NGOs. Also crucial is interaction with the IDPs themselves. The role of the Unit, on the other hand, is to assist the Emergency Relief Coordinator to ensure that operational agencies effectively discharge their responsibilities through the collaborative approach. The RSG's dialogue with governments and all concerned can pave the way for the Unit to build on any resulting opportunities and to then see to it that these agencies intervene accordingly. The Unit can also advise the RSG on situations that might benefit from his dialogue with governments or others concerned. To facilitate this cooperation, the ERC and the RSG have signed a "Memorandum of Understanding" identifying their respective mandates and areas of complement.

It is worth emphasizing that the RSG does not have the capacity to be operational; all he can do is try to be persuasive in his dialogue with all concerned. But OCHA, the Emergency Relief Coordinator, and the Unit that supports him, are tools by which the operational agencies are brought together to see to it that the job is done. There is, therefore, a significant difference between the Unit on the one hand and the mandate of the RSG on the other; however, there is also considerable collaboration, complement and some overlap. [6]

Notwithstanding this growing institutional and policy structure, problems of implementation continue to plague the "collaborative approach" to internal displacement. A series of major UN-sponsored studies of IDP protection, assistance, and institutional structures within the UN and the wider international humanitarian community undertaken in the last year has revealed that existing policies are frequently ignored or not even known in the field. Turf battles among agencies hinder speedy and effective response in some countries and, in others, no agency or organization appears ready to take a major role in assisting IDPs. The coordinating roles of the ERC, Resident Coordinators, and Humanitarian Coordinators have not yet resulted in a predictable and coherent system globally. The UN is currently undergoing an internal process of reform and enhancement of the collaborative approach in response to these studies.

It is important to note that whatever the shortcomings in the performance of the system, the international community has made significant progress in its institutional response. The challenge is to build on this progress and avoid both complacency in satisfaction of the progress made and pessimism in the face of the awesome task ahead.

Contextualizing Displacement Through Country Missions

Country missions are another area where the work of the mandate has focused. These missions are the litmus test of what is being done on behalf of the internally displaced. Statistics become human faces and one witnesses the protection and assistance needs of the displaced populations. Dialogue with governments comes into focus and often is quite gratifying. Of all the missions that I have undertaken, in almost all cases, the results have been significantly positive. In some instances, we have found that, as governments begin to change their policies and as dialogue begins to produce results, humanitarian and development agencies, who are often fearful of the fact that governments regard internal displacement as an area that touches on the sensitive issue of sovereignty, tend to lag behind the changing policy environment. However, performance in this regard is progressively improving. I am finding increasingly that UN agencies on the ground are responding more quickly to the opportunities of changing policies. This is further evidence that the international community is becoming progressively alert to the problems of internal displacement.

There are, of course, countries that are difficult, either because they are in denial of the problem or simply because they are jealously protecting their narrow view of sovereignty. It took me a number of years to secure invitations from some countries, among them Indonesia, Turkey, Mexico and the Russian Federation. But in all these countries, once I was invited and undertook missions, the dialogue with the authorities was constructive and the outcome positive. The challenge in front of me then was to move the operational agencies to catch up with the positive developments and to cooperate with the governments in responding to the needs of the internally displaced. And then there are problems of implementation of recommendations. Sometimes we get positive feedback on implementation, but quite often there is a gap between the encouraging results of the missions and the level of implementation and follow-up activities. This, I fear, is quite common to all human rights mechanisms. Nevertheless, the fact that governments initially respond positively to the conclusions and recommendations of the missions means that there is a common ground for on-going dialogue to bridge the gap of understanding with governments and the level of implementation.

Undertaking Research Projects

Through the Brookings-SAIS Project on Internal Displacement, studies are undertaken at the behest of the Secretary-General's request to me to carry out research on the subject. Research within such independent institutions addresses questions of what is displacement, how many people are affected, where are they located, who is meeting their needs, what gaps exist in meeting those needs, and how can these gaps be bridged—not only by mobilizing the UN system but also other intergovernmental agencies and NGOs. Since then we have produced volumes of text on various aspects of internal displacement.[7] We have recently begun to probe into more difficult and controversial issues, such as the role of peacekeepers in protecting IDPs, measuring national responsibility, dealing with non-state actors, protecting voting rights, ensuring access to education; protecting property rights, developing criteria for when displacement ends, monitoring development-induced displacement; and maintaining efforts to develop a more comprehensive protection regime for IDPs and refugees. It is important to stress that these are policy-oriented studies whose findings are capable of practical application in the field.

Linking Levels of Action

An important aspect of what we have found in our work is the linkage of various levels of action. When we remember that the problem is inherently internal, then the distance between global concerns and local conditions becomes obvious. Working through regional organizations and local communities down to the ground level is crucial. For example, the Brookings-SAIS Project has worked with the Consortium of Humanitarian Agencies (CHA), based in Sri Lanka, to develop a tool kit and a practitioner's kit on return and resettlement for use in the work with IDPs at the local level by the government and non-state actors. The Project not only conducts and commissions research on various aspects of the problems of internal displacement, but also organizes seminars at the national and regional levels, and cooperates with community leaders, research institutions, academicians, and other experts around the world. In addition, the Project has assisted the work of the IDP mandate in forging cooperation with regional organizations.

The need for regional cooperation emanates from the fact that these problems usually spill over the borders and therefore problems of one country become shared by the region. By the same token, there is a mutual interest on the part of governments to work together in addressing their problems cooperatively. Over the years and as noted earlier with respect to the promotion of the *Guiding Principles* , the Project has forged relationships with regional organizations around the world, including the Commonwealth, the Council of Europe (COE), the Economic Community of

West African States (ECOWAS), the Inter-Governmental Authority on Development (IGAD), the Organization of African Unity (OAU, now the African Union (AU)), the Organization of American States (OAS), and the Organization for Security and Cooperation in Europe (OSCE). We have also found that it is important to see IDPs not just as victims of humanitarian crises, but as citizens with rights who are capable of resourcefully responding to their situation. The *Guiding Principles* are proving to be potentially significant in turning what would be an expectation of welfare, to demands of rights by IDPs. Ensuring that IDPs can access and use the *Guiding Principles* is one of the reasons why they have been translated into many languages.

STIPULATING SOVEREIGNTY AS RESPONSIBILITY

The fundamental norm of sovereignty as responsibility that has guided my work on internal displacement is, in significant part, the result of post-Cold War developments. As the Cold War era was beginning to unravel, it became necessary to speculate on the implications of the emerging new order on perceptions of national and regional conflicts. It was obvious that these conflicts would no longer be viewed in the context of the proxy confrontation between the super powers. But what new conceptual framework would influence response to these conflicts in the post-Cold War era? I was fortunate to be involved in two initiatives that would help shape my perspective on the emerging challenge. One was the development of an African Studies Project as a branch of the Foreign Policy Studies Program at the Brookings Institution. The other was participating in the initiative of the former Head of State of Nigeria and now the twice-elected President, Olusegun Obasanjo, toward a Helsinki-like Conference on Security, Stability, Development, and Cooperation in Africa–CSSDCA.

Our Brookings Africa Project began with a conference that made an overall assessment of conflicts in Africa and the challenges of the post-Cold War era. The conference papers were edited and published by Brookings under the title: *Conflict Resolution in Africa*.[8] Following the publication of the conference papers, we undertook national and regional case studies to deepen our understanding of the issues involved.

Several publications resulted from these studies.[9] A synthesis of these case studies led to the main conclusion that as conflicts became internal, they also primarily became the responsibility of governments to prevent, manage, and resolve. National governance was perceived primarily as conflict management. State sovereignty was then postulated as entailing the responsibility of conflict management. Indeed, the concluding volume in the African series at Brookings was titled *Sovereignty as Responsibility*. The envisaged responsibility involved managing diversity, ensuring equitable distribution of wealth, services, and development opportunities, and participating effectively in regional and international arrangements for peace, security, and stability. A subsequent volume, *African Reckoning*, tried to put more flesh on the skeleton of the responsibilities of sovereignty, building largely on human rights and humanitarian norms and international accountability.[10] As noted earlier, since internal conflicts often spill over across international borders, their consequences also spill across borders, threatening regional security and stability. In the "apportionment" of responsibilities in the post-Cold War era, regional organizations become the second level of the needed response. And yet, the international community remains the residual guarantor of universal human rights and humanitarian standards in the quest for global peace and security.

The development of the Helsinki-process for Africa was motivated by the concern that the post-Cold War global order was likely to result in the withdrawal of the major powers and the marginalization of Africa. It was, therefore, imperative for Africa to both take charge of its destiny and observe principles that would appeal to the West and thereby provide a sound foundation for a mutually agreeable partnership. This was found in the Helsinki framework of the Economic and Security Cooperation in Europe, ESCE, that became the Organization for Security and Cooperation in Europe, OSCE. A series of meetings culminated in the 1991 Conference in Kampala, Uganda, which was attended by some 500 people, including several heads of state and representatives from all walks of life. The conferences produced the *Kampala Document*, which elaborated the four "calabashes," so termed to distinguish them from the OSCE "baskets," and give them an African orientation. The calabashes are: security, stability, development, and cooperation. The adoption of the CSSDCA by the Organization of African Unity was initially blocked by a few governments that felt threatened by its normative principles. When Obasanjo returned to power as the elected President of Nigeria, he was able to push successfully for the incorporation of CSSDCA into the OAU mechanism for conflict prevention, management, and resolution.[11]

In connection with these initiatives, I began to focus attention on promoting the need to balance conventional notions of sovereignty with the responsibility of the state to provide for the protection and general welfare of citizens and all those under state jurisdiction.[12] Given the sensitivity of the mandate on internal displacement, I felt that the way to bridge 1) the need for international protection and assistance for the internally displaced and 2) the barricades of the negative approach to sovereignty, was to build on the fundamental norm of sovereignty as a positive concept of state responsibility toward its citizens and those under its jurisdiction. In my own experience, this approach has been quite effective in creating dialogue with governments. Of the 30 missions I have undertaken around the world, no government authority has ever argued: "I don't care how irresponsible or irresponsive we are, this is an internal matter and none of your business."

The principle of sovereignty as responsibility has been strengthened and mainstreamed by the Canadian sponsored Commission on Intervention and State Sovereignty.[13] The real question now is how the international community can reinforce, strengthen, and make effective the application of the principle of sovereignty as responsibility, building on the national, regional, and international apportionment of responsibility. With respect to IDPs, the question is whether governments, in partnership with the international community, are effectively addressing the crisis of internal displacement and meeting the needs of the affected populations. Here, there is clearly a major gap between what "ought to be" and what "is."

The challenge that postulating sovereignty as responsibility poses for the international community is that it implies accountability. Obviously, the internally displaced themselves, marginalized, excluded, often persecuted, have little capacity to hold their national authorities accountable. Only the international community, including sub-regional, regional, and international organizations, has the leverage and clout to persuade governments and other concerned actors to discharge their responsibility or otherwise fill the vacuum of irresponsive sovereignty. This, too, need not be seen in confrontational terms. Often, the fact is that governments of affected countries, even if they wanted to discharge the responsibility of assisting and protecting their needy populations, lack resources and the capacity to do so. Offering them support in a way that links humanitarian assistance with protection in a holistic, integrated approach to human rights should make the case more compelling. No government worthy of the title can request material assistance from the outside world and reject concern with the human rights of the people on whose behalf it requests assistance. Doing so would be like asking the international community to feed them but not ensure their safety and dignity.

CONCLUDING REFLECTIONS

I would like to conclude on two themes: the need to address the root causes and some personal reflections on the legacy of Sergio Vieira de Mello and the role he played in facilitating our work.

In my statements on the crisis of internal displacement, including during my country missions, and in my reports to various organs of the UN system, I always end on the challenging note of seeing the crisis as offering opportunities for addressing the root causes of internal displacement. Displacement is only a symptom of the causes reflected mostly in conflicts and human rights violations, which are themselves symptoms of deeper rooted problems, embodied in diversities characterized by acute disparities or inequalities in the shaping and sharing of power, national wealth, public services, and development opportunities. Discrimination on the basis of race, ethnicity, religion, culture, or gender means that there are those who are "in," enjoying the dignity of full citizenship and those who are "out," marginalized to the point of virtual statelessness.[14] Unless these inequities are affirmatively addressed, these countries will have a hard time achieving peace, security, stability, and development.

Ironically, while conflicts, displacement, and the resulting violations of human rights and humanitarian standards are rooted in gross inequities, displacement itself exposes the disadvantaged to conditions in the more privileged areas, which sharpen even more the citizens' real-ization of how marginalized they really are. Even if peace is achieved and the displaced are able to return to their areas of origin, they cannot be expected to go back to the conditions of dire poverty and lack of essential services, employment opportunities, and prospects for eco-nomic, social, and cultural development. Not only should they be guar-anteed a safe and dignified return, they also need to be provided with assistance for their general welfare and sustainable development.[15]

Let me conclude by reflecting very quickly again on the role Sergio Vieira de Mello played in facilitating our work. As explained earlier, because of the fears and concerns about sovereignty, I see our task as pri-marily one of persuading governments of our respect for their sover-eignty, but also challenging them by interpreting sovereignty not as a barricade against international involvement, but as a positive concept of state responsibility that protects and assists needy citizens and all those under its jurisdiction. Sergio, to me, represented that approach. He was someone who engaged governments diplomatically, with due deference to their sensitivities, but at the same time with firm principles and with a clear view of what was expected of them. An example in this respect was the manner in which he promoted the *Guiding Principles* on Internal Dis-placement. As noted earlier, under his leadership, IASC endorsed the *Principles* and called upon the agencies to bring them to the attention of their governing bodies and direct their field staff to use them in their oper-ations. Since that time, the impact of the *Guiding Principles* has been quite remarkable. Once endorsed by the IASC, the Commission on Human Rights recognized that the *Principles* were already in operation, and could no longer deny the practical importance the operational agencies attached to them in their work. And so, in that respect, Sergio offered far-sighted leadership to the service of the UN and humanity.

A glance at the many countries in which Sergio served indicates that he was interminably associated with all aspects of the challenge inter-nal displacement presents to the international community. Indeed, it is necessary to see the problem and the response to it holistically. Inter-nal displacement challenges the international community with the need to develop ways of preventing the arbitrary displacement of popula-tions, responding to the protection and assistance needs of those already displaced and finding durable solutions in the form of safe return with dignity, alternative resettlement, and social reintegration and development. Beyond that, it requires addressing the root causes of displacement to create conditions of a just peace, security, stability, and development, which would, in turn, prevent or discourage displacement. In other words, internal displacement is not only a humanitarian and human rights crisis, it is also a political and security issue—a challenge to nation-building.

To end on the personal note with which I began, Sergio Vieira de Mello was not only an exceptional international civil servant and leader, he was a very dear colleague, whom I am proud to call a friend. Needless to say, it was devastating to get the news of his death. In the African indigenous religions, perception about the life-hereafter combines with an aspect of immortality that is founded on the memory of the departed by the living: family, friends, and all those whom one has touched in one's life. It is through the living that the identity and influence in this world are maintained. As the conference and this volume demonstrate, his name and his accomplishments will continue to be a source of inspiration to all those who are called upon to serve the United Nations and the cause of humanity.

Humanitarian Action in a New Barbarian Age

David Rieff

IF THE HOPE for human progress and for a better world can be said to rest on anything, it rests on the great documents of international law that have been promulgated since the end of the Second World War. These include, first and foremost, the *United Nations Charter* and the *Universal Declaration of Human Rights.* But while these two documents offer a global vision of what might be if humanity is lucky, it is the corpus of international humanitarian law, that is, the rules governing armed conflict, that have actually proved their utility over the course of the past half-century. The four *Geneva Conventions* and their *Additional Protocols,* the *Genocide Convention,* and, more recently, such initiatives as the ban on landmines, are no mere pious sentiments. They have saved innumerable human lives. Think, for example, of the fact that since the adoption of the international treaty that banned the use of poison gas as a weapon of war, gas, so ubiquitous in the trenches of the western front during World War I, has probably only been used a handful of times since. Norms, it seems, can sometimes influence realities.

That said, it would be a misreading of history, and, perhaps, a culpable exercise in self-flattery as well, to make a fetish of the law and imagine that realities will invariably or inevitably migrate toward norms. Over the course of the past half-century, there are examples where they have and examples where they haven't. The full legal emancipation of African-Americans in the US Civil Rights Movement of the 1950s, 60s, and 70s is an example of a law-based reform or, to put it differently, a normative transformation that did end up transforming American social reality even though at least a significant minority and possibly even a majority of Americans were against such decisions as Brown v. Board of Education when they were first handed down. And yet, in contrast, normative changes related to the status and treatment of children encapsulated in the UN Convention on the Rights of the Child have had limited impact outside the developed world despite the best efforts of many dedicated activists and political figures.

In other words, the record is mixed. Those who believe that human progress is inevitable would doubtless describe this as a matter of "two steps forward, one step back." Even among those of us for whom the Classical Greek vision of history as cyclical seems to conform better to the realities of our sad world than the Christian, Marxist, or, indeed, liberal expectation that progress in the moral order of the world is as bound to take place as progress in scientific understanding, we would hardly want to do away with the notion of progress altogether. As the great liberal realist, Raymond Aron, once put it, "if one is not [an advocate of progress], what is left?" Humanity, he added, had no hope for survival "outside of reason and science."[1]

Aron's conclusion in large measure amounted to insisting that one had to be optimistic in spite of what one knew—"despite the twentieth century, I remain an advocate of progress," was the way he put it. This is not to be confused with the more self-congratulatory fables that have captured the imagination of too many decent people in the contemporary world that revolve around the notion that a "revolution of moral concern"—the phrase is that of the Canadian writer, Michael Igantieff—began in the aftermath of World War II, gave rise to the United Nations system as well as to the transformation of both the concept of state sovereignty and the reach of international law, and promises to usher in a better world in which the worst human cruelties and historical tragedies—another World War I, Shoah, or Gulag Archipelago—will not be permitted to unfold and whose perpetrators will not enjoy the impunity that they have throughout most, if not all, of human history.

Aron was not an optimist. Nor, when all is said and done, were the founders of the United Nations. But if an Eleanor Roosevelt or a Gladwyn Jebb viewed the nascent world body as a means of preventing the kind of descent into the inferno that the Nazi experience had revealed to be a constant human possibility rather than as a means of inducing any ideal world order, their successors gradually became more optimistic. A document like Secretary General Boutros Boutros-Ghali's 1991 "An Agenda for Peace" described a world that really might be perfectable. And the final documents that accompanied the decade-long extravaganzas of UN conferences of the 1990s had a similarly utopian tinge to them. Poverty would be halved by a date certain; states that abused their own populations would be forced to desist because the Westphalian order, with its culture of impunity, was fading and we were entering the age of rights. War would be limited in scope, with limitations on what weapons could be employed when and where, steadily expanding protections for non-combatants, property, and cultural and religious sites growing in scope.

This would happen, activists often argued, because of the transformation and expansion of legal norms and the campaigning of civil society groups. The context for the change would be the UN, which was viewed (and, indeed, for all its faults continues to be viewed in this way by many people throughout the world) as the sole legitimate authority for international rules that could apply to all of humankind. The fact that the UN was an institution without much real power and that the term civil society is so nebulous as to be more a socio-political Rorschach blot for campaigners and activists than a term that has any real specific gravity passed largely unnoticed during the 1990s—that 'silly season' of the inflated expectations. (Otherwise, why is Human Rights Watch, which has no democratic accountability, viewed as an emblematic institution of civil society while the US National Rifle Association, with 4 million members, is viewed as something else?)

Instead, there was the very real expectation that the world was becoming a more civilized place. Again, why the same decade that witnessed the Balkan catastrophe and the Rwandan genocide could interpret itself as a period of enormous promise is a question for psychiatrists, not political analysts. But that optimism was real. And the creation of the International Criminal Court, which was heralded as the first institution that promised to genuinely promise an end to impunity for war criminals, served as the capstone for these generous and well-intended expectations of decent people around the world.

As Undersecretary General for Peacekeeping, Kofi Annan had presided over the two worst failures of the United Nations during the first post-Cold

War decade. But as Secretary General, Annan not only acknowledged the UN's failures—however belatedly, and, in the case of Rwanda, not until 2004 on the eve of the 10th anniversary of the genocide, ambivalently—but made the UN Secretariat a bully pulpit for this 'revolution of moral concern' and for individual human rights as finally 'trumping' state sovereignty. Annan's UN was a place in which international law, above all international humanitarian law—that is, the laws of war—was viewed as the essential component for building a more decent world order. And in speech after speech and document after document, UN officials from the Secretary General himself on down emphasized the need for states to comply with the obligations they had under the various international treaties and conventions to which they had signed on. The problem, UN officials repeated, was no longer one of first principles; the transformation of the normative environment had seen to that. Rather, the question was now one of making these norms binding—in short, of enforcement.

In retrospect, this approach begged at least as many questions as it answered. There was the uncomfortable question of why, if the norms were so terrific, the reality of the world was so dire? But at least that objection could be answered by saying that just as it had taken a great deal of time and struggle and false starts to get the norms right, so it would take a long period before effective modalities of enforcement were arrived at. And activists could point to studies ranging from the report on UN peacekeeping by the former Algerian foreign minister, Lakhdar Brahimi, to the Canadian government-sponsored document on humanitarian intervention, "The Responsibility to Protect," as examples of serious efforts to think about implementing the new norms and of, in effect, institutionalizing and reifying that 'revolution of moral concern.'

More difficult was the issue of what possible motivation could impel states to act out of essentially altruistic motives, which, however much they had been weakened by the realities of globalization, were still the fundamental constitutive elements of world order. That is, why would great powers intervene to prevent genocide in places of little economic or geo-strategic significance to themselves except very rarely and inconsistently? One did not have to be a Kissingerian realist, or the reincarnation of Lord Palmerston, to conclude that states had never behaved in this way in the past. And if their previous conduct had been fundamentally determined by interests, rather than ideals, what, if any-thing, had changed? Was the human rights revolution of the second half of the twentieth century really that compelling? Or, as the British diplo-mat, Robert Cooper, argues in an influential book, *The Breaking of Nations: Order and Chaos in the Twenty-First Century,* did the fact that a successful global economy required a rules-based order really imply a commitment to a human rights rule as well?

On the face of things, that appeared unlikely. Africa, where most of the crises that might require so-called humanitarian intervention were occurring, was by the turn of the millennium almost irrelevant to the world economy except for certain key resources like oil that could be extracted even during civil wars and famines. At a generous estimate, it accounted for some 3 percent of world trade. The Balkans, East Timor, Haiti: they were similarly marginal in geo-economic terms. This reality, which is as undeniable as its elaboration is unpalatable, threw the debate back into the context of morality. And if the 1990s had proved anything, it was that where morality was concerned the so-called international com-munity was highly selective in its commitments. The British might decide to do something about their ex-colony, Sierra Leone, but even the highly interventionist Blair government was at pains to point out that its deploy-ment was not to be construed as the first of many. There would be no British troops sent to Zimbabwe on human rights grounds although the tyranny of Robert Mugabe was almost as destructive to its own people as the Revolutionary United Front had been in Sierra Leone (the Mugabe government simply used hunger as a weapon, rather than muti-lation). The Clinton administration made the same point after the US-led war in Kosovo in 1999.

Of course, had the great powers been willing to give the UN a stand-ing force and the authority to deploy it, as the UN's own Sir Brian Urquhart had once suggested, the dilemma might not have been so acute. But the great powers found a weak UN exactly to their liking, while, in much of the developing world, the critique of absolute state sovereignty that Kofi Annan had pursued was viewed as a way of legit-imizing neo-colonialism rather than guaranteeing or helping to secure people's human rights. Inevitably, instead of being narrowed, the gap between the new norms of international humanitarian law and realities on the ground began to widen. The fact that some humanitarian interventions, notably the one in Kosovo, were undertaken without UN approval only increased skepticism in the developing world about possible hidden agendas in the revolution of moral concern.

Perhaps, had the September 11 attacks not taken place, some consensus might have been arrived at. Possible, but not likely. While the attacks on the World Trade Center and the Pentagon did transform the landscape of international relations, many of the contradictions between norms and realities that September 11 put in such sharp relief were already part of the geo-strategic landscape. It is just that, like icebergs in the North Atlantic, they lay largely submerged and out of view.

So many factors militated against norms becoming reality. First and foremost, the UN had no real power to set the agenda anywhere except where the great powers had no great interest in setting one themselves. Thus, before September 11, the UN view on Tajikistan carried some weight, but once the US decided to invade Afghanistan the UN was relegated to the sidelines. Second, there was no appetite in the rich world for the kind of redistributive justice that would have begun to address the underlying inequities that were at the root of so many so-called humanitarian or human rights crises. The refusal of the European Union nations to radically overhaul their policies of massively subsidizing their own agricultural sector was one illustration of this. The comparative failure of the debt relief movement to sway Washington in any truly significant way was another. Third, despite what Third World intellectuals might imagine, there was no appetite in Western Europe, Japan, or the United States, to 'recolonize' the world. The logic of Secretary General Annan's speeches might sometimes seem to imply endless wars of altruism, but neither Washington nor Brussels was prepared to make any such commitment or to facilitate and subsidize a UN force that would.

The September 11 attacks only exacerbated these trends. But they exacerbated them to a remarkable degree. Confronted by terrorism, whether or not it was appropriate to call the necessary response to it a 'war' as the Bush administration did, it was the politics of that most profound and essential interest—existential security—that was at the fore of policymakers' calculations, not elective wars in the name of humanitarianism and human rights. At the same time, much as had been the case

during the Cold War, states threatened by terrorism were not only immediately engaged in curtailing domestic civil liberties but tended to be
more willing to overlook human rights violations, even on a massive
scale, by states that might play a strategic role in the anti-terrorist campaign. The American government's volte face on Uzbekistan—surely one
of the most abusive regimes on the face of the earth—because the Kari-
mov dictatorship had facilitated US operations during the invasion of
Afghanistan was a case in point. In fairness, human rights concerns have
always been ignored—as much if not more so in Europe as in the United
States—when major commercial interests were at stake, as the case of
China has demonstrated all too vividly.

Senior UN officials were perfectly well aware of these trends. But since
it has little real power (to use Joseph Nye's categories, it has no hard
power and only a small amount of soft power), and since its legitimacy
is derived so importantly from its commitment to the primacy of international law, the world organization was hard-pressed to 'shift gears' to
somehow respond to or at least accommodate these new realities. Perhaps, had it done so, it would have destroyed its own *raison d'etre*. But
by not adjusting, the UN found itself wrong-footed by the new world dis-
order that the rise of Islamic terrorism and the international response to
that terrorism had brought into being. In effect, it believed it could
remain a 'non-combatant' in that struggle. But neither the terrorists, nor,
for that matter, the Bush administration, was prepared to concede the
UN the right to maintain such a stance.

Sergio Vieira de Mello was without question the most brilliant UN
diplomat of his generation, a throwback, in terms of charisma, dedication, intelligence, and drive, to such figures as Fulke Bernadotte and
Brian Urquhart. But when he reluctantly accepted Secretary General
Annan's plea to becoming the UN's special representative in Baghdad
after the overthrow of Saddam Hussein, de Mello never seems to have
imagined that the anti-US insurgents and terrorists would view the UN
as aligned with the US invasion. In a sense, he was right: institutionally,
the UN had opposed the war. As de Mello saw it, he was trying to help
the Iraqi people, not serve the US occupation authorities. As the UN
report on his death concluded, neither de Mello nor his colleagues seem
to have fully taken in the fact that to the Iraqi guerrillas, the UN was just

as much the enemy as the US was. And de Mello was not so much wrong—what else could he have done? To have hunkered down in a bunker, as the Americans did, would have been to betray everything the UN and he personally stood for—as overtaken by a colder world. Faithful to his ideals, he died for his belief in the UN, which, whether one shares it or not, ennobles his sacrifice. But it is by no means clear that those ideals can be held on to.

The ways in which the United States has turned the international order on its head in the aftermath of September 11 are obvious. By eschewing any serious commitment to the multilateralism that lies at the heart of international law, the future of any viable world system, however embryonic, in any usable time frame, is open to question. But terrorism also throws that future into question. For terrorism, by definition, challenges the state's monopoly on force which must lie at the heart of any international system worthy of the name. It also deforms, if it does not negate entirely, the soldier-civilian distinction that lies at the heart of international humanitarian law. To be sure, that distinction was already under threat from the revolution in military technology of the last decade. A guerrilla force cannot fight a modern army equipped with night vision equipment (this has deprived guerrilla forces of their strongest traditional advantage, the night), thermal imaging, GPS, smart weapons, drones, and satellites. Or, rather, it cannot fight such an army while obeying the laws of war. To the contrary, it must employ perfidy, pretending until the moment it attacks that its fighters are non-combatants, and it must employ terror, because while it cannot hope to challenge a modern army on the battlefield, it can hope to demoralize that modern army's citizens back home.

The idea that guerrilla forces would simply bow to the superior technology of modern armies from developed countries is as utopian as the expectation that war itself has been superseded. An American judge once remarked famously that the US Constitution was not a suicide pact. By the same token, for the guerrilla fighter neither are the laws of war. And from Gaza to Iraq, the force of that reality is becoming plain.

Of course, where this leaves an international system (a sounder concept than international community) that is law-based is very much an open question. And it is hard not to feel that a new barbarian age is upon us—and that one of the first victims of that age was Sergio Vieira de Mello.

Post-Conflict Transitions and Working with Local Communities to Create Leadership and Governance

In this section five remarkably experienced humanitarians share the lessons they have learned working to rebuild communities in post conflict situations.

Mark Malloch Brown emphasizes the absolute necessity of proceeding only with local support: "Reconstruction and the choices that are made about priorities and the allocation of resources between different communities must be made by local or national government entities that enjoy local legitimacy. When foreign aid agencies seek to make these choices, however fair-minded they might appear to be, they generate controversy around the justice and legitimacy of the actions taken." Arthur Dewey emphasizes the necessity for greater integration in every phase of a complex emergency: "Integration, particularly the inclusion of a military component, carries risks, but none so great as sacrificing integration itself on the altar of humanitarian purity. Integration in the interest of humanity is no vice. Humanitarian exclusivity in the interest of purity is no virtue." In a challenging chapter, Ghassan Salame warns of the dangers of rigidly defining post-conflict situations: "When does a conflict *really* end and when does a post-conflict situation *effectively* start? Is what we call post-conflict a mere lull in the fighting? Is it only the passage from one sequence to the next in a chain of wars? I tend to believe that being truly in a post-conflict situation should remain an open-ended question and not a for-granted one." In two

complementary chapters UN Undersecretary-General Shashi
Tharoor and Ambassador Roland Eng from Cambodia consider
the impact of local media in post-conflict transitions. Tharoor
notes, "By giving voice and visibility to all people—and especially
the poor, the marginalized and the minorities—the media can
help remedy the inequalities, the corruption, the ethnic tensions
and the human rights abuses that form the root causes of many
conflicts." Ambassador Eng illustrates his message within a context of experiences he shared with Sergio during the reconstruction of Cambodia after the genocidal reign of the Khmer Rouge.

Post-Conflict Transitions: The Challenge of Securing Political, Social, and Economic Stability

Mark Malloch Brown

WHEN I THINK of all that Sergio's life encompassed—his life-long work to assist the world's most vulnerable people in times of crisis—I know that he would have been pleased that the arrangements to remember him are not solely focused on his achievements, extraordinary though they were, but on taking forward the debates about humanitarian activities in today's difficult environment. He would consider that a proper and appropriate way of honoring his life because in all the years he worked in this field, he was always asking questions, always wondering "what next?"

In fact he quietly chided me when I first returned to the UN after many years outside it, and made the complaint that there were "no new ideas" in the issues that mattered to humanitarianism. He confirmed that I was right at one level—the debates about internally displaced persons; the interventions that made for successful post-conflict recovery; the continuing erosion of the status of refugees—that all of these problems, and others, have been with us for many years. But as he also pointed out, the context in which we have sought solutions for them, and therefore the solutions themselves, have changed dramatically. And they continue to change today.

Two particular events stand out today in terms of the changed environment in which we must now revisit humanitarianism. The first was the tragedy of September 11, which changed utterly the international political context in which we must operate. The second was the incident that took Sergio's own life: the bombing of the UN Headquarters in Baghdad on 19 August 2003.

While the first event reoriented much international political life around the fight against terrorism, the second spoke to us of the consequences of the 'war on terrorism.' The fact that, unintentionally, both sides of this war had adopted a symmetrically similar position: "you're either with us or against us." In that context, the neutral space for humanitarianism and its apolitical character, the space that we had all taken for granted, was drained along with the belief that all combatants in a conflict situation understood and respected the context in which we operate.

These events are now forcing us to revisit the very premise of how we operate in post-conflict situations.

In the short term we need to reduce our exposure in countries such as Iraq or Afghanistan by limiting the number of expatriates and ensuring that they operate in a more low-key way. We also need to build a wider set of relationships with local combatants in crisis situations in order to recover, in some part at least, some shredded part of the mantle of a security arrangement which depends on trust in us from different parties to a conflict.

This in turn has consequences for the next phase, the post-conflict phase of reconstruction, where that deepened relationship with local partners allows us to press ahead on the key issue of local ownership of the process. Reconstruction and the choices that are made about priorities and the allocation of resources between different communities must be made by local or national governments and government entities that enjoy local legitimacy. When foreign aid agencies seek to make these choices, however fair-minded they might appear to be, they generate controversy around the justice and legitimacy of the actions taken.

To realize goals of UN legitimacy and worker safety, many of the difficulties of the past that were not related to these situations on the ground, but rather to the institutional relationships or turf fights between different NGOs and the UN and other international and donor entities, have been largely resolved. Indeed, I think it is one of the many legacies of Sergio that during his tenure as the Head of the Office of the Coordinator for Humanitarian Action (OCHA) he was able—working with myself and the United Nations Development Program (UNDP), and with our colleagues in the Department of Political Affairs and the Department of Peace Keeping, as well as many NGOs and bilateral donors—to settle the issue of conflicting mandates: to create a unified, broadly agreed division of labor between the actors and therefore a united response that was not competitive or dysfunctional in character. That progress has allowed us to focus even more clearly on the real issues: countries in conflict and how to manage the aftermath of conflict situations.

More than a Peace Treaty

Too often the UN and other partners have pulled out the champagne at the moment that a peace treaty is initialed, failing to understand that the history of peace-making points clearly to the fact that initialing the peace agreement is the beginning not the end of the process.

As Paul Collier, former Director of the Development Research Group at the World Bank, and others have so persuasively argued, post-peace-agreement countries have a disproportionate propensity to revert to conflict. The correlation between that propensity and how long they've been kept out of conflict is also important, because the risk goes down the longer there is peace. It's like the heart attack victim who has a high risk of a second heart attack in the immediate period after the first, but as time elapses, the risk decreases. Conflict after a peace agreement follows the same lines. It becomes enormously important, like a good doctor in a cardiac ward, to have early, effective intervention to a patient during that period of maximum risk. And yet, the whole organization of international intervention around broader development issues is still set up to deal more comprehensively with the later rehabilitation period, when the phase of greatest risk has passed.

In order to embark on genuine peace building and sustain the peace agreement, it is imperative to intervene quickly, decisively, and effectively to create real momentum and a peace dividend for those emerging from conflict. Sergio himself saw that the first part of this was to move as rapidly as possible to strong local control of the recovery process. The role of international actors is to support, not substitute, that control—a lesson now being learned in Iraq and one that Sergio himself had cause to learn in East Timor when he arrived as administrator of that territory in a role not too dissimilar to the one Ambassador Paul Bremer played in Iraq until June 2004.

The fact is that Sergio, even with a strong multinational UN mandate and the full support of the people of East Timor, found that there was a real, perhaps inevitable, impatience to assume self-government: a goal that the East Timorese had fought for and given their lives for over many years. Therefore Sergio moved quickly to ensure that, even ahead of the dates mandated by the international agreement concluded with Indonesia at the time of East Timor's secession, East Timorese officials were as involved as possible in the government of their own country. No one knew better how vital local ownership is to peace building efforts, or was more skilled at reaching out to local communities to help build it, than Sergio.

So from that starting point, let me set out an agenda for successful, sustainable post-conflict governance, which I place under three headings: the political, the economic, and the social.

THE ROLE OF POLITICAL FACTORS

The only long-term basis for effective, peaceful civilian governance is legitimate, representative local and national institutions—and that means much more than just holding elections. We need a broader set of democratic features in post-peace agreement countries, which allow a free media to hold the executive to account; which allow strong parliamentary scrutiny and oversight of the behaviors of the executive; and which ensures that there is a system of law that produces justice in a reasonable time for the poor so that they see these institutions as representing them rather than—as is too often the case— them being perceived as having narrowed their interest base to that of a self-seeking political class alone. This set of broader democracy issues does not come easy, but without it there is limited scope for peaceful competitive democratic struggle.

There are two ways of addressing this. One is to try to strengthen democratic governments. And this is the nuts and bolts of what UNDP does all over the world: from helping run effective elections, to strengthening parliaments and supporting more transparent policymaking and judicial reform. But in crisis situations, where people have fundamentally lost trust in their institutions for whatever reason, there is sometimes a need for

temporary dialogues that are extra-institutional in nature, namely mechanisms that bring together partners from different stakeholder groups.

This is something UNDP has been pioneering in Latin America, working in several countries with churches, labor organizations, business
organizations, and civil society, to form a dialogue that also involves
politicians, but which the institutions—the politicians, parliaments and
parties—are not able to legitimately carry out on their own.

But while these are proving to be extraordinarily important means of
trying to rekindle conversation and dialog at a time when it appears that
everyone is polarizing into potentially conflicting camps, we at UNDP
do worry about the consequences of them becoming a substitute for formal institutionalized democracy. They have value as a short-term substitute when democratic institutions are failing, but a way has to be found,
as quickly as possible, to channel political participation back into re-
ignited, re-invigorated formal democratic institutions which permit both
the competition of ideas and their peaceful resolution, and the emergence of a consensus to govern the affairs of that country.

In addition to democratizing the peace building process, the other big
political issue that needs to be dealt with relatively early in post-conflict
situations is rule of law: the urgent need to create a justice system that
offers justice to the winners and losers in the aftermath of conflict, but
which over time, also offers justice for crimes committed in the past,
which is such a critical part of the broader reconciliation process. As UN
Secretary-General Kofi Annan has said: "rule of law delayed, is lasting
peace denied." Political and legal institutions that ensure accountability—
accountability of today's government, accountability for past government, and accountability of a future government—are vital because they
are the basis on which people cease to be combatants and, as citizens,
recover their trust in national institutions.

The Role of Economic Factors

It is clear that what is increasingly fueling conflict is the issue of control
of national resources and economic wealth, particularly in resource-rich
countries. More often than not these conflicts are fueled by economic
inequality or what is viewed by people as uneven access to the economic

wealth of the country. Regarding the issue of resource control in countries, particularly resource-rich countries, petroleum has arguably become the single greatest driver of conflict today.

Clearly we do have some development-related activities, which can make a very significant difference on this issue. The first is better resource revenue management, and here the most important starting point is a transparent system of demonstrating to the citizens of the country, wherever in that country they live, how that revenue is being used. The World Bank's efforts, pushed by civil society, to help create such a regime for the Chad-Cameroon pipeline, were an early important example of that. And there are other examples, now in Kazakhstan and elsewhere in Central Asia, of governments trying to demonstrate open, transparent, democratic accountability for oil funds by isolating them from other government revenues, reporting on how they are used, and allowing some international monitoring or oversight of that effort.

A second priority is to ensure that macroeconomic policies are not so restrictive on public spending that critical peace dividends are not put in place: that armies are not too quickly disbanded because salaries are considered unaffordable; or that health and education systems or public employment schemes are not held back, thus denying benefits and opportunities to ex-combatants. And linked to this is the vital task of removing small arms from communities through disarmament, demobilization, and reintegration programs (DDR). The greatest threat today to renewed conflict in places such as Liberia is young men with guns who have not been quickly disarmed and given alternative economic livelihoods.

When any of these policies are under-funded for shortsighted reasons of macro-economic stability, it can very quickly become self-defeating, leading to a resumption of conflict of which among many other victims, the earliest is macroeconomic stability itself. In that context, I welcome the growing international commitment to assist vulnerable crisis and post-conflict countries in this area, as seen in schemes such as the World Bank-led Low Income Countries Under Stress (LICUS) Initiative, which is providing much-needed support to promote improved delivery of basic services, primarily health and education, in countries where very weak policies, institutions, and governance hinder the ability of countries to deliver these services themselves.

The Role of Social Factors

Finally, in addition to the economic and political steps needed to assist countries in post-conflict recovery situations are social factors.

Socially inclusive development policies and programs that offer educational and healthcare access to all irrespective of ethnic, social or political affiliation, are vital paths to bridge building. Establishing an environment where the poorest and most vulnerable groups, especially women, can make choices that secure their lives and livelihoods are the essential social building blocks that lay the foundations for peace and prosperity, which more often than not, also serve to address the build-up of insecurities that can cause, trigger, or re-ignite conflict.

More broadly, social and demographic factors play an important role in the development or re-ignition of conflict. Poor people rarely start conflicts; it is more often the children of the middle-class, claiming to speak for the poor, who are the leaders. But nevertheless, the major common demographic fact of so many of the countries that are recovering from conflict or at high risk of future conflict is an exploding youth, without economic opportunity and often without a political voice.

Across a great swath of countries, from Pakistan moving in an arc across to West Africa, many countries are confronted with a huge youth unemployment problem, and beyond that, a youth participation problem. Already, a majority of the developing world is under the age of 25. We will add another billion people to that age group by 2015. It is a striking demographic. Combine this with economic systems that are not producing growth or jobs at a rate to absorb them into the labor market, political systems that are not genuinely participatory and representative and that deny them a voice in their own future, as well as continued migration from countryside to city, away from the more controlled social structures of the countryside to the more anonymous urban lifestyle, and it is clear how an explosive cocktail is being created.

While youth employment is almost certainly not the kind of issue that has a role in a short-term conflict prevention strategy, if we are to make sure that conflict becomes less a part of our lives in coming years, we have to possess an effective strategy for dealing with the wider issues. This is a strategy contained in the "Millennium Development Goals," agreed in the *Millennium Declaration* just over three years ago, to work to ensure that globalization works for the world's poor.

In conclusion, none of the points I've made here are original, but they are the issues that Sergio grappled with every day of his life as he managed the transition of countries from humanitarian crisis to a stable path of peace building. Sergio had a great track record. In so many of the countries in which he was involved, we have seen successful outcomes. That is why we can learn a lot from what Sergio did and we all have a lot to learn from how he operated. Conflict has, sadly, become an ever-bigger part of national life in many countries. Finding the interventions and means of supporting local leaders to resolve these conflicts must remain an absolute global priority, not just for those citizens directly affected by conflict, but for all of us, arising out of our common humanity and global citizenship.

Humanitarian Action and the International Response to Crises: The Challenges of Integration

Arthur Dewey

IN A STATEMENT at United Nations (UN) Headquarters in New York, U.S. Secretary of State Colin Powell described Sergio de Mello as "a soldier in the cause of peace." He was indeed, in all of his awesome humanitarian duties. He was also one of humanity's great captains—and he joins that short list of eminent crisis managers and civil administrators. Each of these great captains had a technique that marked them and made them great. One of Sergio's greatest legacies will be the "Sergio Technique"—in sum, a magnetism that brought all the parts together—especially the people parts at every level. The challenges of integration in responding to a complex humanitarian emergency were not lost on Sergio.

As a former UN Deputy High Commissioner for Refugees (UNHCR) and a forever member of the UNHCR family, I had the honor and privilege to work with Sergio Vieira de Mello through much of the mid-1980s. Now I am serving as the Assistant Secretary of State for Population, Refugees, and Migration in the U.S. Department of State. Between these two assignments, my time with Sergio as a friend and colleague spanned well over 25 years. In a meeting with Sergio in Baghdad, only a short while before the tragic bombing of the UN headquarters there, I joined those who had urged him to stay on in the Iraq post. His last words to me were vintage Sergio. He said, "I can't, Gene. Human Rights is my post, and I've got to get back."

The Bureau of Population, Refugees, and Migration at the U.S. Department of State is multilateralist in humanitarian action—not because we are idealistic "UN-huggers." We are multilateralist because it works. It works for financial burden sharing because UN consolidated appeals permit the U.S. taxpayer to bear only 25 percent of worldwide refugee program costs—as opposed to 85 to 100 percent if we were to act unilaterally. Multilateralism also works better for the victims of complex emergencies. This is possible because serious supporters of the UN, such as our part of the U.S. State Department, are literate, competent, and oriented toward making the most of the entirety of the multilateral humanitarian system. We do it behind the scenes. We do it with daily intensive engagement in Washington, at multilateral headquarters such as New York and Geneva, and wherever the UN is engaged in the field. By tying in to the tested competencies of the UN, the U.S. can accomplish its humanitarian objectives with a smaller investment than were we to go it alone; and we can do it with a major economy of resources.

U.S. multilateralism not only ties into the burden sharing economies, and the operational competencies of the UN system, it also permits the integration and unity of effort that is made possible through the mutual reinforcement and interoperability of UN agencies. It is the values and self-interest benefits of multilateral action that drive and define the approach I take to integration and cohesion in humanitarian action.

We have to look at integration in terms of what constitutes the total effort. The total effort should be seen as fundamentally a civil-military effort, but broken down into discrete political, security, humanitarian, and development components—plus human rights efforts as a vital part of the humanitarian component. The full range of players, operating under their competencies and mandates, are what constitute the total effort with respect to integration and cohesion. Thus I feel justified in making a strong case for integration and cohesion.

From the practitioner's standpoint, I believe there are six major principles necessary to achieve effective integration and cohesion.

1. *Comprehensive Planning.* Planning is second nature to military personnel. The military is very good at planning, and at changing plans and adjusting plans that are always out of date. And they have campaign plans. But what military personnel are not as good at, and that perhaps

no one is as good at, is *comprehensive* campaign planning. The State Department calls it political-military planning. Experienced humanitarians prefer to call it political-military-humanitarian planning. The value of comprehensive planning is that it provides a logical vehicle to include and to orchestrate all of the essential actors. It becomes a software kind of portrayal of the critical path from the start-state to the desired end-state of a complex contingency operation. Use of this template permits positioning each of the key players on the critical path at both the point and time in which they must appear to achieve an integrated operation.

Such comprehensive planning is indispensable, but almost unheard of in terms of actual practice. During the tenure of former U.S. President Bill Clinton, the State Department received "Presidential Determination 56 (PDD 56)," which mandated a political-military plan for any major complex contingency operation. But we never got a political-military plan in time for actual effect and benefit to operations in the field during that time; and we still haven't even today. Some plans have been written but they are always late. They tend to become an interagency least common denominator and fall short in terms of clarity and adequate provision for each phase in the life cycle of a complex contingency operation. This planning process illustrates as much as anything the challenge of integration. Just trying to get a plan cleared in an inter-agency process as complex as the one in Washington is a Herculean task. And then, if you take into account the total constellation of players—including those in the UN and the international system as well—then it tends to become a plan too far. But it was Dwight Eisenhower's view of planning that should keep us going: "A plan is nothing; planning is everything." It is this process of comprehensive planning that is needed to bring civilian planners up to the level of planning rigor that military persons take for granted. It could avoid some of the major oversights and miscalculations that have popped up with both civilian and military planners in past contingency operations and interventions. The value of such planning is illustrated in the way things have proved to be difficult in Afghanistan, and how they have proved to be more than difficult in Iraq.

In our Bureau at the U.S. State Department, I asked our people to write a comprehensive campaign plan for the major emergencies such as Afghanistan and Iraq. I did so to realize a benefit from the rigor of forcing ourselves to think our way through the critical path that leads to the desired objective. The genius of this is in the process, even if it doesn't result in official doctrine or a blessed statement of purpose or plan on the part of the U.S. government as a whole. It helps us enormously in prioritizing our own resources, and in exercising a serious strategic player role with respect to other colleagues at the U.S. State Department, elsewhere in the U.S. Government, and in the international community.

In Afghanistan this kind of planning was helpful, however, in terms of achieving an exceptionally successful transition through the fundamental stages leading ultimately to indigenous rule. There has been a lot of superficial and ill-considered criticism of how things have worked out in the case of Afghanistan. In my view, the glass is far more than half full. What has been neglected in the public view is the vital role that the UN has played in the transition from the end of the military operation to continuing the work that the UN had done for years in Afghanistan. Through the genius of something called the Program Secretariat Process, the UN Assistance Mission in Afghanistan was able to start and continue transferring the sinews of public services to the Afghan authority. This was done through implementing those services initially, but then as fast as feasible, handing over to Afghan ministries and the Afghan authority the governance processes of planning, programming, and eventually budgeting.

When I was in Afghanistan in July of 2002, I was struck by the potential of this process. I was also struck by the imperative to neutralize opposition to this process that came, unfortunately, from some of the senior leaders in the Afghan government. There was also the need to counter and neutralize a strong anti-humanitarian mentality at the top of the Afghan government, as well as a counter-productive anti-UN mentality. For Afghanistan to receive maximum benefit from the UN, there had to be a conscious effort to reduce these obstacles. We succeeded in doing that by pointing out that this opposition was a train wreck we could not afford to have happen. Serious watchers of events in Afghanistan began to see a shift in Kabul. Trashing humanitarian action and complaining about the "high overhead" UN and NGOs soon led to the applauding of humanitarian action and to recognizing the vital contribution of international organizations and NGOs while the new Afghan Government was trying to get on its feet.

This effort, springing from the U.S. State Department, paid off. The Afghan transition experience stands as a model for the vital role the UN can play in most nation-building situations. That role is to act as an essential "half-way house" in the post-conflict phase while simultaneously delivering governmental services and transferring those responsibilities as rapidly as possible to indigenous authorities.

2. *Need for a Humanitarian Impact Statement.* I believe that thinking through the humanitarian impact of actions taken, or not taken, is vital to a clear understanding of what coherence and integration means. We have an impact statement for everything else; we have it for small business, we have it for gender, and we have it for the environment. But most important is having it for *people.* We demonstrate time after time that we are better at "tree-hugging" than at "people-hugging. Let us look at five examples to underline the importance of humanitarian impact.

First, look at the Balkans: the failure to assess the impact of not acting in the early 1990s to ethnic cleansing should haunt us all our days. The fact, and the realization that should have been on everyone's mind there, was that we could not afford to not act, and that we would need to act at some point to avoid a second twentieth-century Holocaust.

The second illustration of the need to calculate humanitarian impact was the invasion of the Krajina in the summer of 1995. A few humanitarians were saying: If you invade the Krajina, you are going to have 150,000 innocent people displaced; you ought to look at that humanitarian impact and get the UNHCR ready, and get relief articles ready to deal with a visible, realistic contingency. That impact was never calculated nor operationalized at policy circles. Rather the key people in charge then—and they included both American and German officials— overlooked the humanitarian impact and focused on the advantages of using the invasion to readjust the map of Bosnia. The numbers of innocent civilians impacted were actually much greater than humanitarians predicted—200,000 people, maybe more, were displaced. Most still remain displaced.

Then with the NATO bombing of Serbia in 1999, we witnessed the lack of humanitarian assessment, the cost of not acting on the intelligence that once that bombing started, you would have massive movements of people that had to be assisted. The failure to link this information with the organization responsible for coping with this massive people move-ment—UNHCR—represents one of the major failures in humanitarian assessment in modern times. There was a lot of criticism of the High Commissioner for having performed in a substandard manner in the Kosovo operation. Doubtless some of this was justified. But a significant responsibility for that substandard performance rests heavily on the shoulders of those who did not share the information with those capable of acting on it, and upon those who failed to calculate the inevitable humanitarian impact of not being prepared. When the bombing com-menced, and masses of people started to move, major donor states failed to contribute sufficient funds to the accountable UN agency—UNHCR—to respond adequately. When tempted to heap most of the blame on the UN, it is healthy to recall that *we* are the United Nations. Drawing on the cartoon character Pogo, when we meet the enemy, it is sometimes us.

Those are three examples from the Balkans. Now two additional examples from Africa are related:

The one that should haunt us always is the genocide in Rwanda's Tutsi and Hutu that commenced on 6 April 1994. Once the killings started, it became a kind of sleepwalking into an apocalypse that any honest observer could see coming. There was a horrifying reluctance and state of denial by most large UN member states, including the United States. Similar failures at UN headquarters have been detailed in the inquiry commissioned by the UN. Inaction, delayed action, and insufficient action resulted in the horrific slaughter of 500,000 to 1 mil-lion people. Official protests asking "What could we have done?" or apologies after the fact do little to wash the hands of those officials from whom much more should have been expected.

Next, there was an obvious disaster in the making when approxi-mately 1 million displaced persons marched from Southwest Rwanda into Eastern Zaire starting on 14 July 1994. Ironically, the march began on Bastille Day when the French pulled out of Operation Turquoise—an umbrella that provided counter genocide protection for the Hutu peo-ple. However unconscionable the pullout, the French at least put the world on notice that they were going ahead with it. The humanitarian world knew it was coming, and knew that it would indeed be a human catastrophe of epic proportions. But what these humanitarian leaders neglected to acknowledge was that even epic disasters respond to basics. The month-to-six-week warning that we had before this million-person march started offered time to plan for the first priority—water. There was even time to plan for the allocation of food shortages already ravaging refugee pipelines in Africa to give at least some attention to the impending food needs around Goma, Zaire. The common excuse for doing nothing was that it was too big to handle. It was left to an NGO in the United States, in this case the Congressional Hunger Center, to mobilize action, to prod the U.S. to do its part, and to get the U.S. to urge the UN to pick up its responsibilities. Goma, Zaire, in July 1994 is one of the saddest testimonies to the consequences of failing to calculate humanitarian impact of actions taken, or not taken.

These terrible examples, and one could cite several more on top of them, underline the importance of having a humanitarian impact assessment of what we do and what we fail to do. This ties directly to the imperative for integration and cohesion in international humanitarian response—the need to bring to bear all the tools in the toolbox that are essential to make such a response possible.

3. *Comprehensive Mission Planning.* This is a process that, again, military personnel take for granted. They do it all the time. But either by preference or default, they tend to do it in isolation from civilian planners and policy makers. It is rare for civilian planners, or any of the key civilian players, to sit down with military planners, and provide their input—their political, economic, and especially humanitarian impact information—into the mission planning process. So the result is that you often have a deficient mission—a mission that is wrong-headed, or a mission that is sub optimal, or a mission that cannot be accomplished. While mission planning is a rare process, it is one that I believe we need to look at seriously and try to operationalize in an integrated, cohesive way with all key civilian and military players. We also need to look at accessing the outside players that have useful input to planning our mission, our objectives, and our end-state. We need to find ways to reach out to the UN and NGO players, to facilitate their input to mission planning. The lack of precedents, and the lack of checklists, for such comprehensive mission planning make it a daunting exercise. But the potential value of the process makes it absolutely imperative.

4. *Civil-Military Planning for Specified and Implied Tasks to Support Humanitarian and Nation-Building Objectives.* This principle is related to comprehensive civil-military mission planning. But it goes beyond that planning to scope the range of specified and implied tasks that military forces *could* be called upon to perform in support of the humanitarian or nation-building effort. This principle was practiced for the first time for Iraq. Well before the operation started, civilian planners worked together with military planners to lay out who would do what and how coordination would be achieved.

For the Iraq humanitarian contingencies, this planning was quite thorough and comprehensive. Civilian planners reached out early to senior UN officials to attempt to paint a common operating picture of likely contingencies and how to deal with them. Although these UN planners, almost to a person, objected to the idea of any conflict in Iraq, the support that all the agency heads and the head of the task force in the UN, Louise Frechette, the deputy secretary-general, provided was magnificent. They did everything they could as far as preparedness, pre-positioning, staffing, and spending money. They were concerned enough to prepare for, and hopefully prevent, a humanitarian crisis. From our Bureau at the U.S. State Department, and from USAID, we did everything we could, and spent everything we had, to make it work.

That kind of planning did, indeed, avert a humanitarian crisis in Iraq. But beyond this coordination at the top of the UN, there was a need to acquire input from individual UN agencies and from the NGOs on individual support measures that they might need security forces to provide. This input was needed to establish the range of implied and specified tasks that the military force, the coalition military force, could be called upon to perform to support the civilian and humanitarian operation.

We had good cooperation from the NGOs, sitting down with them and going over the range of tasks they envisaged might be needed. We came up with three or four pages of specific tasks. We obtained similar input from UN operational agencies. Then we took that input to the military planners in the field, in Qatar and Kuwait, sat down with these planners, and laid out the full range of concerns drawn from the civilian humanitarian community. A few events were missed, including the looting of the Baghdad museum (other agencies pointed that out, so it was not totally missed). The major omission as we now know it was the persistence and the intensity of the resistance of the Baathists and the Fedeyeen. We foresaw the chaos, the lack of public safety, and the need for robust civilian policing linked to a justice system. We knew that shortfalls in these areas would produce major problems. But this pre-conflict planning went a long way to avoiding other major problems. Most notable, was the fact that such unprecedented planning avoided having to face a humanitarian crisis at any stage during the period following major military operations.

5. *Pre-Deployment Huddling.* A vital fifth principle is the need to undertake a pre-deployment workshop before pursuing these interventions. The only precedent for this kind of pre-deployment "huddle" of all the players is the interactive, participatory workshop that Special Representative of the UN Secretary-General Martti Ahtisaari conducted for the UN Transition Assistance Group for Namibia prior to the civil-military deployment to that country in 1989. And if you ask Ahtisaari today why this was one of the UN's finest hours, he would acknowledge that they gathered the whole team together—the civil-military team—and went to where Namibia is on the map, where you are, to whom you report and who reports to you, what your job is, who is on your flanks, what you can expect from him or her and what he or she may need from you. Ahtissari attended every session during this two-week period. He used it to build the team, generate loyalty and *esprit de corps,* and provide the best possible opportunity for integration and unity of effort.

Such teambuilding contributed enormously to the success of that operation. We should have applied that lesson learned to Afghanistan. For Iraq teambuilding occurred through what the military calls a "rock drill." But the pre-deployment rock drill was very short. It did identify critical gaps, labeled show-delayers or showstoppers, but there was insufficient time to deal with these gaps. The rock drill was conducted with the best of intentions, but fell short of realizing the full potential of such a pre-deployment huddle.

6. *Real-Time After-Action Review.* The sixth principle is the need for all the key players to conduct individual and joint assessments of how the operation is going, virtually as it unfolds from day to day. Such real-time assessments permit greater optimization of the integrated

approach. They suggest and permit necessary adjustments—both civilian and military—to personnel, priorities, and procedures. The U.S. military does this; they did it in Iraq, and they credit much of their success to the rigor of this running-during-action review. There was no comparable civilian assessment going on, by the Office of Reconstruction and Humanitarian Assistance, or the CPA, the Coalition Provisional Authority. It is hard to do. But to maximize the benefits of an integrated approach, this kind of running assessment needs to go beyond the military to include all parts of the operation so that timely adjustments can be made. This includes civilian adjustments in particular, whether it concerns civil affairs, police and justice, human rights, or infrastructure. Whatever it is that is breaking down, and wherever it is breaking down, underlines the value of daily assessments so that integrated, comprehensive adjustments can be made.

CONCLUSION

Integration, particularly the inclusion of a military component, carries risks, but none so great as sacrificing integration itself on the altar of humanitarian purity. Integration in the interest of humanity is no vice. Humanitarian exclusivity in the interest of purity is no virtue.

Humanitarianism's Age of Reason

Ghassan Salamé

IN POST-CONFLICT SITUATIONS, the first challenge is to identify the sequence of events preceding conflict resolution, and how you classify what has apparently ended is of utmost importance. Was it really a conflict? Then, what kind of conflict was it? An international police operation, a foreign aggression, a regional war, a civil war, a state collapse, all of the above, none of the above? Depending on the answers to these questions, humanitarian conditions, popular perceptions, and the kind of post-conflict settlement one should work to devise and implement are substantially different in each case.

The Germans at the end of World War II were in a completely different mind set than, say, the Somalis after the collapse of President Siad Barre's regime in 1991. Both cases could equally qualify as post-conflict situations; actual needs and perceptions were, however, extremely different in an industrialized country, the epicenter of a world war, from what they were in a marginal underdeveloped one, torn apart by small armed gangs.

One of the most common misunderstandings that confound post-conflict resolution is perspective: How do humanitarian agencies assess post-conflict situations versus how do the nationals describe what they have been going through? We think our interlocutors are coming out of a civil war while they view themselves as victims of a foreign aggression; or we think they are happy because a dictatorship has fallen while they complain about the collapse of a reassuring order. We are compassionate with their past sufferings, but they seem happy to have won their battle against some enemy group. We are motivated by the immediate past, but they have a better, deeper, somehow obsessive, grasp of history. And, looking for immediate remedies to pressing problems, we easily become fed up with history, while our interlocutors seem to have made of it their single, possessive, teacher!

Hence one of the most immediate and unnerving challenges one faces, paradoxically, deals more with the past than with the future: How far in history must we walk back and which lessons should we draw, and for what use, today and tomorrow? The easiest answer I hear is "let bygones be bygones, we are here to help you build another, brighter, future." Although such a stand is politically correct and definitely pragmatic, individuals and groups may think you despise their past, because you do not want to take it into consideration. Especially following civil wars, where to start in your narrative is crucial because at some point one group was dominating the other, before having the latter take revenge. Once, in 1975, while visiting a small Christian village in a mainly Druze area in Mount Lebanon where the people were being asked to avoid buying arms and to eschew any kind of military confrontation with their (more numerous and better equipped) neighbors, I was told: "Last time we did not arm ourselves and we lost 17 victims." "When was that?" I asked. A chorus of village dwellers replied, "In 1860!"

Given the above information, three attitudes are thus possible for humanitarian agencies to assume. One can consciously or unconsciously listen too much to one party and end up adopting its narrative; this happens more often than not. In fact, I have encountered dozens of peace-keepers and humanitarian activists who are sometimes consciously, and at other times unconsciously, pure partisans of one party, repeating its narrative without restraint. This is a recipe for disaster that strips us of our credibility and makes us a party to the conflict. The second, opposite, attitude is to ignore the past, and concentrate on the future by basically telling your interlocutors: "Your past is your property, you deal with it as you wish, we are here to help you build your future." This is certainly a more prudent stand, but somehow naïve (in view of the groups' attachment to and pride in their own past) and somehow patronizing ("We are modern and you indulge in archaism."). The third and best attitude, in my view, though the most difficult as well, is to be as knowledgeable as possible about the past. Making the effort to comprehend the history of the conflict sends a clear message that we really care about them, that we are able not only to listen, but able to develop solutions to partisan narratives of the past, that we know enough of what happened before we arrived to prevent a repetition of past tragedies. Such a stand gives us a much better standing with the various parties. Being respectful and wise enough to study their history lends to being determined to help them build a new history, not because you are ignorant of key events but precisely because you know it too well.

This has been confirmed by many studies on post-conflict situations. A knowledge of history will help identify local actors, beyond the present, always troubled circumstances, will also help understand their reactions to your proposals and therefore would help in your facilitation efforts. How many times were we faced with local leaders shouting at us: "But here it is different!" Too much reliance on your past experiences in conflict resolution can become an impediment in your dialogue with local actors. They may be ready to acknowledge that we have accumulated experience from other conflictual situations, but we also have to modestly acknowledge that no post-conflict situations are really similar, that local conditions are crucial, and that our experience drawn from past involvements all over the world is only of relative value. Packages built on your past experiences are to be tested against the peculiarities of the local conditions and possibly forgotten when faced with a new challenge.

Our characterization of the latest conflict in date is therefore crucial. Those who went to Afghanistan in 1988 and described the situation there as mainly a post-foreign-occupation situation missed the complexities of the Afghan domestic tensions and rivalries below the occupation/liberation paradigm. Those who went to Iraq and missed the complex history of that country and their even more complex fabric of society remained prisoners of the dictatorship/democracy paradigm. This is important to realize, but is certainly not the exclusive or even the most important paradigm needed to build a better future for Iraq. The durability of the settlement will depend on a number of variables drawn from each country's history. Has there been a tradition of authoritarian rule or, on the contrary, a competition between an authoritarian rule and a parallel tradition of mutual accommodation among the warring groups? Were alignments dominated by ideological factors (as in the Greek or Spanish civil wars), by social and economic interests (as in many African civil wars), by identity issues (as is often the case in the most recent civil wars in the Balkans and the Caucasus) or, more generally, by a *sui generis* combination of all these ingredients?

Politically, in Iraq, a post-conflict situation was officially declared the day a statue of the past president fell down in one Baghdad square. But it soon appeared that, from a military point of view, Iraq was entering into a state of (geographically concentrated but nationally disrupting) insurgency that was to take the lives of many more Iraqis and foreign troops than the war itself. From a humanitarian point of view, Iraq was neither in a new conflict nor in a post-conflict situation. Rather the conflict was in a stage of post-sanctions. One's view depends, of course, on perspective. My outlook is based on a deep feeling developed in Iraq that politically, even though wars have been terrible in the daily life of the population and authoritarianism has been the lot of Iraqis for decades—before as well as during Saddam Hussein's era—in the collective mental framework, sanctions have been much more harmful to daily life, the general well being of the population, and the very survival of the middle classes, than the successive wars that have hit the country or dictatorship itself.

Iraqis have known the taste of wars, harsh repression, and authoritarian nepotism long before Saddam, although he had practically three decades to excel in each of these fields, especially in his last decade in power. Still, the long years of UN-imposed sanctions appear to have been the most destabilizing factor in the Iraqis' daily life, public values, professional activity, and view of the world. Sanctions deconstructed a rather thriving economy and, more importantly, a lively, talented, upward-moving society. Sanctions produced a new, flawed, almost cynical and substantially arbitrary relationship between state and society. Ask Iraqis when their country's infrastructure began to collapse. Ask them when their salaries lost 90 percent of their value. Ask them when lawlessness became rampant, when tribalism began to surge. Ask them when civil administration became widely inefficient and corrupt. Ask them when social ills such as prostitution, disinterest in education, and lack of solidarity among family members became evident. In all cases and they would answer almost invariably: "When the sanctions were imposed on our country." I dare to add that, twenty years from now, collective Iraqi memory will probably keep sanctions as the worst source of modern misery and sadness. They may differ on the identity of who to blame for that sudden misery: the fallen regimes, world powers, and even the UN. Iraqis still have yet to see how external, government and nongovernmental actors are integrating this factor in their approach to present-day Iraq.

Again, any generalization would be dangerous. Elsewhere sanctions might have been more useful in bringing about positive change without having the same devastating effects on the society (South Africa, for example). Mentioning sanctions leads to a wider issue—the proper characterization of the fallen regime. When leaders have been around for ten, twenty, or thirty years, they tend to operate within developed successive forms of rule and control. How many times were we told that the post-Kuwait, post-sanctions Saddam Hussein was radically different from the pre-1990 Saddam? One has to develop a clear idea of the evolution of the fallen regime. In Iraq Ba'thists would be the first to recognize that the regime that fell on 9 April 2003 was very different from the one their party had built in 1978 and even farther from the one they thought they would be building. The regime's last decade in power was indeed marked by a rapid, deep, disturbing deterioration of the state/society contract: The regular army had been sidelined and the regime was relying instead on a number of competing praetorian guards to protect itself; The party was weakened by tribal and semi-religious forms of mobilization that utterly contradicted the principles upon which the Ba'th party had been established; Saddam's sons, too young to play a role before 1990, became the pillars of the latest configuration of power; Sectarianism, muted for a long time in view of the regime's secular orientation, became devastating after the savage quelling of the 1991 shi'i *intifada;* Kurdish nationalism, for which Hussein himself was willing to give substantial concessions in the 1970 Status (something for which he had been criticized by many in the Ba'ths own ranks), became radically different after the attack on Halabdja and the 1991 campaign of repression. By ignoring the crucial fact that the regime that fell in 2003 was radically different from the one pre-war American and British propaganda portrayed, as well as from what the regime had been at its inception, very serious major mistakes have been committed by the Coalition in the post-war era, including a reckless disbandment of the army at a time when it could have been used in imposing law and order, a sweeping, indiscriminate, revengeful deBa'thification that fed the insurgency with new recruits and aggravated sectarian feelings, and a poorly inspired *tabula rasa* policy in public administration that disrupted the daily life of a weakened population.

Then comes a second, no less crucial question: When does a conflict *really* end and when does a post-conflict situation *effectively* start? Of course, the line is blurred and you very rarely have a conflict that suddenly stops at a single point of time to be followed by peace. Uncertainty about the mere beginning of a post-conflict situation is an organic ingredient of such a situation and that's why we are generally unable to name it and content ourselves by saying this is the period of time that comes after a conflict is apparently over. Still, the question begs to be asked in Congo as well as in Sierra Leone, in Burundi as well as in Iraq. Is what we call post-conflict a mere lull in the fighting? Is it only the passage from one sequence to the next in a chain of wars? Is an ongoing insurgency a mere sequel of the past or the first steps in a future wide-scale rebellion?

Having witnessed a 15-year conflict in my home country of Lebanon, it was the case over and over that we would falsely think that we had reached a post-conflict situation when militias were, in fact, preparing themselves for the next phase in their fighting, when foreign powers were preparing themselves for a new kind of interference, when arms dealers were secretly making new juicy contracts. I tend to believe that being truly in a post-conflict situation should remain an open-ended question and not a for-granted one. More often than not, a post-conflict situation is viewed by local actors as one in which winning parties try to consolidate their grip on power and on resources and defeated groups prepare themselves for a new round of conflict, while neighboring countries are reassessing the situation. And, if any of the actors think that the new *status quo* is detrimental to their interests, they try to favor acts of destabilization directly or through proxies. That's why a post-conflict situation for some is viewed may be seen as a pre-conflict one as well.

Such a contrast in perceptions, of course, affects our willingness to invest in infrastructure rehabilitation, the selection of local interlocutors, the timeframe of our mission, not to mention the very essence of that mission. Are we doing what can be done before the country enters a new phase of a protracted conflict or are we, on the contrary, starting to rebuild the country because fighting is over? Our analysis will have crucial personnel, financial, and programmatic effects. But your analysis should always take into consideration the way nationals view their situation. Having ignored that in the past, a number of humanitarian missions have ended up indirectly, though substantially, helping armed groups prepare themselves for the next battle. This has especially been the case in Africa. For having mistaken a truce for a post-conflict situation, a lot of people looked naïve to the local population and/or wasted precious resources on already doomed projects. Any humanitarian mission, in such uncertain times, needs to prepare for the worst while trying to persuade the communities that conflict, like all human endeavors, is not a fatality. Working with local communities, especially when people think that foreigners are better informed, means telling them the truth while encouraging them to seek and long for more peaceful times.

One should however never underestimate the fact that while reconstruction is important in and for itself, it is also a message of confidence in the future of peace. It is therefore a bet and when, in hesitation, the bet should be positive as often as possible, especially when resources are available. Postponing reconstruction does not only mean a delay in the rehabilitation of equipment or in restoring basic public services and utilities, it also implicitly means that foreigners (governments, international organizations, NGOs) are too skeptical concerning the country's immediate future or the chances of peace for them to invest energy and resources. If only to avoid giving the locals such an impression, taking an uncertain bet on the future of peace is never too expensive: even in doubt about Israeli intentions, rebuild Gaza airport; even in fear of new fighting, build roads to connect cities in Congo, even when Taliban are active again, build the Kabul-Kandahar highway. A balance is, of course, to be found between available resources and the need to reassure locals on your confidence in their immediate future. A haste to do things may squander your funds, but too much reluctance will certainly fuel more pessimism and despair.

What is the situation in today's Iraq? Yes, it is a post-conflict situation, which means that an invasion took place and that a regime change has been imposed. There are, however, reasons to believe that resisting the invasion was merely postponed by the fallen regime until the occupation was completed, because it knew it had not the means to oppose the progress of the US troops. Its leaders chose instead to make the invader's stay extremely costly, waiting to absorb the initial shock before launching counterattacks. The Coalition war on Iraq was not a conflict but a regime change by force. The regime collapsed and the Coalition tried to impose a post-Saddam order. In the process they unleashed new forms of insurgency against the new order, incited new forms of external interference by state and non-state actors, and possibly opened the door to new forms of domestic instability. To be in a post-conflict situation is, at the time of this writing, an assumption, a bet on the Coalition's capabilities of imposing a post-Saddam order as well as a regime change that will benefit the Iraqis and produce a stable, prosperous new Iraq.

Hence a nagging issue: Should we, in the UN, really help in imposing that order at the risk of antagonizing those who oppose foreign occupation? How do we label those who challenge the new order: as resistors? insurgents? armed groups? terrorists? The same pointed question has been in post-Idi Amin Uganda, in post-Mobutu Congo, in post-Khmer Rouge Kampuchea, in post-Taliban Afghanistan, not to mention post-Saddam Iraq or even, with some provisos, in Chechnya. Here again some conciliation between one's beliefs and the population's feelings is always necessary. You do not want to adopt their vocabulary but you cannot hurt them. I understand that humanitarian action seeks to avoid such issues as much as possible, but one has to understand that local communities can be highly interested in national politics and that this is, after all, a basic right of theirs. They may think nationally, but you need to work locally and expect some tension between the two outlooks, especially when rejection of a fallen regime does not automatically translate into an acceptance of foreign occupation, as is largely the case in Iraq. Those who thought that these two concepts were synonymous are still paying for their mistake. Anyone given the responsibility of managing a post-war situation should ask every morning: "Am I doing the right thing so that a conflict is not replaced by another? Am I stabilizing the country or helping fuel another war?" Poor post-conflict management in Colombia (1957) led to a new civil war a few years later. Poor management of unity in Yemen between 1990 and 1994 led to a bloody North-South military confrontation The conclusion of the Taïf Agreement in Lebanon induced an intra-Christian civil war in its wake. Poor management in Iraq led to fueling the insurgency and *ad infinitum.* Most important is to remind oneself that past exclusion-prone, predatory elites can sometimes be replaced by equally exclusion-prone, predatory groups. Mobilization clichés against a rogue regime are of no use in dealing rationally with post-conflict situations.

Reconciling differences of perspective between the victors of the conflict and the people who live in the supposed post-conflict situation, leads naturally to another concept. I, of course, have strong reservations on "creating leadership and governance." A more modest, and certainly more efficient, way of approaching local communities is first and foremost to identify forms of leadership that are already there. I really do not know leaderless local communities. You may not be aware of those existing leaders, you may not like them, or you may not share their views, but they are always there and often where you do not expect them to be: heads of tribes, bearded clerics, more or less recycled warlords, traditional urban notables. What do you do with them? Do you recognize them although you hate their politics? Challenge them by supporting contenders closer to your heart? Try to weaken their impact among those you are helping?

A conceptual issue is central in this respect: civil society is never exactly the one you think of. There has been a wide, and very debatable, infatuation with the concept that strengthening civil society institutions is, for many, the remedy to all ills. But is this really the case? In situations of state collapse (some fifty states are more or less in this situation), the most urgent task, precisely in order to protect the society, is to rebuild a state apparatus or at least to maintain the existing one and gradually, patiently, reform it. No peaceful society can survive without a minimum of state institutions and politically recognized legitimate order. Many societies, torn apart by years of civil war long principally for the restoration of legitimate authority as a prerequisite for the restoration of civil peace. What happened in Central and Eastern Europe cannot be transplanted everywhere. When the state apparatus has been very strong, well entrenched, totalitarian in nature, building up civil society organizations in post-conflict eras is the primary task. Elsewhere, indeed in most conflictual cases in Asia and Africa, the state's weakness is much more of a problem than an asset. Reinforcing the state becomes a popular demand and an objectively urgent task as well. There is a thirst for a regularly operational, efficient, clean state that is somehow omnipresent in post-conflict situations in the developing world. External helpers, too much obsessed with civil society, often tend to ignore this. "Bring the state back in" is a rallying cry some are still not ready to hear. It is time they do.

The most crucial challenge is therefore to distinguish between the state apparatus and the political regime, avoiding an all too common temptation to identify one with the other in a *tabula rasa* approach. Conflating the two would paradoxically vindicate the fallen regime, who often tried to legitimize itself by identifying its rule with the proper, neutral, non-political functioning of a public administration. A more exhausting, time-consuming, but certainly better approach is to impose a clear difference between party and government, regular army and intelligence agencies, national police and praetorian guard, etc. Post-conflict emerging elites may not help in this endeavor, because like their nemesis, they have learned to mistake a political regime for a legitimate state. Hence the looting of public offices once a regime falls, from Mogadishu to Monrovia and from Kinshasa to Baghdad. A third party should distance itself from these easy, dangerous associations. An effort to gradually patch up elements of the defeated elites with elements of the emerging ones should then begin, as a first step toward national reconciliation. Government agencies, by allowing bureaucrats, experts, and civil servants to somehow merge in order to produce a new order that is based on some continuity of the state apparatus and on the introduction of new blood, should be a pioneering example for the society to start thinking about peaceful coexistence of various groups in a stabilized country. One common error is to mistake the management of post-conflict situations for an all-encompassing revolution. No one has a mandate to help run Iraq the way Republicans ran France in 1789, or Maoists ran China in 1949, or Khomeynists ran Iran in 1979!

Then comes the issue of what is the first thing you should think of doing in matters of governance. Elections are the answer most often heard. Let me be frank and say this is not (more precisely, not in most cases) my view. First because, more often than not, people do not call for elections as an urgent task to perform and, second, because elections are often very hard to organize in a proper way during the first phases of a post-conflict situation. Poorly timed, improperly prepared, or insufficiently credible elections are the source of new tensions and of new forms of exclusion. One should never forget that by elections, you may mean a proper way of leadership selection while others may consider elections as a way of pursuing the conflict by other means. In cases such as Iraq, elections are primarily perceived, at present, as a way of transforming a sociological majority into a political one. Which is fine with any democrat, but then, it is hard to convince other groups that elections are not primarily a way to consolidate and aggravate their exclusion. It is therefore crucial that a number of measures be taken to instill a democratic definition of the election process and to introduce safeguards that prevent elections from becoming synonymous with a rampant coup d'etat (Algeria, 1991, where the army reacted by brutally stopping the process) or with a collective punishment of a previously dominant group. As Arend Lijphart, Theodor Hanf[1,2] and many others have convincingly written, multi-confessional, multi-ethnic, multi-linguistic societies cannot be ruled through elections by a mere application of the one-man, one-vote principle. Westminster is great where it is, it is not necessarily a successful ready-made product.

To elaborate, ethnocentrism can be fatal. In societies where individualism has been the dominant political and social value for centuries, the Westminster or American type of democracy easily fits. In other societies where recently emerging individualism is still in competition with well-entrenched forms of family, tribal, or other bonds of collective solidarity and mutual help, one has to balance individual human (and voting) rights with the group's fear of losing their political standing, or even their mere existence. To organize electoral systems that prevent an automatic, brutal transformation of an ethnic majority into a legally dominant hegemonic group through the electoral process, you need time, subtle yet often complex legal techniques, and visionary, cooperative local leaders. These essentials are not necessarily available the very first day (or month, or year) the guns fall silent. Elections can be facilitated quickly, but only if they clearly are part of the solution and not part of the old problem or the source of a new one.

Governance often means the drafting of a new constitution. Of course constitutions and other basic laws can be written in a few hours, as we are often told by supposedly smart "experts." But here the process is almost as important as the end product. That is why it is crucial to help create the proper conditions for a truly national, transparent process by which a consensus can emerge gradually so that the drafting process of a constitution acts as a unifying rather than a divisive process. A truly legitimate process cannot be rushed. Various political and/or ethnic factions, leading and recognized legal experts, secular and religious leaders, and the population at large should be given a real chance to appropriate the process. Haste to impose drafts by winning groups, exclusion of large sectors of the society, drafting in closed rooms by unknown local and foreign experts, and brutal transposition of models adopted elsewhere often mar a constitutional process, affect its durability, and can incite new forms of armed rebellion.

One important factor is to be humble enough to leave it to the nationals to devise their own political future. Do not underestimate the quality of professional expertise in legal and other matters one finds in most war-torn countries. We should not rush to propose our own expertise in constitution drafting, or in other topics, in countries with an educated elite, many decades-old law schools, and/or a very politicized population. They need us to amplify their influence on events, to prop them up against warlords and thugs, but they know the country's needs much better than we do.

We can offer expertise if requested; we can play the facilitator if we are neutral; we can help devise a proper drafting process if locals feel they have reached an impasse. But those who invaded Iraq with an already written constitution in their pocket while entering Baghdad were adding insult to injury in the home country of many notable jurists, some of whom had been helping build legal regimes in neighboring countries. I fully understand that the days of absolute sovereignty are behind us and I applaud the most recent evolution in our interpretation of the concept. Still, this evolution should never reach the point where the sovereign right of a people to choose a political regime of their liking is properly denied, a position which is even less acceptable than the absolute exercise of sovereignty by authoritarian leaders.

The fine line between (an old) regime change and (a new) regime imposition by force was not really crossed in Afghanistan. It probably was in Iraq. While regime change as a superpower's policy is highly debatable—at the very least, especially when it has not been explicitly authorized by the UN Security Council—the imposition of a new political regime, constitutional arrangements included, is a clear violation of a people's right to self-determination, which is not to be confused with old-school obsessive sovereignty. Persuasion, facilitation, and mediation by foreign actors are acceptable in constitution-drafting. Beyond that, a foreign actor is merely imposing a foreign will.

In many (though not all) post-conflict situations, of much more immediate relevance than the organization of elections or the drafting of a new constitution are three tasks, equally essential for civil peace. The *first* is to ensure the establishment or the reform of national police. In order to push for an early, peaceful start of the reconstruction effort, security of the civilian population is of the essence in the immediate post-conflict period. What about existing national police? What about militias attempts to impose themselves as local police? What about the role given to the military in domestic security? What role should occupying and/or peacekeeping forces play in ensuring urban security? What about dealing with spontaneous *ad hoc* organizations practicing a police role on the local level? It is dangerous to come out with a one-size-fits-all formula in view of the substantial differences one finds from one country to the next. Sometimes there is no such a thing as a national police. In other cases, the police have been so tainted with past illegal practices and/or human rights violations that there is no other solution than to disband them; in some cases, police can be salvaged with another leadership and, more importantly, another code of conduct.

If there is one single rule in this respect, it would be to take the civilian population's fear of aggression, looting, theft of property, kidnapping, etc., very seriously. It would not be enough to put the blame on the past regime, competing militias, or even the supposedly "natural right" of some to express their newly acquired freedom by attacking their neighbors. Of course, politically motivated saboteurs may have a free run; professional criminals and recently liberated prisoners can wreak havoc in uncertain times. Still, human nature being what it is, normal people, with no crime antecedents, can and do behave inappropriately in transitional times.

In Iraq, "transitional" has a name: *Farhoud*—a time when anyone may do anything. Post-conflict transitions have a history and, fearing these special days, Islamic legal experts of the past have come to the very extreme conclusion that "a hundred years of arbitrary rule are better than one single night without a ruler." Poorly inspired attacks on government buildings have to do with a deeply flawed confusion of a fallen regime with public-sector property. By taking revenge on the state, people ignore the fact that they are hurting their future more then punishing their fallen rulers. Attacks on private property are even less excusable. Hence the importance of rapid police redeployment, a task that must be tackled empirically depending on the case, but one that should always be given the highest priority.

A *second* immediate task is justice. I am writing here of regular, ordinary, tribunals. Civil peace often depends on the rapid reactivation of the judicial system in order to settle civil disputes on property, on disappearances of heads of families, on inheritances, on pensions, on labor conflicts, etc. Clear examples showing that tribunals are operational, that justice is no longer constrained by vested interests nor by political pressure, are important early on in the process. This rebuilds confidence in the state and does not rely upon private justice or illegal (re)appropriation of property. This challenging task may be much less spectacular than the prosecution of war criminals, but it is much more vital in the rapid rewriting of a new social contract between state and society.

Grandiloquent speeches on rule of law remain useless if the population does not develop a rapid, sincere, confidence in its country's judicial system. Although repression and authoritarianism are the curses of many a country in the developing world, the failure to provide proper civil judicial courts is much more common, even in relatively peaceful and/or democratizing countries. And while the quality of the political regime is of the highest concern to those who are politically motivated, the quality of the judicial system is of utmost importance for every single citizen. It is particularly sensitive in matters of real-estate ownership.

In so many conflicts, personal property issues are intertwined with polit-ical/ethnic considerations. Sometimes personal lust has prevailed, and with others, it is collective punishment against a group. These are issues for which people are ready to die . . . and to kill. A very prudent approach should be followed (although I am not sure all international organizations were very prudent in Iraq). Real estate is not going to dis-appear, so a gradual, slow, approach is important, with a growing involvement of the national reconstituted judiciary in settling first indi-vidual cases and, later, collective cases.

Transitional justice is equally important, even on the local level. Post-conflict situations are full of acts of revenge (Frenchmen killed by their fellow countrymen after France was liberated; Algerians suspected of collaboration were killed by other Algerians in 1962; death squads belonging to various factions are operating in Iraq . . .). One is often faced with the very destabilizing factor that you cannot entirely prevent people from taking revenge on those who harmed them, but you need, on the other hand, to develop a spirit of reconciliation. Things are, of course, much easier when national institutions are still operational and can take care of these issues. But if this is not the case, acts of revenge can incite the frightening climate of a witch hunt, of collective indiscrim-inate punishment, or of new ethnic tensions.

A lot of skepticism envelops transitional justice in most post-conflict situations. In most cases, it is viewed as the victor's justice. Hence the crucial importance of international norms, so that crime is not followed by revenge and that the doors to reconciliation are left open. In general, international/national tribunals, open/closed prosecutions, and death/jail sentences are already hotly debated, and it is not my purpose to engage those debates here. They may be spectacular, and they are always highly political ("The Hague" is a *word* with so many contradictory meanings in today's Balkans!). One thing, though, is certain. These issues are much less important for most people than the settlement of judicial civilian cases that are much more vital to them. A reconstituted independent civilian judiciary, a less spectacular endeavor indeed, is the much more urgent task.

A *third* immediate task is the preservation of civil society's acquired rights. While one crucial challenge in Afghanistan has been to reintroduce women's rights, which had been suppressed under the Taliban, the main challenge in today's Iraq is to preserve the substantial progress in women's rights acquired in the past five or six decades and now challenged by some opposition forces. Civil society is not necessarily made up of liberated anti-veil women, well-shaven and environment-friendly young men, and modernistic, multilingual, intellectuals and poets. Civil society leadership is mainly made up of people who have influence unrelated to their position in the power structure. One has to be sure that a civic culture is not thrown away with a fallen regime. Many regimes have had the ambition to modernize their societies while imposing their own authoritarian rule—two mutually supportive tasks. Authoritarianism was used to destroy, or at least weaken, traditional loci of influence or power, which had the perverse effect of strengthening dictatorial rule while opening venues for non-traditional forms of group solidarity. Infatuated with their "creative chaos approach," post-modernists tend to reject both modernity and authoritarianism. The gender issue points to a wider problem. The real challenge is to maintain and reinforce the modern sectors of the society—even if they were introduced by authoritarian leaders—while also introducing democratic reforms to the political domain.

While no two cases are absolutely similar, it is natural and useful to learn from past experiences. But, then, which past experiences should we to learn from? More often than not the references are so distant that we add to the problems rather than settling them. The obsession with 1945 Germany in understanding present-day Iraq is one case among many. My view is blunt. Mistaking Baghdad for Berlin, 2003 for 1945, the Ba'th Party for the Nazi Party, Saddam for Hitler, and the Middle East for Central Europe has been and still is one of the most important US blunders in Iraq. It has unnecessarily made the US actions in Iraq much more difficult, not to mention harmful to the Iraqis themselves. This simplistic approach led to a number of unfortunate decisions such as the indiscriminate, deBa'thification that weakened the state apparatus and disrupted public services and the disbanding of the army, which beefed up the ranks of the insurgency with disgruntled officers.

I am certainly not a culturalist. I do not think that civilizations really exist as political actors, that cultural identities static, or that cultural, linguistic, or religious borders are able to prevent the dissemination of human ideas, values, or institutions. Cultural borders are real, but they keep moving. They are always relative and have a strong tendency to collapse before new ideas. Cultural identities are real but they are never reduced to one religious, professional, or cultural ingredient. They are a combination of all these. Identities are also in a permanent flux of deconstruction and reconstruction and they tend to admit, in such a process, foreign as much as domestic inputs. Cultural boundaries are thus flexible, always reshapable and easy to cross. So to present anybody as Shi'i or Tutsi or Berber as a self-explanatory qualification is, in my view, utterly stupid. As a corollary, to entirely ignore the fact that one is Shi'i or Tutsi or Berber is utterly naïve.

Humanitarian action cannot rely on instant anthropologists, the way Iraq has produced instant Iraqologists and the war in Afghanistan instant Islamologists. It is not because something is daily repeated in the media that it is true. Iraq is NOT made up of Sunnis, Shi'i, and Kurds, people who have reduced the multi-secular fabric to only one of these categories. Iraq is made of Iraqis. The identity of each of them is extremely complex and, more disturbingly, flexible, deconstructed and reconstructed by the day, taking into consideration factors such as their many-generations socialization as national Iraqis, their professional occupation, the urban/rural cleavage, their tribal affiliations, the ethnic-linguistic divide, the sectarian denomination.

That is what makes their society rich and fascinating—that tribes are often divided along sectarian lines, that sects are divided along ethnic or tribal lines, that many families have shifted their tribal or sectarian or geographic allegiances more than once in the past two centuries and, last but not least, and that many have learned to forget all this and define themselves as Iraqis. I never knew the sect of my driver in Iraq. I never asked, and he never told me. Most importantly, from listening to him, I clearly understood that his sect ties were irrelevant to him. It is irrelevant to many Iraqis I have met. The shift, in many western opinion- and decision-makers minds, from a stand where traditional loyalties are utterly ignored in the name of nation-building and modernization to a position where modernization (and its effects) is utterly ignored to the benefit of some post-modernistic infatuation with ethnicity is really disturbing. Does the author (Huntington, 1994) of *The Clash of Civilizations* still remember the fine political scientist who wrote *The Soldier and the State* (Huntington, 1957) and who was an eloquent proponent of (even authoritarian) modernization? Should fashion and/or political agendas prevent us from taking simultaneously the two issues in consideration?

One should never become an accomplice in the ongoing process of overestimating the attachment of people to their religion or the strength of their sectarian, tribal, and other traditional affiliations. I am indeed struck by the easiness with which so many Westerners tend to underestimate the strength of modern, western inspired nationalism in Third World societies. A form of amateurish orientalism, or rather anthropologism dominates the field and so many people think they have found an answer to their questions by the mere mention of some traditional piece of identity they guess in their interlocutor. What you think, or what you say, is now less relevant than what I think you are because I guessed you are Tamil, Sikh, Sunni, or God knows what. Peacemakers would be well advised not to blindly follow these intellectual fashions. We live in a world where modernity is often deeply intertwined with resilient tradition; to ignore either one of these two is to make peace even less likely.

Humanitarianism has hopefully reached its age of reason. It started as a noble sentiment, entered the body of international law a century ago, exploded during the past century's latest decades into a widely shared ideal, drifted into a full-fledged universalistic ideology, and here it is again, back to what could be a long term status not a substitute to politics nor an appendix of it but a useful, indeed indispensable, complement to economic rationality and political activity. Humanitarianism is now a mature self-confident human activity, operating in what still is basically a world of states, now slightly nuanced by limited areas of accepted world governance and of transnational norms.

In his many postings across this vast world, Sergio Vieira de Mello had to face, handle, and help solve these challenging post-conflict dilemmas. I was lucky enough to spend ten weeks with him during his last assignment, Iraq. I was deeply inspired by his juvenile optimism as well as by his quiet wisdom. I admired his open mind as well as his wide experience. Our time together was short, but intellectually intense, full of initiatives. On the second of June, I met a partner; on the nineteenth of August, I cried for the loss of a friend.

The Role of the Media in Promoting and Combating Conflict

Shashi Tharoor

FEW UNITED NATIONS OFFICIALS were more aware than Sergio Vieira de Mello of the extraordinary power of the international media to do both harm and good in the conflict situations into which the UN is thrust. This compilation would not be complete, therefore, without a brief appreciation of the role of the media in both promoting and combating conflict.

At the beginning of September 2002, I was in a television studio in North Carolina, in the southern United States, for an interview about the UN. While waiting to go on air, I was told with pride about a broadcast that the station would air the following day. Called "The Rise and Fall of Jim Crow," it was a searing documentary series about the oppression of blacks in the American south, featuring archival material, photographs, and interviews with black and white Americans who had lived through the period of racial discrimination and segregation. "We cannot understand why we continue to have racial difficulties," said the director, Richard Wormser, "without understanding this period of our history. It is part of my legacy as a white person, as it is part of the legacy of black people."

What is striking is that this series was to be broadcast in a state where the memory of blacks being denied the vote, refused service at white-owned restaurants, forced to sit in separate seats on buses and trains, and not allowed the same educational opportunities as whites, is still relatively fresh in the minds of middle-aged southerners of both races. Now television was helping both blacks and whites to confront the past in order to better understand the present. And North Carolina's schools were embracing the TV show by incorporating it into their social studies curriculums and encouraging students to embark on their own oral history projects.

This was an excellent example of the way in which the media today can—and sometimes does—work to promote understanding and tolerance across a racial or ethnic divide. But the media can also do the opposite. In the wrong hands, or with the wrong motives, it is a tool to incite hatred and violence. In Afghanistan under the Taliban, where women were denied the chance to read, and where all were denied access to alternative sources of information, the media's promotion of the creed of the *Koran* and the Kalashnikov (the *Koran* crudely interpreted, the Kalashnikov crudely made) had devastating consequences for societal well-being and human rights. In Rwanda, in 1994, "Radio Milles Collines" played a chilling role in the fomenting of prejudice, fear, and greed, with a devastating outcome—the genocidal slaughter of 800,000 people. And who can forget the hatred and lies spewed by radio and TV stations of all stripes during the wars and ethnic murders that tormented the former Yugoslavia?

But "hate media," universally detested, is fortunately an aberration. In most countries, the press enjoys a degree of freedom, and that includes the freedom to do good as well as harm. It is not my intention, as a UN official, to prescribe a particular role for the media. On the contrary, an independent media by definition should say and print what it thinks fit, without interference of any kind—a right enshrined in Article 19 of the *Universal Declaration of Human Rights.* An independent, impartial media is one of the quintessential building blocks of democracy. Freedom of the press is the mortar that binds together the bricks of freedom—and it is also the open window embedded in those bricks. By giving voice and visibility to all people—especially the poor, the marginalized, and minorities—the media can help remedy the inequalities, the corruption, the ethnic tensions, and the human rights abuses that form the root causes of many conflicts.

As the senior United Nations official charged with working with the world media to advance the goals and aspirations of the Organization, I am all too aware of the complexity of the tasks facing my colleagues and myself. We cannot afford the luxury of a "message of the day" because each day we are simultaneously putting out several dozen messages everywhere. We deal with a global audience that is both vast and fragmented, whose interests and passions diverge across borders. We try to rouse concern among the rich and the tranquil about the plight of the poor and the strife-torn. We seek to overcome the indifference of the information-saturated while trying not to neglect the needs of the information-starved. We respond to the demands of the sophisticated media of the developed North while trying not to overlook or alienate the media of the developing South. We have to work with journalists and advocates on both sides of every dispute. And we do all this in an uneven global environment, which offers opportunities and pitfalls for us all.

In one sense, globalization, whatever its sins and limitations, plays a positive role. The media bring to our breakfast tables and our living rooms, and increasingly our computers and our mobile phones, glimpses of events from every corner of the globe. Any doubt I might have had about the reach and influence of global mass communications was dispelled when I happened to be in St Petersburg, Russia, for a conference. I was approached by a Tibetan Buddhist monk in robes, thumping a cymbal and chanting, who paused to say, "I've seen you on BBC!" New communications technology has shrunk the world, and in a real sense made it all one. In many ways the information revolution has changed the world for the better, by providing a window that allows for the possibility that people everywhere will better understand their neighbors, and by allowing people who once would not even have known about the possibilities the world has to offer, with a means to take up those offers.

But the information revolution, unlike the French Revolution, is at present one with much liberté, some fraternité, and no égalité. And its twin, globalization, has yet to deliver the goods or even the tools to obtain them to many in great need. The 400,000 citizens of Luxembourg have access to more Internet bandwidth than Africa's 760 million citizens. The dividing line between North and South is not just the poverty line but also fiber-optic and high speed digital lines. If "digital divide" is a cliché of our time, it represents a reality that cannot be denied.

The media is not exempt from the consequences of this divide. While globalization gives us greater opportunities to understand the world around us, the mass media still reflects principally the interests of its producers. What passes for international culture is usually the culture of the economically developed world. There is the occasional third world voice, but it speaks a first world language. As far back as Congo in 1962, the journalist Edward Behr saw a TV newsman in a camp of violated Belgian nuns calling out: "Anyone here been raped and speak English?" In other words, it was not enough to have suffered: one must have suffered and be able to convey one's suffering in the language of the journalist. Are those speaking for their cultures in the globalized media the most authentic representatives of them?

The reality of globalization was also made starkly clear on 11 September 2001. After September 11 there can be no easy retreat into isolationism, no comfort in the illusion that the problems of the rest of the world need not trouble the fortunate few. The world now understands the other old cliché, that of the global village—because a fire that starts in a remote thatched hut or dusty tent in one corner of that village can melt the steel girders of the tallest skyscrapers in the opposite corner of the global village.

And yet the response to terrorism sometimes seems likely to undermine the very institutions of pluralism and tolerance that offer the best alternative to fanatics and killers. The media has a vital role to play in monitoring the efforts of Governments to effectively combat (and prevent) terrorist attacks without simultaneously eroding the human rights of innocent citizens and migrants. UN Secretary-General Kofi Annan has often echoed the observation that those who are willing to give up liberty for security will end up with neither security nor liberty. During the year after September 11, as an increase in hate crimes against brown-skinned minorities in the West was widely noted, there was concern that the issue was being neglected in the mainstream media. The International Council on Human Rights Policy charged in 2002 that the Western media had not done an adequate job in reporting on such hate crimes in Europe or North America. Ironically, when I addressed the South Asian Journalists' Association in New York in September 2001, the convener asked the largely Indian and Pakistani audience whether they had encountered any recent discrimination because of their appearance. Practically every hand in the room shot up.

But I have also been impressed at the way the respectable Western press has made real efforts to avoid falling simplistically into a Huntingtonian paradigm that treats all of Islamic civilization as one undifferentiated terrorist threat. I am impressed by the fact that newspapers in Europe and America (and to a lesser degree television stations) have devoted more space to the problems of Islamic countries and that they have assigned more correspondents to the Muslim world than previously. This is vital, because we all need to know each other better if we are to understand each other.

The media need to recognize that civilizations are not monoliths; each human civilization has a great deal of diversity within it. Religion and culture are merely among the many variables governing the actions and policies of States. Very often States with a common religion may have other differences among them; we just have to consider the contrasting positions taken by different Islamic States of the Taliban's rule over Afghanistan to illustrate the point. Indeed, a large part of today's intercultural conflicts are a result of perceived cultural humiliation. Much of what is happening in parts of the Islamic world, simplistically described as fundamentalism, is an assertion of cultural identities that have been allowed to feel marginalized or thwarted. The answer lies clearly in cultural diversity, and in the development of democracy at local, national and international levels to provide a context for pluralism to thrive. The media is key in conveying the message that it is ultimately diversity that gives the human species its splendor, and has enabled it to make progress, through learning from our different experiences. Every time we fail to respect each other's right to different beliefs, religious expression, and ways of life, our humanity is diminished.

It is only by perpetuating the blind hatred of strangers of an "Other" that terrorism can flourish. Such hatred is in turn the product of three factors: fear, rage, and incomprehension. Fear of what the Other might do to you, rage at what you believe the Other has done to you, and incomprehension about who or what the Other really is. If terrorism is to be tackled and ended, we will have to deal with each of these three factors by attacking the ignorance that sustains them. We will have to know each other better, learn to see ourselves as others see us, learn to recognize hatred and deal with its causes, learn to dispel fear, and above all just learn about each other. We cannot do any of this without the media.

Secretary-General Kofi Annan has suggested that the media consider practicing "preventive journalism" along the lines of the concept of "preventive diplomacy," reporting on potential crises before they erupt, so that the spotlight of the media might prevent an eruption, or mobilize international action before lives are lost. He has not returned to this theme, in part because he does not feel it appropriate to tell the media how they should cover events. But it would be helpful if the media continue to search beyond the headlines, to give attention to conflicts and crises at an early stage, in order to assist and encourage an early response.

The media, along with human rights NGOs, play a vital role in providing early warning of human rights abuses and help mobilize political will to galvanize the international community to take action. The UN itself has developed considerable experience in working with the media to promote reconciliation in divided societies, particularly as part of UN peacekeeping and peacebuilding operations. And the media can also help frame issues in ways that diplomats, trying to bring both sides of a conflict together, cannot. Thus in the Balkans it was the media that gave currency to the odious term "ethnic cleansing" and helped generate sympathy and public pressure for its international denunciation.

Much of the developed world's population obtains its news from television where the motto is all too often "if it bleeds, it leads!" Television is better at conveying image than context. In the process, the search for news, for a good "story," often becomes an end in itself, divorced from the human needs of its subjects. Journalism, that most essential of professions, is also the most predatory; it feeds on suffering, on misfortune, on injustice, all of which it seeks to depict rather than to redress. And yet, without it, no real change would be possible, since change requires awareness, and it is awareness that is the real stock-in-trade of the journalist. In our increasingly interdependent world, it is no longer possible to shelter behind claims of ignorance of foreign lands; news about anywhere is available to even the most incurious, in papers, on TV, and most of all on the Internet. What happens anywhere in our globalizing world increasingly affects us all. As someone once said about water pollution, we all live downstream.

And so it is particularly important that, post September 11, we look beyond violence to the causes of violence, and beyond apparent clashes between civilizations toward commonality and dialog among civilizations. As Socrates taught us, "There is only one good, knowledge; and only one evil, ignorance." By depicting and promoting that vital exchange of ideas and information regardless of frontiers, the media can play its part to make possible a global civilization that is defined by its tolerance of dissent, its celebration of cultural diversity, and its insistence on fundamental, universal human rights.

Earlier in this chapter I disavowed any intention of being prescriptive to the media. And yet, it is hard not to wish that the media devote more time to minorities, their plight and their problems, and to bringing the horrors of racism and religious fundamentalism (of all kinds) to light. To that end, the media can hire more journalists and editors from minorities and can carry out educational campaigns with an anti-racism message. Intolerance cannot be solved through censorship, but through an ever-livelier debate in which the ideas of the hatemongers can be defeated. The media must provide space for such a debate to take place.

At the global level, the media must recognize that there exist, around us, many societies whose richness lies in their soul and not in their soil, whose past may offer more wealth than their present, whose culture is more valuable than their technology. Recognizing that this might be the case, and affirming that cultural distinctiveness is as central to humanity's sense of its own worth as the ability to eat and drink and sleep under a roof, is part of the challenge before the media today.

The only way to ensure that this challenge is met is to preserve cultural freedom in all societies; to guarantee that individual voices find expression, that all ideas and forms of art are enabled to flourish and contend for their place in the sun. We heard nearly a century ago that the world must be made safe for democracy. That goal is vital, and it is increasingly being realized. But it will not be fulfilled unless we also realize that it is now time for all of us to work to make the world safe for diversity.

Creating Local-Level Stability and Empowerment in Cambodia

Roland Eng

Introduction

It was in a tiny jungle hut in Oddor Meanchey Province, along the Thai-Cambodian border, that I first welcomed Sergio Vieira de Mello with a glass of coconut milk. In 1992, the two of us were working there to help repatriate over 300,000 refugees who had been living along the border for over 10 years. Our work was part of one of the largest United Nations missions in history, aimed at bringing democracy to Cambodia after decades of conflict. When I first met Sergio, I wondered whether I was speaking with the right person as he looked more like a movie star with his impeccable hairstyle and perfectly ironed safari suit—than a UN official. As we began exchanging views about the repatriation process in the afternoon heat, I soon discovered that I was working with a most unusual and remarkable man. Sergio held the love and admiration of all those who knew him. Through his dedicated work with local community members and leaders, he helped transform Cambodia from a country devastated by decades of conflict in the 1970s and 1980s, to a nation striving for democratic peace and stability.

As the UN reflects on its ever-evolving role in our world and assesses how it can best assist nations that are transitioning toward democracy in a post-conflict, post-cold war, and post-September 11 world, it is important to understand how people such as Sergio Vieira de Mello helped everyday citizens and communities give life, ownership, and direction to these larger historical movements. While elections, democracy, and state sovereignty once symbolized peace and human security in our world, we now know that local level stability and empowerment are just as essential to keeping the peace. By examining the work of the UN in Cambodia, and in particular, its work at the local level, we can see how it provides us with a new model of what the quest for human security may mean in our globalized twenty-first century.

Historical Background

In 1975, close to 2 million people died as a result of direct killings, disease, and starvation under the revolutionary Khmer Rouge regime as it attempted to turn Cambodia into an experimental, egalitarian society. Between 1975 and 1978 the country's economic, political, and social systems collapsed, and basic services such as healthcare, education, as well as religion were lost. Money was outlawed, the family unit was dissolved, and village governance crumpled. The country fell into ruin. On Christmas day 1978, Vietnamese forces mounted a major offensive on several fronts and ousted the Khmer Rouge from Phnom Penh on 7 January 1979. Yet Radio Phnom-Penh continued to announce important military victories over the Vietnamese right up to 6 January 1979.

Considered by China as a provocative action by Hanoi, at dawn on 17 February 1979, some 120,000 well-equipped Chinese troops crossed the border into northern Vietnam and seized control of several towns. These military actions further strengthened the Vietnamese alignment with the Soviet Union. Meanwhile, over 250,000 Cambodians fled into Thailand, hundreds of thousands wandered all over the interior looking for their loved ones, and famine surged throughout 1979 and 1980. While Cambodia began to recover under Vietnamese rule, times were still harsh as civil war continued to rock the land.

The country became the territory for a proxy war between China, the USSR, and Vietnam. Cambodia was pitted against the United States and China and closely aligned with Vietnam and the Soviet Union. Vietnam's occupation of Cambodia, and later of Laos, represented a direct threat to the Association of South East Asian Nations (ASEAN). Twelve years earlier security concerns and the threat of communism had forced ASEAN's establishment. ASEAN, comprised of Indonesia, Malaysia, Thailand, Singapore, and the Philippines, began to galvanize support to force Vietnam out of Cambodia in exchange for a comprehensive political settlement. All ASEAN members had to cope with domestic communist insurgencies.

As a result of ASEAN's dynamic lobby, the Cambodian issue was raised at the UN General Assembly. After five years of hardship and terror under Khmer Rouge rule, Cambodia, under Vietnamese occupation, was again treated as a pariah state and remained isolated from the world community. But with the collapse of the Soviet Union, Vietnam's foreign aid dried up and its government accepted to negotiate. In 1987 intense and prolonged diplomatic negotiations about Cambodia's future began between Prince Sihanouk and Cambodia's Prime Minister Hun Sen. The first round took place in France and was soon followed by informal negotiations in Indonesia (the Jakarta Informal Meetings, JIM 1 and JIM 2). The large superpowers then entered the negotiations and the UN formally began to address the Cambodia issue. In 1990 Australia drafted a resolution proposing that the UN supervise a transition to democracy in Cambodia. The UN accepted the resolution, as did the four political factions in Cambodia. This proposal materialized as the *Agreement on a Comprehensive Political Settlement of the Cambodia Conflict* or informally, as the Paris Peace Agreements or Paris Accord. It was signed on 3 October 3 1991.[1]

When the UN first began working with Cambodia, its responsibilities were enormous. Its duties ranged from helping Cambodia redefine its geopolitical role, to preparing it for its first national elections, to repatriating the very last refugee. This holistic approach cost nearly $2 billion US dollars. It was the largest reconstruction mission in UN history. Given Cambodia's past, however, one can understand the need for such a huge and integrated reconstruction effort.

THE PARIS PEACE AGREEMENTS

The Paris Peace Agreements were not only an international agreement that negotiated Cambodia's geopolitical role in the world, but also a framework for rebuilding the nation from within. It provided the country with a blueprint for reconstructing its political infrastructure through elections and the drafting of a new constitution, as well as providing practical support in the form of peacekeepers, personnel, and funding. The ultimate mandate of the Paris Peace Agreements charged the UN with establishing a neutral and peaceful political environment within Cambodia so that the nation could decide its political future through free and fair elections. However, establishing such an environment was complex.

The country needed peacekeepers to monitor a cease-fire and to provide basic protection to the population, a newly trained civilian administration to run the country, sufficient infrastructure to provide food, water and shelter to the nation's people, and educational campaigns to prepare for the upcoming elections. In addition, 370,000 refugees had to be repatriated into damaged villages, and long-term problems such as landmine clearance and the rebuilding of schools had to be addressed. Furthermore, the UN hoped to carry out this process in a way that would honor and instill respect for human rights, gender equality, and peace. In these details the Paris Peace Agreement crossed the line from simply being an international peace treaty settling a geopolitical dispute to becoming an international effort to transform the country into a democracy through critical work at both the local and national levels.

The UN designated two important groups to carry out the mandate of the Peace Agreements—the Supreme National Council of Cambodia (SNC) and the UN Transitional Authority of Cambodia (UNTAC). The SNC served as an interim government for the country between 1991 and 1993, and UNTAC, along with its precursor, the UN Advanced Mission in Cambodia (UNAMIC), provided the personnel and resources to carry out the groundwork.

The SNC was chaired by Prince Sihanouk and composed of twelve individuals proportionately representing each of Cambodia's four political parties. In addition, four rotating Cambodian Ambassadors, representing each of Cambodia's political parties, were appointed to New York to facilitate communication with the UN. In the spirit of the peace process, the UN recommended that the group work on a consensus-basis with no single party dominating the process. The UN agreed that it would adhere to any advice given by the SNC, provided it was reached through consensus and reflected the mandate of the Paris Peace Agreements.

The formation of the SNC sent several messages to the world and to the Cambodian people. On the one hand it symbolized Cambodia's newly found sovereignty and voice in the international arena. At the same time, the SNC addressed important domestic and local needs by keeping the peace among the country's diverse political parties, and served as an apparatus of communication between the UN and the Cambodian people. In this sense, it was a way for the UN to communicate with and involve local people in the implementation of the Paris Peace Agreements, while simultaneously learning about problems on the ground.

While the SNC helped organize the transition at the national level, UNAMIC and UNTAC implemented the mission at the local level. The UN first sent UNAMIC, a team of 268 UN personnel from 23 different countries, to monitor the cease-fire, scout out the situation in Cambodia, and further define the UN mission in Cambodia. Using the information of UNAMIC, the Security Council then created UNTAC, a team of 20,000 UN personnel, in 1992, charging them with the broad mission of dismantling 70 percent of Cambodia's armed forces, organizing a free election, and repatriating over 350,000 refugees along the Cambodia-Thai border. All this had to be completed within eighteen months, in time for the national elections.

The UN's work in Cambodia was not only its largest and most ambitious mission to date, but represented a turning point in how the organization structured its operations. The UNTAC mission had seven distinct operational components—Military, Civilian Police, Civil Administration, Electoral Preparations, Rehabilitation, Repatriation, and Human Rights. Of these seven units, six were civilian in nature and primarily focused on local and community level work, suggesting the UN's evolving understanding of peacekeeping as a combination of local, national, and international level work, as well as military and non-military involvement.

THE UN TRANSITIONAL AUTHORITY IN CAMBODIA

The UNTAC mission served in Cambodia from 1992 to 1994 and had seven objectives: 1) monitoring a cease-fire within the country, 2) preparing for the 1993 national elections, 3) rebuilding infrastructure destroyed by the war, 4) repatriating 370,000 displaced persons, 5) supervising and training a civilian administrative structure, 6) training a police force of

3,600 civilians in human rights and professional development, and 7) setting up a system to monitor and protect human rights within the country. To carry out these goals, UNTAC personnel had to understand the local power structures at the village level, and work effectively with the Cambodian people throughout the country. This was quite challenging, as previous years of conflict had altered traditional structures of power within the country, and it was difficult to determine which individuals and groups were most interested and capable of supporting the mandate of the Paris Peace Agreements.

When UNTAC first entered Cambodia, local decision-making power in the villages typically centered around six patron-clients, kinship-based domains—the administrative domain, the religious domain, the knowledge domain, the spiritual domain, the economic-political domain, and the development assistance domain. The administrative domain encompassed local-level government officials hired by the state to run the villages. The religious domain revolved around the monks and the monasteries. The knowledge domain centered on schools, teachers, and doctors. The spiritual domain included traditional healers. The economic-political domain encompassed wealthy villagers who employed other villagers. The development assistance domain focused on new power structures within and outside the villages that foreign aid and nongovernmental organizations were creating.[2]

Throughout the years, the role and degree of power held by each of these domains changed as different governments and economic ideologies transformed the country. When UNTAC began work in Cambodia, it had to decide where its efforts would be most effective, and which methods of engagement would be most transformative in these constellations of local power. Ultimately, UNTAC chose to work primarily through the administrative domain, the newly forming development assistance domain (which it played a primary role in creating), and to some degree, the political-economic domain. In addition, UNTAC attempted to reach citizens in ways superseding these power structures by directly reaching people through media efforts such as UNTAC radio. These methods met with various successes and challenges in each of the UN's operational components, but played important roles in shaping democracy at the local level.

MILITARY PEACEKEEPING

The UN deployed nearly 16,000 armed and unarmed blue helmets for peacekeeping and monitoring the cease-fire in Cambodia. According to the UN, these troops were deployed in over 650 separate locations, and worked with over 250,000 local Cambodian militias in the villages. The blue helmets were divided into several units, including a headquarters staff in Phnom Penh (204), a military observer group (485), an infantry element (10,200), an engineering element (2,230), an air support group (326), a signals unit (582), a medical unit (541), a composite military police company (160), a logistics battalion (872), and a naval element (376). Over 350,000 weapons, 10 fixed-wing aircraft, 26 helicopters, and a handful of sea and riverboats accompanied them. Their duties included verifying that all foreign forces departed the country, supervising the cease-fire, beginning the military demobilization and cantonment process, and implementing weapons control and mine clearing. Attempting to contain the country militarily proved to be especially challenging, as many military members also worked in jobs in the country's agricultural and economic sectors. Hence, in order to save the country's fragile infrastructure, the peacekeepers had to intervene in the most gentle of ways.[3]

Judy Ledgerwood, a fellow at the East-West Center in Hawaii who served with UNTAC's Information and Education Division, notes that these peacekeepers gained the trust of the local population in several ways. First, their multinational nature illustrated their intentions to truly serve as peacekeepers rather than as a manifestation of any one nation's self-interest. Ledgerwood notes that when the peacekeepers arrived, Cambodians saw a multinational force of "Uruguayans, Pakistanis, Dutch, Indians, French, and so on. German military doctors provided medical care. Russian civilian pilots flew the helicopters. Australian signal men handled communications, and the roads were repaired by Chinese, Japanese, Polish and Thai engineers.[4]" Not only were different nationalities represented in the country overall, but each unit was also mixed. This prevented the targeting of certain nationalities, such as UNTAC's fifty US soldiers, hence avoiding situations such as that which occurred in Somalia. This mixing of nationalities additionally avoided communication and decision-making problems that might arise in command structure if units were divided by nationality.

Ledgerwood also notes that the UN peacekeepers were viewed as legitimate because they truly played a neutral role in Cambodia. UNTAC troops never once fired on any of the factional forces except in self-defense, and restrained themselves from entering Khmer Rouge territory. Consequently the Cambodian people came to view them as true facilitators, interested in helping them create their own future. While this behavior instilled trust and a sense of security in Cambodians, it was also problematic, as some groups labeled UNTAC troops "cowards" for not dealing militarily with the Khmer Rouge. Throughout the cease-fire, the Khmer Rouge were not viewed as upholding their end of the Peace Agreements and eventually pulled out of them and attempted to hinder the elections. [5]

Because of this, some people view the military component of UNTAC's mission as a failure. Raoul Jennar claims that the peacekeepers actually only enforced the cease-fire for the first three months after the Paris Peace Agreements were signed. Consequently, the Khmer Rouge doubled the territory they occupied and preceded to blow up bridges around the country, on average one every two days.[6] Ledgerwood also believes the fact that the Khmer Rouge were allowed to remain armed and prevented other factions from fully disarming, hence paving the road for future violence within the country, especially in terms of political violence during future elections. At the time UNTAC was fully aware of these troubles, but decided to proceed with the elections, believing that the support of the Cambodian people, the full-fledged support of the international community, and the goodwill of the remaining factions would be enough to carry the country through.

During these times, efforts were made to continue a dialog with the Khmer Rouge while simultaneously calling on them to not impede the work of UNTAC or the elections in any form. UNTAC also attempted to isolate them by restricting the flow of petroleum products into their territory. They were unsuccessful in controlling the Khmer Rouge, however, and the elections, while still held, were marred by incidents of political violence.[7]

The peacekeepers also encountered trouble in other unexpected ways. According to Ledgerwood, local Cambodians complained that

UNTAC troops lived boisterous social lives, drinking heavily, visiting brothels, and causing traffic accidents. Evidence exists that UNTAC troops, through the frequenting of brothels, exacerbated the spread of HIV/AIDS in Cambodia. While the peacekeepers played a vital role in stabilizing Cambodia, and succeeded in carrying out the elections, some of the mistakes they made at the local level still have serious consequences for the Cambodian people today, both in terms of continued election violence and social problems.

THE CIVILIAN POLICE FORCE

The UN assigned over 3,600 personnel to supervise the local police force, conduct professional training, and protect human rights in preparation for the 1993 elections. These personnel worked with over 50,000 local Cambodian police, and operated out of one central policy and management office, as well as 21 provincial and 200 district-level offices. While sixty percent of the staff was involved in the voter registration process and election monitoring, their daily duties also included dealing with traffic control, human rights abuse, and riot control. While this group had a tremendous opportunity to interface with Cambodians at the local administrative level, Ledgerwood claims that this was one of the least successful components of the mission. Unfortunately, the majority of UN personnel was not trained properly in their roles, did not possess the language capabilities to conduct their work, and did not understand Cambodian social customs. Ledgerwood strongly emphasizes the need to provide social customs training to all personnel who will be interacting closely with the local population.[8]

CIVIL ADMINISTRATION

UNTAC brought in over 224 specialists and 84 international support staff to work in over 21 government offices dealing with foreign affairs, national defense, finance, public security, information, and other areas that would deal specifically with the implementation of the peace agreements or the elections.[9] The Paris Peace Agreements vested UNTAC with complete control over these offices, including unrestricted access to information and administrative operations, the power to remove or reassign specific administrative officers, and the ability to take remedial action against any complaints received. While UNTAC staff was vested with considerable power over their Cambodian counterparts, their twenty-one offices were set up as mirror images to Cambodia's already existing administrative structure, and the group worked closely with the SNC national government. Their duties included working with the SNC on developing a framework for freedom of association and the right to assembly in Cambodia, working with judges and police to help redesign the Penal Code, working with banks to overhaul the financial system, continuing the process of property privatization, and organizing the technical and administrative needs of the media and radio. UNTAC's work with the civil administration sector was extremely important in that it redefined the roles that individuals could play in Cambodian society, and allowed them new ways to participate in the reconstruction of their country.

REHABILITATION

Rehabilitation was one of the major challenges in Cambodia. As Grant Curtis writes, ". . . the destruction of Cambodia's physical infrastructure during the Khmer Rouge regime, followed by more than ten years of isolation, deterioration and neglect, demanded that Cambodia undergo extensive rehabilitation and reconstruction before the country could proceed on a path to sustainable development. Yet in Cambodia, everything was seen as a priority, with everything needing to be done at once, and everything dependent on something else."[10] In Cambodia, rehabilitation during UNTAC's mission included serving basic humanitarian needs, such as providing food, housing, and health assistance, as well as helping former military members and refugees reintegrate into society. Rehabilitation also included rebuilding infrastructure—important not only in the physical restructuring of the country, but beneficial as a source of employment. Unfortunately, the funding for this component of the mission was raised through international donors, who were not as dependable. While the various countries pledged over $800 million in contributions at the Ministerial

Conference on the Rehabilitation of Cambodia in Tokyo in 1992, only $120 million of this was actually collected by the end of 1993.[11] Curtis also notes that because there were so many essential and immediate needs, the Cambodian government could not decide what to prioritize when spending the money. Consequently foreign aid donors and outside consultants were in charge of the reconstruction process. Some argue this led to a foreign-aid dependency problem in Cambodia, and is an example of the loss of local and national control of the peace process that still leads us to troubling consequences today.

REPATRIATION OF REFUGEES

While the military and civilian police force components of the mission focused on working with the local level government structures, UNTAC engaged with more traditional sources of village power when dealing with the repatriation, elections, and human rights aspects of the mission.

When UNTAC entered Cambodia in 1992, over 370,000 refugees were living along the Thai-Cambodian border, two-thirds of them having lived there for over ten years. Ninety percent were under the age of forty-five, and half of them were children under the age of fifteen. Under the Paris Peace Agreements, these refugees had the right to return to any place of their choosing within Cambodia, and were guaranteed human rights and fundamental freedoms in the process. Returning these refugees to Cambodia involved ensuring that they had an adequate place to live that was free from political oppression, that they had access to safe food and water, that they had a year's worth of rations, and that they had an agricultural piece of land that they could cultivate. This was quite difficult given that the country was littered with land mines, and that many refugees were returning to areas of high conflict where armed local warlords still wielded significant levels of power.

Furthermore, this work was to be completed under a difficult time constraint, given that UNTAC was hoping to repatriate the refugees in time to participate in the national elections. The UN designated the UN High Commissioner for Refugees (UNHCR) to head this project.[12] It was in situations such as these that people such as Sergio Vieira de Mello, head of the repatriation process, made a significant difference.

Sergio was able to carry out his task by truly working at the local level, by spending a great deal of time talking with individual refugees and learning about their challenges and preferences. He also networked with local leaders, village chiefs, and even negotiated with the warlords in areas where refugees needed to resettle. He made village chiefs sign agreements officially allowing refugees to return to their villages, and he negotiated with warlords to ensure their safety. By working with all those wielding power in the refugee communities, and by learning about each of their concerns and needs, he was able to get results.

In addition, Sergio seemed always able to deal with the many unexpected problems that surfaced during repatriation. For example, after the process had started it was discovered that there was simply not enough land to repatriate all refugees. UNTAC was able to increase the land slotted for repatriation and developed non-agricultural solutions for some refugees. These included provision of a housing plot or a cash grant. Over 80 percent of those repatriated chose the cash grant.[13] In addition, UNTAC worked with villages, drilling new wells, building roads and bridges, and providing other forms of infrastructure to ease the absorption of thousands of people. It was this flexibility and long-term thinking that played such a key role in the process.

Sergio's success illustrates how an approach that does not promote top-down change, but rather gives communities an opportunity to be part of the decision-making processes, can work. While his willingness to work with the warlords may have been controversial, he recognized that they were part of Cambodia's long-term landscape, and that including them as stakeholders in Cambodia's reconstruction process would produce more sustainable results.

ELECTIONS AND HUMAN RIGHTS

Managing the national elections also required intense creativity to ensure the involvement of local populations. UNTAC not only had to effectively manage the logistics of the elections, but also had to convince the Cambodian people to participate in them. In terms of logistics, the UN appointed a Chief Electoral Officer who was assisted by 198 international staff based at a central headquarters and twenty-one provincial and municipal centers throughout the country. In addition, over 400 UN volunteers were spread out over 200 districts. Their duties included providing information about the elections, training, communication, and dealing with complaints and coordination. In addition, they were assisted by 4,000 Cambodians who assisted in the registration process (which lasted for three months beginning in October of 1992), 1,000 international supervisors during the elections, and over 56,000 Cambodian personnel organized into 8,000 polling teams that worked in the polling stations during the election. Furthermore, election data and results were handled carefully, using modern, computerized equipment.[14]

UNTAC, by involving the people in the entire voting process, convinced the Cambodians that the elections would be safe, fair, and capable of making a difference in Cambodia's future. Ledgerwood notes that small factors, such as the deployment of many young, altruistic, idealistic people from foreign countries as election supervisors in rural districts, made a difference. For six months at a time they lived in one community, under very basic conditions. Through their dedication and sacrifice they convinced Cambodians of the UN's genuine interest. Perhaps most important however, was the role of Radio UNTAC, targeted directly at educating local communities about the elections and increasing their participation. Radio traditionally has played an important role in Cambodia, given the country's minimal literacy rates, oral culture, and limited access to print circulation and television transmissions.

Radio UNTAC

During twenty-three years of conflict, the Cambodian people had largely been exposed to propaganda rather than to news and genuine information. Both the Khmer Rouge and the Vietnamese government so often used the radio to disparage outside threats to their regimes that communities soon began to view the mass media as a biased source. UNTAC attempted to change the image of the media from an apparatus of propaganda to a source for facilitating meaningful discussion and providing useful information.

Would UNTAC have been such a success without the radio component? I don't think so, and I have always wondered why UN radio did not receive the credit it deserved. Professor Tommy Koh, Singapore Ambassador at Large, noted that one of the most successful aspects of UNTAC was the free and fair election organized by the UN. One of the secrets of that success was the role played by radio UNTAC. It won the confidence of the Cambodian people and was able to get the message out that the vote was secret and that voters should not be intimidated by the Khmer Rouge or by any power play. For the first time in modern history the Cambodians took up the challenge and turned out to vote in large numbers. Tim Carney, Director of UNTAC's Division of Information and Education, deserves much praise for his effort to introduce the spirit of a free press in Cambodia.

On 9 November 1992 UNTAC opened its radio station in Phnom-Penh, and by April of 1993 it had set up enough relay stations to beam the news to all corners of the country. Furthermore, with the assistance of Thailand and Voice of America (VOA), information was also broadcast from Thailand twice per day, reaching people living in the border areas. With the help of Japan, 347, 804 new and used radios (as well as the necessary batteries) were distributed throughout the country by road and by helicopter. At first Radio UNTAC broadcast three times a day, at 5:30A.M., 11A.M., and 6 P.M., based on the Cambodian workday schedule. Eventually this evolved into 15 hours of broadcasting per day during the height of the election campaigns. In addition, district electoral offices in some provinces requested tapes of broadcasts to be played at public meetings.

Initially, Radio UNTAC aimed to educate people about the role of UNTAC in Cambodia, the elections and how the media could serve as an effective tool for managing a nation in a peaceful way, despite differing needs and opinions. According to Zhou Mei, Deputy Director and Chief of Production of UNTAC's Division of Information and Education, UNTAC's programming first included only news headlines and basic features on issues such as the repatriation of refugees, the de-mining campaign, cantonment efforts, voter registration, political party registration, the impact of UNTAC's presence on the local economy, the spread of AIDS, etc.[15] Later, Radio UNTAC covered issues such as the voter registration process, the importance of human rights and the secrecy of the ballot. These topics were often covered using skits and plays. Its work was deemed highly successful, as in the first month, over a million Cambodians registered to vote.[16]

UNTAC also illustrated how the media could serve as a forum for discussion, rather than as a propaganda tool, by regularly playing messages of all twenty registered political parities, and scheduling weekly seminars where parties could state their opinions. In addition, it offered opportunities for individual candidates to respond to each other, and hosted round-table discussions on the air. UNTAC supplemented these radio broadcasts with videos, posters, leaflets, and also made the actual peace agreements available on paper.

Radio UNTAC also made its broadcasts entertaining. According to Ross Howard, of the Institute for Media, Policy, and Civil Society in Canada, Radio UNTAC mixed its shows with popular and traditional music, newscasts, talk shows, drama, soap operas, and free-time political commentary. It became the most popular radio station in Cambodia and encouraged a flood of other independent media sources to develop. During the height of the elections Radio UNTAC received 1,300 letters per day from listeners.[17] In this sense, Radio UNTAC introduced the concept of a free press to the Cambodians and, by offering a forum for expression of opinions, offered an alternative to settling differences through violence.

Radio UNTAC also helped the development of local leaders by working with local branches of political parties in its own office. In *Radio UNTAC of Cambodia* Zhou Mei discusses the many challenges and successes of developing and operating the radio broadcasts. She claims that when she first arrived to work in Phnom Penh, the radio station was simply "a mess." There was no furniture, ambiguous office space, a quarrelling unprofessional staff, and a dysfunctional station due to technical problems. The international staff had been delayed in arrival and foreigners had been hired off the streets of Phnom Penh to run the show. When the international staff did arrive, the two groups had trouble integrating, and an even more difficult time hiring local staff. Not only was it near impossible to find local staff with a background in radio, but those who were hired and seemed to have experience often lied about their previous experience, were caught stealing funds, or did not want to speak about certain political subjects on the air for fear of their safety.

There were also cultural and language barriers between the local and international staff, as well as among international staff themselves. Radio UNTAC dealt with this situation in various ways—several people were fired, and the international staff attempted to train their local colleagues in the skills required for their jobs, including language training, basic radio-producing skills, and typing skills. In order to address safety concerns of the local staff, the international staff ended up covering many of the political topics, while local staff covered such subjects as agricultural, educational, or gender issues. Ultimately, after several difficult months, staff were either able to adapt to their new roles or were fired. In the long run, several dedicated local and international staff members emerged, helping the radio station play a pivotal role in the election process.

Radio UNTAC also played an important role in developing local leadership by teaching political parties about campaigning and the use of a free press. In the weeks preceding the election, Radio UNTAC allowed each of the twenty registered political parties five minutes of airtime. Mei reports that Radio UNTAC was very strict in making these parties act professionally. Any segments that went over five minutes were cut off, and if new tapes weren't submitted each week, the party lost its airtime. Furthermore, no remarks bashing other parties were allowed to air. While the parties were initially angered at the severity of these rules, eventually they came to understand that these were necessary for fair competition, and that a free media meant not favoring one party over another.

In the end, Radio UNTAC, and those who used it, were able to convey a simple but powerful message to the Cambodian people: they would be able to choose who would govern them, and they would be free from the threat of arbitrary exercise of state power. Given the history of Cambodia, it is not surprising that this message was both clearly understood and warmly welcomed, resulting—among other things—in a 96 percent turnout for voter registration. An amazing 89.6 percent cast their ballots over a six-day period from May 23 through 28, 1993, with FUNCINPEC receiving the majority of votes, and the Cambodian People's Party (CPP) closely tied for second.

Radio UNTAC may have been a precursor to what Howard refers to as "transformational journalism," where the media plays an important role in conflict prevention by framing issues in a conflict-preventative way. This form of journalism "is committed to maximizing understanding of the underlying causes of conflict. . . . It is journalism that also seeks to explore the opportunities for resolution." At other times, transformative journalism can mean withholding a certain news story until mediators have had the opportunity to diffuse the situation, or bring together people in disagreement for an on-the-air mediated discussion. In this sense, the purpose of the media is not simply to report what is happening in the world, but to facilitate the process of discussion and dialog in a democratic society. In post-conflict societies that are transitioning to democracy, the media must step beyond the tradition of simply reporting the news, and rather play a pro-active role in creating a space for discussion. In fact, simply reporting facts without providing their context can often incite violence in unstable societies. While we may traditionally understand "objective" news reporting as the reporting of only facts, under the framework employed by UNTAC in Cambodia, objectivity emerged by having the media simply provide space for everyone's voices to be heard. Those voices were then judged by a society that had the means to express their opinions through such mechanisms as elections, exactly as it happened in Cambodia with Radio UNTAC.

The legacy of a free press is visible in today's Cambodia. Although Radio UNTAC shut down after the elections in September 1993, the country has one of the most developed media sectors in the region today. According to the Cambodian Ministry of Information, there are 6 main television stations in Cambodia, 26 radio stations, 125 national newspapers, and 36 international newspapers published or distributed in Cambodia, as well as a plethora of magazines.[18] While the government owns several of these media operatives, and there have been recent accusations of media crackdowns, the Cambodian constitution guarantees all groups freedom of the press. Furthermore, a December 2003 survey by Media Consulting and Development (MC&D) revealed that the Cambodian media has been quite active in its coverage of contentious political and social issues. The survey revealed that 21 percent of media coverage is devoted to political activities, 20 percent to police activities, 12 percent to development issues, 9 percent to economic and financial issues and 5 percent to the arts, culture and entertainment.

Other findings show that the CPP was the party most covered by the press (47 percent of political headlines), but was also the most criticized party (41 percent of the headlines written on CPP criticized the party). With up to 70 articles, the UN was the most widely covered newsmaker among development agencies and private firms. Articles featuring women accounted for 6 percent of the total. Women were mainly portrayed as victims (of rapes, murders, domestic violence, trafficking, and various diseases). In terms of political coverage, the CPP received 47 percent of coverage, while FUNINPEC received 24 percent of coverage, the Alliance of Democrats received 15 percent of coverage, and the Sam Rainsy Party received 13 percent.[19]

While it may initially appear that the CPP received the majority of news coverage, it is important to note that nearly half of its coverage was negative in tone, suggesting that freedom of the press does exist in Cambodia today. While there is still more work to be done, particularly in the area of promoting responsible journalism, the country has come a long way from Radio UNTAC's first troubled months to a society that boasts close to 200 press institutions today.

Conclusion

It has been nearly thirteen years since the UN first began its mission in Cambodia. While Cambodia's government continues its struggle for stability and development, UNTAC was successful in developing local leadership and stability in many ways— from Sergio Vieira de Mello's inclusive work in refugee repatriation to Radio UNTAC's efforts in developing a civil society and free press. While different voices within the country may still be disagreeing upon where its future lies, mechanisms do exist to make these decisions peacefully. This has been the long-term benefit of UN work at the local level in Cambodia. Perhaps the beauty of its work also rests in the fact that the UN provided Cambodians with decision-making power and control over the development and peace process. Cambodians themselves began to shape the work and role of the UN, helping it better understand where its own future and value lie in today's world, and which needs are most pressing for it to address.

It is this combination of local and international collaboration, in a world where local and international issues are intersecting at an increasing rate, which will provide us with the type of human security guarantees that we need today. Why have many important lessons from UNTAC not been heeded in recent years? The critical importance of political neutrality, the integrated approach to peacekeeping, conflict resolution and development, the international composition of a mission's staff, avoiding a top-down approach and ensuring the participation of local communities, are all essential ingredients of a successful approach. One would expect that ten years after Cambodia's first democratic elections these ingredients would be standard components of similar international operations. Sadly, this is not the case.

UNTAC's mandate was established in the early 1990s, a period in recent history when—immediately after the Cold War—there was an almost universal belief in the importance of multilateralism coupled with the conviction that conflict resolution and prevention would become more manageable than they had ever been before. Cambodia benefited from this newly found belief. But in the post-Cold War period the nature of many conflicts changed and those changes became even more pronounced after September 11. Many new conflicts were no longer rooted in different political ideologies but in religious or ethnic tensions. While the UN continued to play a role in conflict resolution and development in places as diverse as East Timor and the Balkans, more often than not the leadership of major operations was provided by one or more major political powers, or by larger coalitions of convenience (Afghanistan, Iraq, Kosovo, and others).

As a result, the political objectives of such operations, many of them short-term, became more pronounced. Other, more longer-term objectives continued to receive attention but not in the same integrated and neutral fashion as had been the case with UNTAC. In his last interview, recorded less than 48 hours before his untimely death in Baghdad, Sergio Vieira de Mello told BBC's *Panorama* that he was convinced that soldiers could not be policemen and that a broader approach to conflict resolution, reconstruction and development was required. "You occupy with a military force but you can't restore law and order with it," he said. "I have discovered in my career, and I've been in six or seven peacekeeping operations, that soldiers are bad policemen, they're not trained for that. And as a rule one should never use the military for law and order tasks. Which is why so many mistakes are being committed here." Commenting on the unnecessarily rough behavior by soldiers in Iraq he also noted that he had often pointed to the importance of respecting local sensitivities, culture, and religion. As the international community is once again forced to rethink its approach to peace making, peacekeeping and development, UNTAC's lessons and the warnings Sergio Vieira de Mello gave in his last interview deserve a good hearing.

Maintaining Humanitarian Space in Conflict Zones

In his long and distinguished career at the United Nations, Sergio Vieira de Mello held many titles; one that was very dear to his heart was Under-Secretary General for Humanitarian Affairs. In this section are chapters by three other international statesmen who have also held that critical post; they offer reflections from the very epicenter of human disaster management. Jan Egeland, Jan Eliasson, and Peter Hansen discuss the historical, legal, and moral bases for securing and maintaining safe, humanitarian space in conflict zones. Jacques Forster, from the International Committee of the Red Cross, ponders the growing dilemma facing humanitarian workers in an era when the rhetoric of "a global war against terrorism" makes the traditional neutrality and impartiality of humanitarian agencies difficult to sustain and even suspect to some.

The Challenges of Humanitarian Diplomacy

Jan Egeland

INTRODUCTION

WHEN MY PREDECESSOR as Under-Secretary-General for Humanitarian Affairs and Emergency Relief Coordinator, Sergio Vieira de Mello, was tragically and senselessly killed on 19 August 2003 in Baghdad, humanitarianism lost one of its finest advocates and practitioners. In a way that few have matched, Sergio combined in one person a deep and noble commitment to humanitarian principles with a hard-headed realism in his work to relieve human suffering in a messy and dangerous world.

This principled pragmatism found its expression in Sergio's efforts to carve out, and maintain, humanitarian space in conflict zones. The dilemmas he faced are ones which he shared with humanitarians all over the world—how to get warring parties to respect humanitarian law; how to work with the military without being identified with them; how to deal with security threats that affect the protection of civilians; how to ensure the security of humanitarian workers; and how to gain broader acceptance of the notion of humanitarianism across cultural, religious, political, and economic divides.

Sergio's death is a tragic reminder that none of this is easy. But his life should inspire in us the conviction that, through human action, the gap between the humanitarian principles and their respect in practice can be narrowed. More often than might be expected, humanitarian space can be maintained in conflict zones.

This chapter explores the notion of humanitarian space—what it means, and what needs to be done to maintain it, particularly in light of the new challenges which we face. I particularly want to explore the tension between the call of principle and the demands of the real world. Humanitarian space requires not only the unswerving devotion to humanitarian principle and the effective utilization of the technical capacities of humanitarian actors, but also effective humanitarian diplomacy. This in turn calls for a well thought through response to old and new challenges that have taken on heightened urgency in recent years.

HUMANITARIAN SPACE

The concept of humanitarian space requires some clarification. At its minimum, it requires establishing and maintaining an environment in which humanitarian agencies can work effectively to assist those who need their support. Such an environment is one where the key principles of neutrality and impartiality are the cornerstones of assistance. It is also an environment where assistance is not a tool of war but is based on need and reaches people no matter what side of a conflict they are on, regardless of military and political action.

Humanitarian space exists when combatants respect humanitarian principles, when humanitarian and non-humanitarian actors understand their respective roles, and when all actors accept their responsibilities within an overall recognized framework. It is an environment of relative security in which civilians are entitled to respect for their lives and their moral and physical integrity. It is an environment that can only exist with broad acceptance of the very notion of humanitarianism.

ENSURING RESPECT BY COMBATANTS OF HUMANITARIAN PRINCIPLES

At the very heart of humanitarianism is international humanitarian law, which imposes obligations on combatants—for instance, to observe the distinction between combatants and non-combatants (civilians), and to allow humanitarians access to civilian populations, both of which ultimately reduce human suffering.

However, in too many conflict zones, combatants not only flout these principles but also actively exploit civilian communities as a weapon of war in various ways—children are forced to take up arms; violence is committed against civilians including sexual violence against women and girls. Furthermore, combatants often deny access by humanitarian agencies to those in need.

Warring parties are often unimpressed by an appeal to the moral force of international humanitarian law: as has been observed elsewhere, morals seldom appeal to warlords.[1] But, to these warring parties, arguments of self-interest can—and should—be made. Indeed, humanitarian law, while morally inspired, also rests on a common interest among warring parties to respect certain limits—lest the other side does not do so. But there are other arguments of self-interest too, and other power which humanitarians may have. Humanitarians have a shared agenda with development and political actors—the agenda of ultimately reaching peace, reconciliation and reconstruction. In focusing on the short-term goal of alleviating the most immediate forms of human suffering, the leverage we have to persuade combatants to observe humanitarian principles can be overlooked, leading to ineffective humanitarian diplomacy.

To combat this tendency to underuse our influence, humanitarians must keep in mind that we are "selling" a moral idea that is formalized in international law, promoting a form of behavior that requires those in power to act in a certain way, and also providing a range of practical services. Humanitarians must be able to understand the particular interests and motivations of their interlocutors, and work out why we would want to change our behavior, what we need to make the change and how we can enable them to make the change.[2] To do this, humanitarians need to actively engage combatants, whether they are state or non-state actors.

For state actors, sovereignty is no longer a sufficient qualification for membership in the international community.[3] States are expected to demonstrate their commitment to uphold international law and respect humanitarian principles. As humanitarians, we must continue to draw the attention of development and political actors to breaches of humanitarian principles and protection issues.

For non-state actors, our approach may be slightly different, depending on the objectives of a given group or organization. For instance, a group with a universal message of solidarity may act differently from one seeking secession or with ethnically based objectives,[4] and may be more receptive to appeals of a moral nature. Even so, various factions seeking international legitimacy should first be judged by their willingness to respect the laws of war. The commitment of combatants to embrace humanitarian principles and human rights can be one of the first preconditions for their involvement in longer-term processes. In addition, we can also work on persuading stakeholders in the combatants' wider network in helping us get acquiescence from the combatants themselves.

This determination to use the "sticks" and "carrots" that we have should not compromise the ideas of impartiality and neutrality, provided we are prudent in observing humanitarian principles and in keeping in mind that the end in view is the ability to provide assistance to populations in need.

MAINTAINING A CLEAR DISTINCTION BETWEEN HUMANITARIAN AND NON-HUMANITARIAN ACTORS AND ACTION

Humanitarians usually operate in environments dominated by non-humanitarian actors, most of whom are armed. In the last decade, military involvement in humanitarian activities has increased and raised issues of principle and policy, in addition to creating operational difficulties. Many humanitarians are concerned that various military actors have gradually encroached into what was traditionally regarded as humanitarian space, imperiling the humanitarian principles of neutrality and impartiality. Others are concerned that in some cases, military actors, by undertaking humanitarian tasks, politicize and devalue the humanitarian "brand," endangering their security and their ability to deliver assistance.

Such concerns have assumed even greater importance in the wake of the wars in Afghanistan and Iraq. These conflicts have brought into sharper focus the explicit linkage between military, political, and humanitarian aims. They have also rekindled the debate among humanitarians on whether humanitarian agencies should advocate for the institution or expansion of military operations, if they believe that this would improve the security of beneficiaries and bring about general stability. There *are* situations where military or peace-keeping interventions will be required to ensure general security as well as access to populations in need. The International Commission on Intervention and State Sovereignty in its report entitled *The Responsibility to Protect,* issued in 2001, suggests a framework for "humanitarian" intervention, which will perhaps lift some of the moral weight off humanitarian agencies who prefer to opt out of debates on intervention for fear that it may affect their neutrality and impartiality.

Humanitarians can question the legitimacy or wisdom of particular military actions, but once they have been instituted, they can find themselves working in complex military environments. This is, after all, the age of complex UN peace-keeping and peace-building operations, and of a whole series of comparatively new military players—ISAF, ECO-MOG, EU forces, and Occupying Powers to name a few. Humanitarian agencies have still not fully established the appropriate mechanisms for relations with all of these new players.

It would be a mistake to assume that these actors will all automatically share the views of humanitarian agencies on the delineation of roles in humanitarian operations. For example, in crisis situations these military players may be more concerned about the rapid deployment of personnel, equipment, and supplies and less intent on ensuring that the right perceptions are created on the ground.

Here, too, effective humanitarian diplomacy is vital. Every effort should therefore be made to try to clarify these relationships in advance and anticipate possible problems on the ground. Equally important are efforts to communicate with and educate these new constituencies of the importance of respecting humanitarian principles, and of how this is done practically.

In the last few years, the distinction between humanitarian and non-humanitarian actors has been further complicated. In addition to armed actors, there has been increase in the importance of another set of non-humanitarian actors, namely civilian contractors implementing aid programs funded by the military. Civilian contractors are more difficult to distinguish from humanitarian agencies: after all, they do not carry arms. They are civilians and may appear to implement programs that are similar to those of humanitarian agencies. The challenge humanitarians face with their key constituents is differentiating themselves from civilian contractors, particularly given the superficial similarities that exist between the two. The importance of this issue may grow in future complex emergencies where a sizeable amount of bilateral aid available may attract more of these actors.

An important response to this range of challenges was the formulation of *the Guidelines on the Use of Military and Civil Defence Assets (MCDA) to Support United Nations Humanitarian Activities in Complex Emergencies.* The *Guidelines,* which were officially launched in June 2003, are the result of nearly three years of deliberations between Member States, International and Regional Organizations, and Agencies from both the humanitarian and military communities. This generic document is meant to provide the framework for drafting guidelines for particular operations in specific emergencies.

One such guidance paper was the *General Guidance for Interaction between UN Personnel and Military and Civilian Representatives of the Occupying Power* that was prepared by the Office for the Coordination of Humanitarian Affairs (OCHA) for the Iraqi Crisis. Based on the MCDA document, it was adapted to the realities and requirements of the particular situation in Iraq and provides clear guidance on permissible and non-permissible actions of humanitarian actors in their contacts and interaction with military forces in Iraq.

Humanitarians within the United Nations system are in a unique position in their ability to use humanitarian diplomacy to promote humanitarian space. They can—and must—use the institutional authority of the organization, and the very principles on which it is based, to articulate and promote principled humanitarian action, and to try to infuse those principles into political and peace-keeping activities.

However, their very relationship with other parts of the UN system—particularly the political and peace-keeping actors—can affect perceptions and blur the distinction between humanitarian and relief and political or peace-keeping action.

Humanitarians therefore walk a fine line between leveraging different aspects of the UN system and promoting humanitarian principles. They need to continue building on the complementarities of character between the different facets of the organization. They must also use their unique position to advocate that humanitarian assistance and humanitarian actors only provides temporary relief to human suffering. Humanitarian efforts cannot and should not be used as an alternative to political action in countries that are not seen as strategically important as a lowest-common-denominator alternative to political action or as a cover for a lack of political will to resolve conflict.

ACCEPTANCE OF RESPONSIBILITIES IN RELATION TO HUMANITARIAN SPACE

The effectiveness of humanitarian action does not exclusively depend on the work of humanitarians. It hinges on the acceptance of a framework of responsibilities in relation to humanitarian assistance by different actors whose actions affect humanitarian space. So while humanitarian agencies have the responsibility to assist wherever there is need, governments, local authorities, and *de facto* authorities also have a responsibility to facilitate access and security to populations in need.

Humanitarian agencies are denied access to affected populations in too many crises where they are deployed. Today, there are over twenty countries where access to civilian populations in need is in some way restricted. For instance, in Uganda today, outside the main northern and eastern towns, access has been dramatically reduced by the increased activity of the Lord's Resistance Army (LRA). Some 1.3 million people have been displaced by the war. Many of these people are living in "resettlement camps" in inaccessible areas, with severely limited access to their lands, their livelihoods and to humanitarian assistance. In these circumstances, food aid provided through the World Food Programme is saving more than 80 percent of the population from starvation, but even this food aid is vulnerable to looting during LRA attacks. Humanitarian access is entirely dependent on limited and unreliable military escorts provided by the Ugandan government.

In the occupied Palestinian territory, humanitarian access continues to be a cause of serious concern. Recent developments, including the construction of the Israeli security barrier, will only serve to further limit the access that affected communities have to humanitarian assistance, essential services, and their livelihoods.

Humanitarians must work with governments and non-state actors to systematically address restrictions on access. Humanitarian diplomacy is crucial in ensuring humanitarian access by promoting and ensuring the acceptance of responsibilities in relation to humanitarian assistance. Just as there are places where these responsibilities have not been accepted, there are areas where humanitarian diplomacy has been successful. Take the work of the UN led by Sergio in the Democratic Republic of Congo (DRC) in 1996. In negotiations with the Congolese government, the UN persuaded the government to waive its concerns over national sovereignty and allow humanitarian agencies to access people in need in eastern DRC by the most practical route.

The Challenge of Security Threats

There has been an evolution in the nature of security threats—new weapons, new ways of conducting wars, new ways of inflicting violence, and new ways of deterring those who would keep the peace and those who would bring assistance. This lack of security cannot be viewed as a static problem, but rather as a shifting series of challenges that we must all address with innovative policies and tools—one of which is more effective humanitarian diplomacy.

Security threats directly impinge on humanitarian space in two ways: they obstruct humanitarian access and the protection of civilians; secondly, they affect the security of humanitarian workers.

Humanitarian Access and the Protection of Civilians

The experience of humanitarians in Namibia and Angola shows us that human rights abuses are more likely to take place in geographically isolated areas where humanitarians are denied access or where the deliberate erosion of security is used as a pretext to deny access to humanitarians.[5]

In northern Uganda, where humanitarian access has been severely limited because of security conditions, more than 10,000 children have been abducted by the LRA over the past 12 months alone, and forced, through brutal means, to become child soldiers, laborers, and sex slaves. Fear of abduction by the armed groups has created tens of thousands of "night commuters" throughout the north and east of Uganda—children who walk up to three hours to the major towns every evening before dark, simply to avoid abduction. The recruitment and use of child soldiers is a problem mirrored in many other conflicts and one that requires security, access to, and protection for children.

A lack of security also raises other protection issues, such as increased sexual violence in armed conflict. The fact that women continue to constitute a large part of civilian victims in armed conflict demands urgent and vigorous attention. Rape and other forms of sexual violence continue to be used as brutally devastating weapons of war—in the Democratic Republic of Congo (DRC), Burundi, West Africa, and far too many other conflicts around the world. In DRC, in particular, extreme crimes of sexual violence—described by some as "sexual torture"—have taken place on a chilling scale.

The example of the DRC shows us what the return of a measure of security can mean for restoring humanitarian access. The turning point came with a strengthened peacekeeping force and the political commitment of the government and the regional actors, supported by the international community, to a peace process which has begun to take hold. As a result, humanitarian access has begun to improve after years of deterioration, in turn improving humanitarian conditions in areas where peace-keeping forces have been deployed. In eastern DRC, increased access has inevitably revealed greater need and the need to provide more physical protection for civilians, particularly women who were subjected to sexual violence.

These are but two examples of the protection issues that arise in insecure environments where humanitarian access is limited or non-existent. As the improvement of security conditions largely depends on political or military actors, humanitarian diplomacy is one of the tools humanitarians can use to negotiate for improvements in security conditions. Humanitarians should also use humanitarian diplomacy to bring about more accountability, particularly of those who perpetrate these violations, through the right to protect framework as part of humanitarian principles. Despite the inherent risks in these fragile situations, the international community must recognize its responsibility to ensure adequate and timely resources to bring about peace and security.

Security of Humanitarian Workers

Security threats do not only endanger the people that humanitarians seek to assist. Security threats also affect the overall security of humanitarian workers. In the past year alone, humanitarian workers have been killed or abducted in Afghanistan, Cote d'Ivoire, Iraq, Liberia, the Democratic Republic of Congo, the Occupied Palestinian Territory, Somalia, and the Sudan.

Humanitarian emblems have provided humanitarians with a certain protection, based on an understanding and acceptance of their humanitarian mission. This has now been tragically challenged in Iraq and Afghanistan.

One of the particular security concerns for humanitarian workers has been the ferocity of terrorist attacks against them. Unlike other state and non-state actors that can be involved in different ways, as outlined earlier, terrorists pursue a completely different set of objectives which are unknown to us and in which, presumably, humanitarian principles are irrelevant.

These challenges point to the need for more robust international response to crises. They also increase the importance of humanitarian diplomacy. Humanitarians must encourage the Security Council, through its various mechanisms, to continue to stress to all parties to armed conflicts their obligation to ensure the safety and security of humanitarian personnel and to ensure that those responsible for attacks are brought to justice without delay. Member states must be encouraged to not only pinpoint but to tackle some of the possible root causes of terrorism: alienation, desperation, failures of political processes, and disenfranchised constituencies.

BROADENING THE ACCEPTANCE OF HUMANITARIANISM

The challenges to humanitarian space outlined above require broadening the acceptance of humanitarianism which rests on three key pillars: 1) the universal acceptance of the humanitarian idea, 2) a greater involvement of local communities, and 3) a geographically more diverse support base.

Universal acceptance of the humanitarian idea is particularly important in light of the very northern and western footprint of humanitarianism. This geographic bias feeds perceptions of humanitarianism as a Western campaign, resonant of missionary efforts in the last century. The success of being able to cut across traditional divisions hinges on actively involving non-traditional participants, such as Islamic welfare and relief agencies, not all of which have the same views of humanitarian principles, structures or resources as their northern counterparts.

There has also been another cause of this misperception of humanitarianism—the belief that people are most likely to help their "dearest and nearest."[6] also called by some, "a doctrine of 'cultural proximity.'"[7] Humanitarians must restore value to interaction with people, by continuing to raise the awareness of their domestic constituencies, to crises where there are not necessarily political, economic or strategic interests.

The *involvement of local communities* as well as beneficiaries in this dialog is crucial. The security of humanitarian workers often rests in the hands of local communities and depends on their trust in the intentions of humanitarians; they also play an important role in influencing non-state actors, either through their social or economic influence. Humanitarians must more vigorously pursue a dialog with local institutions; they must foster incremental engagement, taking on board the concerns of stakeholders and finding better, more precise definitions of humanitarian space.

Finally, humanitarians must *increase the narrow base* that supports international humanitarian action. Since there are no assessed contributions for humanitarian activities, as there are for political or development activities, humanitarians inevitably face alternating ebbs and flows of contributions to humanitarian assistance, often based on the political interests of a handful of countries. This overall decrease in multilateral aid and the increase in bilateral aid may indicate waning interest in multilateralism.[8]

Broadening our support base by engaging more donors, humanitarian personnel, and NGOs from the South is vital. We cannot allow multilateralism to wither—we have to demonstrate and promote the value of multilateralism to develop new partnerships with new donor countries such as the growing economies of Asia, Latin America, and Eastern

Europe. We also have to be more effective in enlisting new types of part-ners, such as the Diaspora to provide resources and know-how for humanitarian solidarity.

All of these are concrete, practical steps we can take to promote a moral and ethical transformation in international relations and domestic politics and power struggles—one that ensures that we, as humanitarians, have the capacity to act always and everywhere in accordance with our humanitarian principles and in support of humanitarian space.

CONCLUSION

Challenges to the support and implementation of our programs present at an opportune time of technological advancement that enables rapid response to developing crises. We have tools, logistical capabilities and early warning systems. We can provide relief and expertise and opera-tional leadership to disaster-stricken areas within hours nearly anywhere in the world. Our assistance has become more operationally effective, timely, and targeted.

But what good are stand-by arrangement for relief goods and person-nel if humanitarian space is not respected? What good can humanitar-ian workers do if they are deliberately targeted by political actors or terrorists? What good are our logistical capabilities if we do not have broader support for our actions?

If we are to use this capacity to achieve humanitarian outcomes we must use humanitarian diplomacy to bridge the gap between humani-tarian theory and practice.

Humanitarians need to engage with all actors, clearly laying out the humanitarian principles involved, and pointing out the benefits that can accrue from those principles being observed. In their dealings with all parties, they need to be scrupulously impartial and principled, and build their credibility accordingly.

Sergio Vieira de Mello was the quintessential diplomat and one of the most accomplished practitioners of humanitarian diplomacy. He instinc-tively understood the negotiations that were required to create the cir-cumstances and conditions for effective humanitarian assistance. Sergio showed us that, in addition to being master planners, sharp analysts, adaptable logisticians, and articulate advocates, humanitarians also need to be determined diplomats. To further humanitarian action, we need to foster a culture of influencing debates and being aware of proposals, concessions, bargaining tactics, keeping in mind that humanitarian principles are our non-negotiable bottom lines.

Passion and Compassion

Jan Eliasson

I WOULD LIKE to pay tribute to Sergio Vieira de Mello by first offering a brief historical note to the rules of law that should have protected him on his final mission. Then I shall pose a number of challenges that continue to face humanitarians in conflict zones.

During the summer and fall of 1991, the international debate on humanitarian action was intense. Paradoxically, the end of the Cold War in the late 1980s led to more civil wars and internal strife both in the Balkans and in Africa. Conflict resolution became even more complicated and civilian casualties even more extensive. Dealing with conflicts inside nations triggered fundamental questions of sovereignty. I chaired the United Nations General Assembly Working Group on Emergency Relief, formulating a humanitarian mandate for the UN in December 1991. UN Resolution 46/182 established the position of Under Secretary General for Humanitarian Affairs, a UN position I was honored to initiate, and which Sergio eventually held.

Bernard Kouchner of France carried the torch of *"ingerence humanitiere,"* humanitarian intervention, which was met with strong suspicion and criticism from many developing nations. Was this not in fact a humanitarian Trojan Horse hiding political schemes of overturning distasteful governments in the developing world?

This type of reaction clearly influenced the negotiated text of UN Resolution 46/182, which stressed the responsibilities of sovereign states, underlined the requirement of consent, and limited UN action to humanitarian crises and natural disasters. No one during these negotiations in 1991 used the term humanitarian intervention or dared speak about intervening against grave human rights violations.

How much has changed since the adoption of Resolution 46/182 and the establishment of Department of Humanitarian Affairs?

Many challenges and critical tasks remain; they are both short-term and long-term, both concrete and conceptual. First of all, there is an immediate and urgent task to deal with security, physical security. We must find ways to assure respect for international law, humanitarian law, which is the responsibility of all governments, as well as all parties in a conflict. There exists a document that outlines UN policy on keeping its workers safe known as the *Convention on the Safety of United Nations and Associated Personnel of 1994* (see appendix). Although we have instruments in place designed to prevent events such as the tragic bombing of UN headquarters in Baghdad, to be realistic, we must recognize that there are some groups who function outside a formal government's control.

I think it's very important to put a strong pariah stamp on any action against humanitarian workers, and let it be known that those who are part of supporting or helping movements that attack humanitarian workers will be clearly labeled with that same pariah stamp. We have to be able to reach out to those who cannot sign the conventions.

Another part of the security problem is one that goes to the deeper issues of the political arena. The United Nations, and all humanitarian workers, must be careful to define the mandates under which they serve. One can see the difference between the clear mandates for Afghanistan, UN Resolutions 1300 and 1373, and the situation in Iraq, where we have already paid the price for an unclear mandate. Where the mandates are unclear, it is very difficult for humanitarians to maintain neutrality.

No doubt there has been progress in awareness of humanitarian issues. To place the human being in the center has been a positive result of the end of the Cold War. Nations are no longer seen as pawns in geopolitical chess games—they are societies, composed of individuals with rights and needs.

UN Secretary General Kofi Annan has played a crucial role in moving forward humanitarian concerns as well as the global community's responses to gross violations of human rights. Standing up for the individual's dignity so sharply and courageously, as an African, as the most prominent international civil servant, Annan has contributed more than anyone else to dispelling the notion that humanitarian action, or even intervention, is a North/South issue.

Also the awareness of an urgent need for prevention and preventive diplomacy has tangibly grown in the last decade. During my years at the UN, particularly dealing with the crisis in Somalia from 1992 to 1993, I increasingly felt frustration, anger, and despair over late responses, neglect of early warning signs, and passivity facing emerging crises. In fact, when I left the UN in 1994, I went to Uppsala University as a Visiting Professor to deal more deeply with the fundamental issue of preventing violent conflicts. Many shared my reaction to the raging humanitarian disasters of the early 1990s. Our aid workers were like firemen who were on day shifts as well as night shifts and who, all too often, came to houses that had already burned down.

Both inside the UN, among governments, and in the important NGO community, the advocacy for prevention was impressive in the 1990s. The Center for International Health and Cooperation published a seminal text *Preventive Diplomacy,* in 1996.[1] The Swedish Government adopted an Action Plan for Prevention in 1999. The European Union established a similar program in 2001, encompassing the fifteen member states and the European Commission. Within the UN, the General Assembly, the Security Council and the Secretary General all have underlined the need for early action, coordination, and comprehensive approaches, deeming them important elements in maintaining humanitarian space in conflict zones.

Still, I must say, we have a long way to go.

Enhanced awareness is always an essential first step. But it must be followed by concrete and rapid action, and by adapting the responses to the need for coordinating such action. Coordination in today's world means close cooperation, not only within the UN and the Bretton Woods institutions, but also between other international organizations, governments, and NGOs. Progress is being made, but not enough.

Someone has said that democracies do not prepare well for things that have never happened before. The pessimist would say that even if we go through disasters, lessons learned seem hard to come by. We still lack political will and the optimal organization to react and react early. When did we last see the headline, "The Disaster Did not Occur"?

We are now seeing an impressive mobilization to deal with the humanitarian challenges in Afghanistan. If we are to learn anything as humanitarians from the Afghanistan crisis, we should now urgently identify other nations and places where conditions are such that not only humanitarian disasters but also political extremism can evolve. Somalia is a case in point. A massive effort in dealing with the long-standing Somali humanitarian crisis could mean the difference between life and death for hundreds of thousands of people, the difference between peace and war, and the difference between economic development and political disintegration.

Earlier I mentioned "the human being in the center" as becoming an increasingly accepted humanitarian aid strategy. Still, I cannot hide my deep disappointment over the rampant disregard for human life, both when it comes to civilian populations and to aid workers in armed conflicts today. Far too often, we see breaches of international law, including the violation of humanitarian neutrality. Far too often we see civilians and humanitarian workers become hostages or victims in political or military crossfires. World leaders and world public opinion must rise against such unacceptable violations of international law and of human dignity.

One of the more hopeful developments today is the acceptance that effective action means coordinated and global response. Even hard-core critics of multilateralism—and there are many, not least being the United States—are agreeing that no one can fight terrorism, money laundering, and organized crime alone. There has to be effective international cooperation. This change of attitude, brought home by the September 11 tragedy, could, and should, spread to other areas such as migration and refugee issues, health and development, arms control, and the environment. Indeed, we may face a historic opportunity to make international cooperation a natural reflex of enlightened self-interest.

But if we do not want to add this opportunity to history's long "List of Missed Opportunities," we have to make sure that there is an institutional framework, a structure, which is strong and flexible enough to deal with the complex issues facing us. Furthermore, we must develop a political framework that provides—with the UN in the center—the mandate and authority to act quickly and decisively in early stages of conflict. Here governments and NGOs have important roles. Political acceptance of substantial, far-reaching multilateral cooperation is necessary and sorely needed. The absence of cooperation and failure to preserve the safety of humanitarian space resulted in the death of Sergio Vieira de Mello. Yet his legacy inspires others to carry on this noble work.

Sergio was very much the ideal of both a diplomat and a humanitarian. He was so well spoken and versed in his profession, that he was as at home with the Presidents as he was with those who did the most menial field tasks. He always put problems in the center, not the institutional structures. The problems are here; how do we deal with them? he would ask. Today we still have many frustrating limitations, and depressing realities, but we also have new possibilities, new opportunities, and we have the potential to do more, to do better. This applies to governments, the NGO community, international organizations, and, last but not least, the essential organization, the United Nations.

Maintaining humanitarian space requires the support offered by international law. For example, there are conventions, treaties, and laws that assure humanitarian access to civilians in conflict zones, that uphold the right of innocent individuals to protection in conflicts, that preserve the rights of minorities, and that guarantee respect for religious minorities, ethnic, and racial groups. In humanitarian work, in conflict resolution, and in reconciliation, an absolute respect for cultural sensitivities is also indispensable, and that was just a portion of the genius Sergio brought to his work.

Finally, I want to end by remembering two facets of Sergio's personality. He was a person who combined passion and compassion. Without passion, nothing happens in life. Without compassion, the wrong things happen. In the end it is human beings who move the world, and it is those human beings that we are trying to help with both passion and compassion.

Preserving Humanitarian Space in Long-Term Conflict

Peter Hansen

INTRODUCTION

WITH VERY FEW EXCEPTIONS, it has been considered self-evident among those in the humanitarian community that to achieve a reasonable measure of success humanitarian action in conflict zones should be predicated upon notions of neutrality and impartiality. In recent years, particularly following the outbreak of numerous local and regional armed conflicts in places such as Angola, Afghanistan, the Balkans, Iraq, Sierra Leone, Burundi, Ethiopia and Eritrea, Chechnya, Colombia, and East Timor, an increasing number of observers have challenged this traditional presumption of humanitarian action, arguing that "humanitarian actors are deeply involved in the political sphere."[1]

For anyone familiar with the humanitarian imperative that has come to define so much of what the United Nations (UN) has stood for since its founding, the implications of this challenge are great. If humanitarian space is purposefully compromised by assuming a political character, the risk of that space collapsing altogether becomes all too real and dreadful as a prospect. Some have suggested that the attack on UN headquarters in Baghdad in August 2003 was the result of "a dangerous blurring of the lines between humanitarian and political action" and "the consequent erosion of the core humanitarian principles of neutrality, impartiality and independence" of the UN humanitarian mission.[2] This line of thought maintains that the gradual erosion of humanitarian space in Iraq has been the result of the "choices made" (i.e. policy choices) by the international community through the UN since 1991, beginning with years of hard-hitting sanctions imposed by the Security Council, followed by "the lack of a clear UN mandate" in the aftermath of the US invasion and occupation of Iraq in 2003.[3] The conceptual dilemma it presents is something that would seem to require the careful consideration of all who find themselves on the front-line of humanitarian action in conflict zones, particularly at this critical juncture in the history of the humanitarian enterprise.

This chapter examines what is meant by the concept of humanitarian space, and how such space is best maintained in conflict zones while taking into account divergent views on the subject. To this end, I explore how the largest humanitarian actor in the Middle East—the United Nations Relief and Works Agency for Palestine Refugees in the Near East (UNRWA)—has struggled to maintain its humanitarian space in a particularly volatile conflict zone for over five decades. It is hoped that the international humanitarian community will find UNRWA's experience useful in navigating the conflict zones in which they operate, to be better able to maintain their humanitarian space and to continue to better serve their beneficiaries.

HUMANITARIAN SPACE: PRINCIPLES, CHALLENGES, AND UNRWA's EXPERIENCE

In his 1995 Annual Report, former Secretary-General Boutros Boutros-Ghali noted that "[s]afeguarding both the concept and the reality of 'humanitarian space' remains one of the most significant challenges facing the humanitarian community."[4] But what exactly is meant by the term humanitarian space? It has been variously described, *inter alia,* as follows:

- "Humanitarian space is more than a physical area; it is a concept in and through which impartiality and non-partisanship govern the whole of humanitarian action. . . . in moral terms," [it is] "a space that is not delimited, that is made up of tolerance and respect for each and every individual once they are wounded or captive, and displaced persons or refugees, no matter to which side they belong."[5]
- "If we assume that war and violence are extensions of the political, then we understand the traditional description of humanitarian space as an area separate from the political."[6]

- "Humanitarian space is a dynamic term. Far from being like a walled room of fixed dimensions, humanitarian space . . . expands or contracts depending on circumstances. It may be circumscribed—or expanded—by the actions of political and military authorities; it also may be enlarged—or contracted—by humanitarian actors themselves. In short, humanitarian space is neither durable nor transferable but elastic."[7]
- "Humanitarian space is that space where humanitarian assistance is provided on the basis of need and is delivered with impartiality. Humanitarian space is 'owned' by humanitarian agencies and actors and extends from their inherent values of independence and impartiality. Military forces must minimize any movement into 'humanitarian space.' Any such movement serves to blur the distinction between humanitarian and military actors . . . ."[8]

It is apparent from the preceding characterizations that humanitarian space is based upon two central assumptions. First, it exists simultaneously on both a physical and moral plane. Accordingly, medical relief convoys and hospitals are as much a part of humanitarian space as the awareness by military and para-military actors that refugee camps must be respected as violence-free civilian areas. Second, humanitarian space is predicated on the need to maintain designated areas that are neutral and impartial within larger spaces that are inherently political. For example, in the heat of a military conflict between two or more combatants, the provision of medical aid to civilians and other non-combatants in designated health clinics must be protected and respected as inviolable by all parties. Historically, especially over the course of the twentieth century, the concept of humanitarian space has evolved in response to the increasing level of violence experienced by and directed towards civilians and other non-combatants in times of war. In answer to the need to provide protection and assistance to such vulnerable populations in conflict zones, neutral and humanitarian institutions such as the International Committee of the Red Cross (ICRC) and the UN were established, and the international community promulgated an extensive body of international humanitarian law,[9] central tenets of which have been the concepts of humanitarian action and humanitarian space. In the context of the Arab-Israeli conflict, UNRWA has maintained a humanitarian space over its 53-year history that is unique in the UN system. From focusing in its very early years on refugee reintegration activities, UNRWA has developed into a multi-faceted organization that provides essential education, health, relief and social services, and micro-credit, to over 4 million Palestine refugees throughout its areas of operations. In addition, the vast majority of the over 24,000 agency staff are Palestine refugees themselves, which itself uniquely marks the humanitarian space that UNRWA occupies.

Because of the highly volatile and prolonged nature of the conflict in which it operates, UNRWA has been compelled to maintain its humanitarian space in a wide variety of "conflict" situations, including periods of war (1956, 1967, 1973, and 1982), periods of limited and prolonged occupation (1950–1966, 1967–present in the West Bank and Gaza Strip; 1982–2000 in Lebanon) and periods of insurrection (1970 in Jordan; 1987–93, 2000–present in the West Bank and Gaza Strip). In each of these periods, UNRWA has faced numerous challenges to its humanitarian space, including: threats to the physical safety and security of its staff and pupils; the detention without charge or trial of its staff; curtailment of the freedom of movement of its vehicles, goods, and staff; the misuse, damage, and/or demolition of its installations and premises; and the damage and/or destruction of refugee shelters.

While UNRWA has exerted great efforts to maintain its humanitarian space over the years, the period since September 2000—the month in which the current intifada in the Occupied Palestinian Territory (OPT) began—has presented some of the most difficult challenges in its history. Limitations enforced on UNRWA's humanitarian space have been numerous, and have included severe access restrictions and armed attacks on its personnel and installations.

Many of these limitations on UNRWA's humanitarian space have contravened applicable principles of international law, including the *Charter of the United Nations,* the 1946 *Convention on the Privileges and Immunities of the United Nations,* the *Fourth Geneva Convention* and the 1967 bilateral exchange of letters between UNRWA and the Government of the State of Israel (known as the Comay-Michelmore Agreement). More importantly, these violations have contributed to the development of what the Secretary-General Kofi Annan's then Personal

Humanitarian Envoy, Ms. Catherine Bertini, termed a serious "humanitarian crisis" in the OPT during a visit to the region in August 2002.

In addition to the Arab-Israeli conflict, armed conflicts in other regions in recent years have given rise to a debate as to whether humanitarian action must be neutral and impartial in order to be effective in meeting its goals. According to Weiss, a number of developments in the 1990s—including "the complete disregard for international humanitarian law" in conflict zones, "the direct targeting of civilians and relief personnel," and "the protracted nature of many so-called emergencies that in fact last for decades"—has split the humanitarian community into two groups.[10] On the one hand are the traditionalists who "believe that humanitarian action can and should be strictly insulated from politics," and on the other are the "political humanitarians, who believe that political and humanitarian action cannot and should not be disassociated."[11] This split has been exacerbated by the international community's increasing willingness to deal with humanitarian crises as threats to international peace and security, most particularly in high profile cases, allowing for the simultaneous and at times combined deployment of military and humanitarian personnel in conflict zones.[12] This incremental integration of the military with the humanitarian witnessed in recent years has brought into sharp relief the dilemmas of humanitarian action and the maintenance of humanitarian space in the contemporary period, and "carries crucial policy and institutional implications for the humanitarian enterprise."[13]

A good example of a recent conflict that captures the essence of the debate and the resulting dilemma is the war in Kosovo. For the traditionalists, the widespread reference to that war as "humanitarian" was regarded as a particularly striking, if not offensive, oxymoron. As noted by one traditionalist:

> . . . how can a war—essentially something that causes destruction, losses and unspeakable suffering—be 'humanitarian'? Even if the motives are of a humanitarian nature—defending the basic rights of any human being—war itself cannot be 'humanitarian.' This most inappropriate libel . . . has been very detrimental to the humanitarian concept itself, and to humanitarian action as such. The 'merging' of military and humanitarian operations has been facilitated by this gross contradiction in terms, and the ensuing confusion has grown exponentially.[14]

For the "political humanitarians" such "confusion" was a welcome development. In their view, the simultaneous bombardment of Serb forces along with the provision of relief assistance to Kosovar refugees made it possible to stop even greater atrocities before they took place, thereby saving more lives as well as bringing about conditions for a relatively quick political settlement. In this sense, the resort to force was the lesser of two evils, and one that better served the ultimate objectives of humanitarian action.

To the traditionalists, because humanitarian space is neutral and impartial, its proper maintenance depends upon its separation from the political and violent. Because such space is viewed as finite, traditionalists hold that if it is increased there is necessarily less space available for the political/violent and vice-versa.[15] Warner has noted that this "zero-sum" relationship has particular "implications for the occupation of a bounded area," [16] such as during a state of belligerent occupation. For example, if a legal aid center run by a humanitarian agency is raided and shut down by an occupying power, or the protection afforded to refugee camps is violated by military or para-military actors, the total area of political/violent space has increased at the direct expense of the humanitarian space formerly maintained by the humanitarian actor. Such has been the case on a number of occasions where UNRWA installations in the OPT, schools and health clinics among them, have been forcibly commandeered by Israeli military forces for use in military operations, or when both the Israeli military and Palestinian militants violated the humanitarian space of the refugee camps in the OPT by conducting armed activities in them.[16]

For political humanitarians, on the other hand, humanitarian space and the political/violent do not operate in a zero-sum context. They argue that the expansion of humanitarian space allows for the parties to the conflict to avoid having to reach a swift political settlement, ultimately resulting in greater civilian suffering. As Warner notes:

> The recent rise in interest in humanitarian affairs is an abnegation of responsibility by those in power. That is, instead of admitting that civil wars or outbreaks of violence . . . are very political activities, these outbreaks are termed humanitarian crises in order to avoid hard decisions

about what to do . . . In this sense, upholding humanitarian principles is a *political* move that may undercut the ethical basis of the [humanitarian] organization's activities. [emphasis added][17]

The maintenance of humanitarian space is therefore seen by political humanitarians as an act that effectively shifts "attention away from the politics at the heart" of a conflict, thereby allowing it to continue interminably while humanitarian agencies scramble for limited budgets to dole out "Band-Aid" operations on an ostensibly "temporary" basis.[18] UNRWA has been subjected to such criticism over the years by both parties to the conflict.

On the one hand, Israelis and other supporters of Israel have accused the UNRWA of "keeping the refugee issue alive" by reaffirming Palestine refugee identity and rights, thereby rendering a political settlement of the problem in their view far more difficult to achieve. On the other hand, some Arabs and Palestinians have accused the UNRWA (as well as other international organizations) of providing a "humanitarian cover" for the Israeli occupation, thereby relieving Israel of its humanitarian obligations under international law and enabling what in law is meant only as a temporary condition to remain prolonged and without a final political settlement.

Is the divide between traditionalist and political humanitarian approaches unbridgeable? Is there a more nuanced and less polarized way to approach the maintenance of humanitarian space in conflict zones? It would seem that "humanitarians cannot deny political realties,"[19] and that political actors in a conflict must acknowledge that they too have a vested interest in opening and helping to maintain humanitarian space that is neutral and impartial. As noted by Mary Anderson, the key factor that must be accepted by all humanitarian actors is that, irrespective of motives, the aid they provide has multiple political impacts and can either exacerbate or ease the conflicts amid which they work.[20] For instance, "[t]o the extent that international aid agencies assume responsibility for civilian survival in war zones, the aid they provide can serve to release whatever internal resources exist for the pursuit of the conflict."[21] In this way, it can be said that humanitarian aid carries with it certain "substitution effects."[22] As noted above, in the context of

UNRWA's work, the Agency has been accused by the Palestinians that its vast array of humanitarian and human development aid has effectively underwritten the Israeli occupation, relieving the occupying power of the tremendous financial burden of administering the occupation and enabling it to divert precious resources towards consolidating its military control over the OPT. Similarly, international aid can have "legitimization effects," in the sense that the recipients of such aid may regard the fact of their receiving it as a legitimization of their political cause or struggle. This is particularly true if the recipients are a distinct group belonging to or overlapping with a party to the conflict. Again, in the UNRWA context, it is widely known that the Palestine refugees consider the Agency not merely as an international aid agency providing for their essential needs, but also as the physical/institutional embodiment of the international community's commitment to their welfare. In this way, UNRWA can be said to be perceived by its beneficiaries as "humanitarian plus" in both its role and identity.

Humanitarian aid can also have certain "distribution effects," essentially referring to the divisions that necessarily result among people in a conflict zone when aid is provided to one group to the exclusion of others. As a humanitarian actor charged with the task of assisting the Palestine refugees in areas that include considerable numbers of Palestinians who are non-refugees (in the UNRWA definition of the term), UNRWA has come under the criticism that its humanitarian aid has actually increased divisions among the Palestinians and done relatively little to assist a large sector of the Palestinian population that, in many cases, is as needy as the Palestine refugees themselves. A final impact that exacerbates or eases tensions in a conflict zone is known as "market effect." Because "international aid has a significant impact on wages, prices and profits" in a conflict zone, such aid can "either reinforce incentives to continue warfare or . . . promote and support non-war economic activities."[23] While UNRWA's humanitarian interventions and ultimately its humanitarian space has historically been concerned with focusing on the provision of the essential needs of the Palestine refugees as well as their human development, in recent years the international community through the General Assembly has mandated it to run micro-credit programs with the aim of providing the refugees with the economic incentives not only to build their communities, but also to help increase humanitarian space through the promotion of non-war-related economic activities. This mandate blends in well with UNRWA's socio-cultural contribution to Palestinean refugee society. In addition to its obvious material contributions that UNRWA provides to its beneficiaries, it also contributes to the development of Palestinian society through the passing on of socio-cultural mores and values promoting mutual tolerance and gender parity based on essential principles of the UN organization: freedom, equality, and dignity.

Although Anderson's analysis treats politics as forming an integral part of the role of humanitarian actors, adopting it is not inimical to the core principles of humanitarian space as neutral and impartial. On the contrary, this approach actually demands that neutrality and impartiality continue to form the cornerstone upon which humanitarian space is maintained. Neutrality, in this sense, cannot be understood merely as not taking sides in hostilities or engaging in controversies of a political or ideological nature, as defined by the ICRC, for instance.[24] Rather, neutrality should be the principle by which a humanitarian actor provides assistance in conflict situations where such assistance is objectively required, having no regard to the dictates or political positions of the parties to the conflict. Neutrality cannot mean equidistance between the parties to the conflict, and a humanitarian actor must position himself based on an ethical compass of justice and fairness. Likewise, impartiality must be understood as making no other discrimination in the provision of humanitarian aid other than on the basis of need, giving priority to those most needy. In this sense, identification or sympathy with race, religion, nationality, and other such characteristics must have no bearing on the provision of aid. In essence then, the efficient and effective humanitarian actor must continually act, and be seen to be acting, as making a good faith effort to remain neutral and impartial in situations that are inherently political. This is not an easy task, by any objective account, but it seems to be one that is required if humanitarian space is to be maintained in a world where the tragic effects of war and conflict are increasingly being borne by civilians. As noted by Weiss:

> In today's world, humanitarians must ask themselves how to weigh the
> political consequences of their action or inaction; and politicians must ask

themselves how to gauge the humanitarian costs of their action or inaction. The calculations are tortuous, and the mathematics far from exact. However, there is no longer any need to ask whether politics and humanitarian action intersect. The real question is how this intersection can be managed to ensure more humanized politics and more effective humanitarian action. To this end, humanitarians should be neither blindly principled nor blindly pragmatic.[25]

In addition to the effects of resource transfers on conflict zones listed above, Anderson identifies a number of "implicit ethical messages" in humanitarian activity that also affect conflict. One of these messages is the idea of "impunity" of humanitarian staff who control scarce resources, such as vehicles and fuel, and sometimes "use them for [their] own pleasure without accountability to the people for whom the resources were intended, even when their needs are great."[26] Another such message is the idea of valuing lives differently,[27] highlighted when international aid agencies furnish expatriate staff with supplemental "hazard" pay for serving in particularly harsh duty stations, while failing or being unable to extend similar benefits to local staff. While humanitarian action carries with it a number of other implicit ethical messages, these few examples highlight the difficulty inherent in maintaining humanitarian space without attracting criticism from those who are affected by it. Like many other humanitarian actors, UNRWA has faced criticisms of an ethical nature while seeking to maintain its humanitarian space. For example, funding constraints have prevented UNRWA from extending "hazard pay" to its area staff on a continuous basis, though expatriate staff receive the same.

As noted earlier, humanitarian space is elastic and its contours are continually defined by the parties to the conflict and the humanitarian actors involved in the situation. Special attention must be given to those occasions where a political actor's perceptions impel it to limit humanitarian space to the point where the continued maintenance of that space becomes virtually untenable. Such cases often occur where a party to the conflict enjoys a preponderance of power in a given conflict zone, such that any limitation of humanitarian space by that party is justified under the doctrine of "military necessity" or "national security." Resort to "security" interests provides the disproportionately powerful party to the conflict with a discretion that effectively trumps the efforts of the humanitarian actor to maintain humanitarian space. This problem is compounded by two factors. First, the notion of "military necessity" or "national security" is itself so nebulous as to allow the claimant very wide latitude vis-à-vis the humanitarian actor. Second, the claimant enjoys such overwhelming control over the physical space in which the humanitarian actor operates, that there is usually little that the latter can do to actually reverse developments on the ground. In the OPT, the Israeli authorities often state that the restrictions on UNRWA's humanitarian space are necessary due to considerations of military security or are justified under Israel's inherent right of self-defence. One of the bases upon which this claim is advanced is the Comay-Michelmore agreement which requires the Government of Israel to "facilitate the task of UNRWA to the best of its ability, subject only to regulations or arrangements which may be necessitated by considerations of military security." At no time have the Israeli authorities and UNRWA been able to agree on the scope or application of the language relating to "military security." While UNRWA has taken the position that the term can only be construed narrowly in the specific emergency context of the immediate post-war period in June 1967, and is in any event not applicable by virtue of Article 103 of the *UN Charter*,[28] Israel has taken the position that the term continues to apply to its operations in the OPT, over 36 years after the close of the 1967 hostilities, and has traditionally construed it very liberally. This has resulted in greater limitations on humanitarian space in the OPT than UNRWA believes are reasonably necessary.

When one party to the conflict is so powerful as to enjoy overwhelming control over the physical space in which the humanitarian actor operates, it is useful to consider the options available to maintain humanitarian space. One of the more obvious options is for the humanitarian actor to engage the powerful party in negotiations/discussions on issues of concern, including reference to relevant provisions of international law, status agreements which the humanitarian actor may have with the powerful party, and general appeals to the humanitarian imperative and practicalities. Here, skills of persuasion and diplomacy must be employed in convincing the powerful party that the maintenance of humanitarian space in the conflict zone is ultimately in its own interests, not only military, political, and economic, but moral as well.

When such negotiations/discussions are exhausted, another mechanism that is available is to attempt to persuade the powerful party to cease its limitations on humanitarian space through public pronouncements, either in the media or otherwise. This has been put to good use in many conflict zones in defence of human rights and protection of civilian persons and refugees, among many others. It is a widely accepted form of conflict management and moral suasion that can, if employed properly, can be utilized to great effect. This is particularly so in the current information age, where sources of information are unprecedented and knowledge can be transferred around the world, quite literally, at the click of a button. What must be stressed, however, is that publicity must not be used in a frivolous manner nor resolved to in haste. As in negotiations, good judgment is required in making the decision to "go public" and reticence in doing so is generally to be advised, if only for the sake of maintaining credibility and guarding against any backlash that may result from alienating the powerful party to the conflict. Should publicity fail to render a result, however, the humanitarian actor may look to regional and ultimately international intervention to help maintain its humanitarian space. The increasing number of times the international community has resorted to the use of sanctions and even military force since the early 1990s is well documented. Suffice it to say, that both the Security Council and regional bodies, such as NATO, have been employed in various conflict zones around the world in the name of humanitarian assistance, which itself has increasingly allowed the concept of "humanitarian intervention" to be debated by policy makers, academics, and commentators alike. Of course, humanitarian intervention is a matter which only states—and then only a very limited number of states at that—may initiate, but there have been precedents where humanitarian actors have played a central role in the intervention effort once underway. Examples include the UNHCR's role in repatriating and providing humanitarian aid to refugees in Iraq, Bosnia-Herzegovina, Kosovo, East Timor, and Afghanistan.

For its part, UNRWA has not accepted limitations on its operations and has sought to engage the parties to the conflict in a dialog, at times resorting to publicity in an effort to maintain its humanitarian space. Thus, it has continued to make representations to the Israeli authorities at all levels, including meetings with the Israeli Ministries of Foreign Affairs and Defence, to have constraints on UNRWA's humanitarian space removed or alleviated. As a matter of policy, UNRWA has agreed, without prejudice to its positions of principle under international law, to consider pragmatic solutions that attempt to meet legitimate Israeli security concerns, while easing the movement of its staff members and other such restrictions on its humanitarian space. On other, far more limited occasions, UNRWA has issued public statements on the situation of the refugees (for instance with regard to the demolition of refugee shelters) casting light on the practices of various parties to the conflict and calling upon them to change their behaviour. Finally, on an even more limited number of occasions, UNRWA has relied for support of its humanitarian activities on the international community through the General Assembly and the Security Council, albeit not through economic sanctions and military force, but through the reaffirmation of the need to support UNRWA in ensuring "the safety of civilians" in the OPT and calling on all parties to "respect the universally accepted norms of international humanitarian law" as stated for example in Security Council Resolution 1405 of 19 April 2003. Overall, UNRWA's efforts to engage the Israelis on these issues has been unrelenting and principled in its commitment to core humanitarian values. Nevertheless, the responses of the Israeli government have been grossly inadequate to address these issues. According to a November 2003 status report issued by the Task Force on Project Implementation in the OPT, the "multiple assurances" given by the Israeli government that "humanitarian aid will be fully facilitated . . . contrast dramatically with the facts on the ground," and the "operational environment" has "deteriorated to a degree which many donors consider both unmanageable and unacceptable."

Nevertheless, very serious limitations continue to be imposed on UNRWA's humanitarian space in the OPT, primarily, though not exclusively, by the occupying power. Israeli soldiers throughout the OPT have on many occasions failed to show respect for UNRWA personnel, their vehicles, or their identification cards, as required under international law. On-duty staff members also have been verbally abused, physically assaulted, threatened at gunpoint, and shot at. Since March 2002, eight UNRWA staff members have been shot and killed by Israeli troops, and agency ambulances have been shot at by Israeli soldiers. In addition, there have been many instances where UNRWA installations, particularly schools, have been shot at by Israeli troops, resulting in a number of deaths of and numerous injuries to both school staff and pupils. For their part, the Israeli authorities insist that such shooting incidents occur only because Palestinian militants fire on Israeli positions and settlements from within UNRWA school compounds. While there have been a very limited number of such incidents at the beginning of the current intifada, UNRWA moved to provide 24-hour unarmed guards for all of its facilities and called on the Palestinian Authority for greater police protection. In addition to violating UNRWA's privileges and immunities, even the search and inspection procedures imposed by the Israeli authorities on agency staff in the OPT can pose a threat to their safety and well-being. Such is the case in the Gaza Strip where UNRWA staff and vehicles are required to be searched prior to being allowed to enter the Al Mawasi area. Staff must remove their protective flak jackets and helmets, put this equipment and any other items being carried in their vehicles through a mobile x-ray machine and walk through a metal detector. This process leaves staff members completely exposed to possible gunfire, which periodically erupts in the area, while the Israeli soldiers are protected behind concrete walls or in fortified positions. In addition to shooting incidents, movement restrictions imposed by the Israeli military in the OPT have severely impeded provision of regular and emergency agency services to Palestine refugees. Accessibility to health service installations in the OPT has been hindered for both patients and staff, including those being transported in ambulances and requiring critical care.

In the face of such seemingly overwhelming obstacles, the humanitarian actor must make every effort to engage parties to a conflict that resort to "military necessity" and "national security" grounds on their own terms. As noted, the humanitarian actor must challenge, wherever reasonable, the logic upon which such claims are based. An effort must be made to convince the disproportionately powerful party that its "security" may not reasonably be under threat and that its overall national interests may in fact be better served by helping maintain humanitarian space intact. Such efforts require a good understanding of basic international humanitarian law doctrine such as military necessity and proportionality, and a willingness to engage the political actor on these terms. They also require an acknowledgment on the part of the humanitarian actor that the neutrality and impartiality of the space it aims to maintain sometimes depends on actively engaging with political players, and that given the balance of power on the ground, their efforts may often produce little or no results. Such are some of the pitfalls of maintaining humanitarian space in conflict zones that have been marked by protracted political disputes.

UNRWA's efforts in actively defending and maintaining its humanitarian space in the OPT have encompassed a wide array of activities and programmes. Foremost among them has been its Refugee Affairs Officer (RAO) Programme initiated during the intifada of 1987–1993. Following the request of the Secretary-General to enhance its "general assistance" capacity in the OPT, the RAO programme was launched in 1988 to facilitate UNRWA operations in the difficult circumstances of the intifada and to provide a degree of passive protection to the refugee and non-refugee population of the OPT. The program included a "legal aid scheme" run by UNRWA for the benefit of the refugees. Following the conclusion of the Declaration of Principles of Interim Self-Government Arrangements (DOP) in 1993, the RAO programme was phased out.

During the current intifada, UNRWA launched the Operations Support Officer (OSO) Programme to reinforce its existing operations in the OPT and to help deal with the increasingly severe access restrictions faced by the UNRWA. Like the RAO programme before it, the OSO programme aims to maintain the humanitarian space in which UNRWA operates. It has accomplished this by, *inter alia,* helping to facilitate access of staff members and UNRWA vehicles, reporting on the developing humanitarian crisis in the OPT, and in monitoring and inspecting all UNRWA installations on a regular basis to ensure that they are not being used for any unauthorized or improper purposes.

Another important policy of UNRWA that has helped it maintain its humanitarian space has been the standard requirement of its staff to remain at arms length from all activity, particularly political, that may call into question the neutrality and impartiality of its humanitarian mission. Among other things, agency staff have been instructed to conduct themselves in accordance with established principles and practices of the UN and of the need to refrain from engaging in any activity that is incompatible with their status as independent and impartial UN civil servants. In particular, staff have been informed that they must be scrupulous about the protection of UNRWA installations against any kind of abuse or unauthorized use which may reflect negatively on the agency's position as an independent and neutral body of the UN, including ensuring that political meetings are not held in UNRWA installations, that posters of a political nature are not affixed to the premises, and that UNRWA property, including vehicles, is not in any way used for any purpose unconnected with UNRWA operations. UNRWA staff have been informed that any misuse of their position will—in addition to creating legitimate apprehensions in host countries, in the occupying power, and in donor states, regarding the confidence to be reposed in the agency—result in disciplinary measures being taken against the staff member, including the possibility of dismissal. Although these statements of UNRWA's commitment to neutrality and impartiality have been accepted by its staff, some criticism has been levied by staff members and the wider Palestinian community accusing the agency of attempting to infringe upon the right to free speech of its staff members. This is demonstrative of the tension that exists in the process of maintaining humanitarian space not only in the OPT, but in any conflict zone where local staff strongly identify with one or the other party to the conflict.

What of the future of humanitarian space? Lincoln Chen has noted that "the ultimate shape" of humanitarian space "is being contested by public policies and action on-the-ground," and "will be determined, in part, by new issues, new ideas and new players."[29] One such idea is the concept of comprehensive "human security" which he identifies as having "four basic principles": first, that human security is "people-centered," as opposed to state-centered; second, human security comprehensively promotes freedom "from both violence and poverty"; third, human security is strategically based on protection from the state and empowerment at the grassroots level; and fourth, human security is interdependent in the sense that the security of one can never be achieved at the expense of another.[30] The idea of comprehensive human security meshes neatly with global developments on every score, from the social-scientific to the political, from the economic to the technological.

The tension that has emerged between bilateral and multilateral approaches in addressing humanitarian crises is another issue that will affect the nature and scope of humanitarian space in the future. As noted by Mégarand Roggo, recent years have witnessed a trend among governments indicating a preference for a bilateral approach in humanitarian matters over a multilateral one,[31] despite the fact that such an approach may not be in keeping with the humanitarian goals sought. For instance, following the invasion and occupation of Iraq by a United States-led coalition in 2003, the occupying power set out to provide humanitarian aid to needy Iraqis in order to allow it to, among other things, project itself as a friendly force that had come to serve the best interests of the Iraqi people. This has raised questions of legitimacy and credibility of the humanitarian actor and possibly limited the humanitarian space available in occupied Iraq. Even in the case of UNRWA, despite the credibility and legitimacy it enjoys among the refugees, some donors prefer a bilateral approach to addressing humanitarian challenges. This phenomenon emerged following the onset of the Oslo process in 1993 and the establishment of the Palestinian Authority, further worsening the financial situation of UNRWA.

As noted above, the information age has played a significant role in helping expand and maintain humanitarian space in conflict zones. All signs indicate that the role of media and information in this regard will only intensify as technology and access to it develops. A good example of the use of technology and information to expand and maintain humanitarian space are the specialty websites devoted to the topic of humanitarian intervention and activism, such as the OCHA-run ReliefWeb. This is in addition, of course, to the growing body of academic and specialty journals on humanitarian action, refugees, and other such subjects with a humanitarian focus. For its part, UNRWA has its own website and has regularly made use of the media (through press releases, interviews, and periodic newspaper articles) to help promote its mission among its stakeholders and the international community at large, all of which has enhanced its ability to maintain its humanitarian space.

In conclusion, it can be said that the decade since the end of the Cold War has been an immense challenge for all humanitarian actors. The marked increase in inter-state and intra-state conflict, low-intensity conflict, and the rapid proliferation of non-state actors in conflict situations has caused untold suffering to innocent civilians around the world. These events have posed considerable challenges to the maintenance of humanitarian space in conflict zones. The humanitarian community today has to tread a fine line while adhering to principles of neutrality and impartiality in areas that are inherently political and usually violent. While UNRWA is unique in the UN System by virtue of its organizational status, beneficiary base, and evolution of its mandate, it has faced and continues to face the same challenges in maintaining its humanitarian space that all humanitarian actors now have to deal with. UNRWA's experience with multiple conflict situations, in the OPT in particular, provides a useful example for other humanitarian actors to follow. It goes without saying that the contours of humanitarian space will continue to be shaped by those who are actually engaged in the activity of humanitarian intervention—states, multilateral organizations. and civil society actors. As such, new measures to promote the idea of humanitarianism all over the world, most particularly in conflict zones, should be developed in a manner that highlights the great importance of the values that lie at the core of humanitarian action and space, including neutrality and impartiality, but also encompassing core principles of justice, fairness, equality, and liberty.

Challenges to Independent Humanitarian Action in Contemporary Conflicts

Jacques Forster[1]

Introduction

THE ABILITY of an independent humanitarian organization such as the International Committee of the Red Cross (ICRC) to protect and assist people affected by armed conflict or internal violence depends first and foremost on the acceptation of the organization and of its activities by all parties concerned. Failing that, humanitarian action is either impossible or excessively dangerous both for the persons that are to be protected and assisted, and for humanitarian personnel.

Although the ICRC had experienced severe and murderous attacks on its staff in the past, 2003 was a particularly dark year for its humanitarian activities. Indeed, between March and October, ICRC staff was deliberately targeted in three separate incidents in Afghanistan and in Iraq, causing the deaths of four colleagues. The October 27 attack—a car bomb loaded with one ton of explosives aimed at the ICRC delegation in Baghdad—indicated the perpetrators' intention to reduce to a minimum or to stop altogether humanitarian action. This attack and that which had taken place two months earlier on the UN headquarters in Baghdad, compelled humanitarian actors to analyze more precisely this phenomenon and to reflect on ways and means of maintaining an adequate space for humanitarian action in such situations. The challenge is compounded by yet another difficulty: the tendency for political actors in some conflict situations to combine military and humanitarian activities, arguing that security, relief, and reconstruction are all part of the same process. Under such circumstances, is there still a space for independent humanitarian action?

The answer to this question needs to consider the broader framework of the September 11 terrorist attacks against the United States (US) and the reaction they engendered. These were focusing events of what might well prove to be a new phase in the history of conflicts as a global dimension was added to the already complex maze of local, national, and regional conflicts. A new configuration emerged in which a State declared itself at war with a loosely knitted transnational network conducting or encouraging terrorist attacks in different parts of the world. The greater prominence of terrorist attacks and the response thereto also led to a debate on the qualification of the global struggle against terrorism—is it a war?—as well as on the relevance of the body of law specifically designed for situations of conflict, i.e., international humanitarian law (IHL). Since humanitarian action as conducted by the ICRC is based on the rules laid down by IHL, the present chapter will address both

- the operational challenge of maintaining an adequate space for humanitarian action in situations such as those encountered recently in Afghanistan and Iraq and
- the issues raised by the questioning of the adequacy of IHL in the context of a global struggle against terrorism.

Humanitarian Space and Contemporary Conflicts

The Concept of Humanitarian Space

The concept of "humanitarian" space refers metaphorically to the capability of humanitarian organizations to implement protection and assistance activities in situations of conflict—international or internal—or internal violence. According to the spirit and the letter of IHL this "space" should enable humanitarian action to protect and assist at all times the persons entitled to such protection and assistance (sick, wounded, or captured combatants as well as civilians). Limitations to humanitarian space occur 1) when access to such persons is denied; 2) when an area is out of bounds for humanitarian personnel, and/or 3) when some of the core activities of humanitarian protection and assistance cannot be developed.[2] Larry

Minear notes that humanitarian space "may be circumscribed–or expanded–by the actions of political and military authorities; it may also be enlarged–or contracted–by humanitarian actors themselves." Access, he adds, reflects "not only the constraints imposed on humanitarian actors but also their own ingenuity and resolve in mobilizing and managing humanitarian resources."[3]

Elaborating on Minear's assertion, one could identify four sets of parameters that influence the scope for humanitarian action–humanitarian space:

1. the environment in which the conflict takes place (from the global to the local levels);
2. the goals, interests, and methods of the armed actors taking directly part in the conflict;
3. the policies of actors indirectly involved in the conflict (third States, international organizations);
4. the principles, policies, activities and attitudes of humanitarian actors.

Since Solferino and Henry Dunant's plea to create a space for humanitarian action on the battlefields to assist wounded and sick soldiers, humanitarian action has gone through many phases of expansion and contraction. On the one hand, since 1864 and throughout the twentieth century, one has witnessed a general trend to expand the legal framework of humanitarian action–i.e., international humanitarian law–and its acceptance by States.[4] On the other hand, the last century has also witnessed horrifying events where humanitarian space was totally negated. This can be illustrated by the inability to protect civilians from Nazi persecutions during the World War II and the ensuing Holocaust. "Never again" was the general outcry. Yet, during the latter part of the century, other tragedies, notably in Cambodia and in Rwanda, demonstrated that lessons from the past had not been sufficiently taken into account by the international community of States.

The Contemporary Conflict Environment

The extent to which persons protected under IHL are effectively protected depends mostly on the general attitude of actors of armed violence towards noncombatants in general and civilians in particular. It is all too well known that civilian populations are the main victims, but it must be stressed that in some situations they are the intended targets of armed violence. Attacking civilians, demoralizing them, destroying their dignity, inflicting horrendous mutilations—in brief terrorizing them— have become means of warfare in order to achieve goals of war. This is particularly the case in identity-based conflicts where the objective is to eliminate certain segments of the population or provoke their displace- ment. In such cases, violations of the most basic norms of IHL are not accidental or due to ignorance; they are quite deliberate.

Another feature of contemporary conflicts is their complexity. With a few notable exceptions, conflicts today are internal conflicts in the sense that they are not conflicts between two or more State parties to the Geneva Conventions. These conflicts may display a combination of national as well as local dimensions. They may be motivated by political and socioe- conomic factors and/or include ethnic or religious components.

In many situations, struggles for access to and control of economic resources add to the complexity of wars. International humanitarian law wisely refers to these internal wars as conflicts "not of an international character."[5] Indeed, many of these conflicts that take place on the terri- tory of a single State, also involve weapon bearers (State or non-State) from other countries. They are sometimes called "internationalized inter- nal conflicts," although this qualification carries no legal implications. This complexity also entails a multiplicity and diversity of actors of armed violence, an element that, in itself, makes the task of ensuring respect for IHL more difficult.

Although non-State actors of armed violence are by no means a new occurrence, they have become more numerous and more heterogeneous in the wake of the changes brought about by the end of the Cold War. Their objectives, organization—or lack thereof—and means of warfare have become so diverse, and at times so blurred, that the very concept of "non-State actors of armed violence" is losing much of its analytical value. Indeed, this concept includes "traditional" guerrilla-type opposi- tion groups[6] as well as loosely structured armed bands, roaming about in territories abandoned by failed States. In some instances, using armed force as a means of making a living at the expense of the population becomes an end in itself. Thus, the distinction between political and criminal objectives can be blurred all the more as armed groups may also be closely linked to organized criminals. To be complete, the list would also have to include private militias, who take in their own hands the fight against guerrilla groups, and private security companies that offer, on a commercial basis, a wide range of services, including combatants.

More recently, networks practicing transnational terrorism have also been added to the list of non-State actors of violence following the September 11 terrorist attacks in the US. The importance of this phenomenon warrants a more detailed analysis as these groups are apparently among those who reject humanitarian action and thus attempt to reduce humanitarian space.

The Elusive Definition of Terrorism

Defining terrorism is the initial stumbling block one encounters in any attempt to analyze this phenomenon. This is due both to the very loose manner in which the term is used and to the difficulty in arriving at a universally accepted definition.[7] For some, the concept of terrorism applies solely to attacks using indiscriminate violence to terrorize a population, create a general feeling of insecurity in order to destabilize, and exert pressure of a political nature, usually on a government. For others, a form of terrorism that requires an equally strong condemnation, is that practiced by States using violence and terror against populations under their control. How then is the use of violence—including acts of terrorism—to counter what is perceived as State violence qualified? Perpetrators of a particular act of violence against a dictatorship, in a territory under colonial rule, or in a situation of occupation may be considered as terrorists by some, freedom-fighters by others.

The political component that seems to characterize terrorist acts explains why it has so far not been possible to come to an internationally accepted and comprehensive definition of terrorism. This is by no means a recent problem.[8]

There must be, however, no doubt that possible or alleged political motives in no way justify a terrorist act or mitigate its gravity. Such acts are explicitly prohibited by international law including IHL, largely because of their indiscriminate nature which violates one of the basic tenets of that body of law.

Types of Terrorism

The new wave of terrorist attacks marking the beginning of the twenty-first century gave rise—not surprisingly—to many conferences and publications. Establishing typologies of groups using terrorist methods is an interesting common feature of many of these events as it immediately signals the diversity of the motivations and objectives of those groups.

The 2003 *Yearbook of the Swedish International Peace Research Institute* (SIPRI) thus makes a distinction between nationally or ethnically based terrorism and transnational terrorism. Traditionally, situations in which terror tactics are applied grow from specific historical and political roots. They have also remained within certain geographic limits, mostly determined by the boundaries of Nation States. Nationally based terrorist groups tend to have specific goals (taking power, achieving independence or autonomy). The new phenomenon of transnational terrorism "defies geographical limits in both their methods of organization and their targets"[9] (. . .) "It appears to assail the values, assets, and self-belief of the international system as such."[10] Superimposed links—including practical cooperation—seem to exist between both types of groups.

Another distinction can be made as to the determinants of terrorist acts: An international expert meeting that took place in Oslo in June 2003 dealt with this issue and noted that there is no single cause or common set of causes of terrorism. Terrorists are not "just passive pawns of the social, economic and psychological forces around them. . . . It is more useful to see terrorists as rational and intentional actors who develop deliberate strategies to achieve political objectives."[11] Among the many conditions and circumstances that give rise to terrorism, two strains of the phenomenon appear to be particularly relevant today:

- "traditional strain" in which acts of terrorism are a possible outcome of situations of dictatorship, hegemony of a certain socio-political groups, exclusion or discrimination based on religion and/or ethnicity, colonial situations and situations of foreign occupation;
- a more recent strain can be related to a combination of factors such as rapid modernization processes causing a breakdown of norms and social patterns, making radical ideologies of secular or religious

origin attractive. Situations of failed States—where the State fails to exercise its responsibilities—may also be a facilitating element.

It was also noted in the conclusions of the meeting that addressing the determinants is a necessary but not a sufficient condition to put an end to terrorist acts. Indeed such acts can be sustained for reasons other than those that produced it. Cycles of revenge, the need to sustain the group, and profitable criminal activities are elements that account for the sustainability of terrorism. The same phenomenon may occur in certain armed conflicts.

Clash of Civilizations or of Geo-Political Interests?

Two main interpretations have been given of the September 11 attacks as well as other attacks attributed to the al Qaeda network. They are not mutually exclusive.

- One—following the title of Samuel Huntington's book—refers to a "clash of civilizations" (Western, Judeo-Christian versus Islamic) with different sets of values and to the willingness of extremist groups to conduct an exhaustive fight against Western, Christian influence and values in predominantly Muslim regions. This interpretation is supported by the omnipresence of religious references in statements issued by the alleged perpetrators of acts of terrorism and made by some of those arrested and accused of such acts. There is also a lot of evidence that this is a mainstream interpretation in the United States, judging by official statements and editorial comments of the most authoritative media.[12]
- Another interpretation emphasizes political factors and traces the root causes of the attacks to Western—and particularly US—economic presence, influence, and interests in the Middle East. Governments of the region that condone this presence can themselves also be targeted.

Statements attributed to al Qaeda could substantiate both interpretations as they include political objectives as well as a general aim to promote Islam and to combat "disbelievers."[13]

Terrorist attacks such as those that took place before and after September 11, for example, in Yemen, Kenya, Indonesia, Morocco, Saudi

Arabia, and Turkey fit into the pattern, although regional and local factors doubtlessly also play a role in attempts to analyze their root causes.

As mentioned above, the two interpretations of recent terrorist attacks are not mutually exclusive and possibly not the only possible interpretations. Indeed, the religious/cultural line of interpretation may well serve the purpose of mobilizing broader segments of the society than those aware of the geopolitical stakes. Real or perceived threats to one's identity are often used in identity-based conflicts to muster support for the use of violence.[14] The interpretation given to the terrorist attacks is not without influence on the people the terrorist groups seek to mobilize. The "civilization clash" interpretation and the ensuing policy reactions—sweeping statements on Islam, suspicions based on religion or ethnic origin—can fuel mistrust, fear, and turn into a self-fulfilling prophecy.

It appears important to make a last point on an interpretation of the upsurge of terrorism that links terrorism and poverty. According to this view, poverty and inequalities, without being a direct cause of terrorism, generate frustrations that can only fan hate and violence. In January 2002, the President of the World Bank called for an increase in official development assistance on the grounds that aid is "an insurance policy against terrorism."[15] In the wake of September 11, some aid agencies have presented their activities as aiming at reducing poverty in order to prevent terrorism. Amartya Sen[16] has, however, clearly established that there is no empirical evidence to list poverty as a cause of the use of violence. One could more convincingly argue that violence—notably conflicts—does indeed entail poverty. The link of terrorism with poverty is moreover dangerous in its consequences, as it may lead to a general view that the poor are yet again a threat to the affluent segments of the community (both nationally and internationally).

It is necessary to know more precisely what causes terrorism in order to be able to prevent the continuation and the spread of this phenomenon. Any attempt to analyze the root causes, the precipitating factors, and the declared objectives of terrorist acts, should therefore examine fully the specific socioeconomic and political determinants of each situation, and not be limited to sweeping interpretations based primarily on ideological elements.

HUMANITARIAN ACTION IN JEOPARDY?

According to its mission, the ICRC has to be active in all situations of armed conflict and of internal violence. The objective of its operational strategy is to have access to people affected by armed conflicts and internal violence, wherever they may be, in order to protect their lives and dignity and provide them with life-saving assistance. ICRC's presence and activities on the scene of conflicts cannot be imposed; it must be accepted by all parties to a conflict and be conducted in full transparency. This implies being known, understood and accepted by all relevant actors of armed violence. This requires regular contacts and dialogue with those actors in order to gain this acceptation, to ensure that it is maintained, to inform them of the ICRC's *modus operandi* and activities as well as—if and when necessary—make representations on violations of IHL, in order to induce changes in behavior. By and large, the ICRC succeeds in this endeavor, as attested by the institution's presence and programs in some 75 countries affected by conflicts or internal violence.

At the moment, the ICRC faces a challenge that, although not entirely new, has acquired a particularly critical dimension in some contexts: through declarations and violent deeds some non-State actors of armed violence have clearly indicated that ICRC and other humanitarian actors are not accepted. In 2003, such attacks took place in Afghanistan and Iraq where the ICRC was compelled to limit the scope of its activities. These attacks have had dire consequences for people affected by conflicts in these country, as no other agency was in a position to replace some of the ICRC's activities, particularly the institution's protection programs.

This reduction of "humanitarian space" in some situations of conflict gives rise to many questions:

- on the nature, motivation, and objective of the groups and networks which not only disregard basic considerations of humanity through deliberate attacks on the civilian population but also reject all forms of humanitarian action;
- and on the ways and means of maintaining protection and assistance activities in such situations.

In many conflicts, severe and repeated violations of IHL, terrorizing populations, are a means of warfare, a way to achieve the goals of war. Groups using terrorist methods seek to exert political pressure on authorities who oppose them. These groups are—as we have seen earlier—heterogeneous as to their objectives and as to the reasons that led them to choose terrorist methods of action; a thorough analysis is beyond the scope of this chapter as it would require detailed case-by-case studies.

In 2003 in Afghanistan and in Iraq some humanitarian agencies were the target of deliberate and murderous attacks as part of what appeared to be a strategy to oppose national authorities and occupying forces in Afghanistan and in Iraq. Why? Although the groups responsible for such attacks have not been identified, several hypothetical explanations—not mutually exclusive—can nevertheless be provided:

- The attacks represent a global rejection of humanitarian actors who are perceived as part of a coalition representing the enemy, in political/military terms or in cultural terms, or that are merely seen as representing Western values. The independence and neutrality of the ICRC is not recognized in part due to its perception as a Western institution—by its emblem, the site of its headquarters, its funding, and some of its staff—and rejected as such.
- The attacks represent a determination to disable civilian population (in terms of security, access to basic goods and services) in order to fuel the resentment of the population against those—for example the Coalition forces in Iraq—perceived as unable to reestablish law and order and basic vital services. In that perspective, agencies whose action tends to improve the lot of the population both in material and psychological terms (tracing), are seen as going against such objectives. In Iraq or Afghanistan, the ICRC could be perceived as contributing to the efforts to stabilize the situation and be rejected for what it does.
- The attacks represent a determination to clear a region of all foreign presence in order to control it more effectively. Attacks against humanitarian staff are meant to indicate that all foreign institutions—whatever their areas of concern—as well as their national staff are no longer secure. The media impact of such attacks can also play a role in the selection of a humanitarian target.

These attacks have had two far-reaching consequences. The first one is to create new and severe constraints on humanitarian action that limit its ability to assist and protect the populations affected by the conflict. The second consequence is to reinforce, for reasons related to these security constraints, a pre-existing tendency to combine humanitarian action with military operations designed to win "the hearts and minds" of the population. This tendency, in turn, may render independent humanitarian actors more likely to be attacked because of the confusion between humanitarian and military actors and activities.

As the Cold War ended, States became aware that there was more scope for them than hitherto to engage in humanitarian programs in situations of conflict; and that humanitarian assistance could be included in the "tool-box" of crisis management alongside political, military, and diplomatic tools that came to the fore in the early 1990s. This approach propounded by UN Secretary-General Boutros Boutros-Ghali in his 1992 "Agenda for Peace"[17] report and put this new toolbox into practice in a number of crises, *inter alia* in Iraq, Somalia, and Bosnia-Herzegovina. In this approach, humanitarian assistance is meant to complement other external policy instruments, but it may also be a substitute in situations when the will or the capacity to address the causes of the conflict, or to confront the parties at war, are found lacking.

Even though the present context of the global fight against terrorist activities is different from that of the early 1990s, the tendency to combine military and humanitarian activities has persisted. An example is the establishment in Afghanistan of Provincial Reconstruction Teams. These teams are military units entrusted with civilian tasks such as the rehabilitation of infrastructures or the promotion of "good governance." These tasks are viewed as contributing to improving security of the concerned regions by winning the hearts and minds of the population. The military staff in charge of these activities, known as "civil affairs officers," are assimilated with humanitarian workers thus blurring the distinction between military and humanitarian actors. In such contexts the space left to independent and neutral humanitarian action is very limited indeed; it can be totally denied on the ground that there is no space for neutrality between terrorist groups and those engaged in the global fight against terrorist activities.

An additional source of confusion stems from the policy of certain humanitarian actors—including some components of the Red Cross and Red Crescent Movement—to accept to operate under military protection for the sake of visibility—"at all costs"—or because they give in to pressures from the government of their country.

THE NEED TO UPHOLD A SPACE FOR
INDEPENDENT HUMANITARIAN ACTION

The challenges outlined in the preceding section are quite formidable and an independent humanitarian actor such as the ICRC does not yet—as these lines are written—have all the answers on how to respond to them. In particular, concrete solutions have to be found on the ways and means of carrying out the ICRC's mission of protection and assistance in those adverse circumstances. Experience from the past suggests that it takes some time to analyze every aspect of any new challenge in order to identify and implement consistent and sustainable responses, especially since the specifics of each situation have to be taken into account.

The ICRC is, however, convinced that there is no valid alternative to maintaining and strengthening independent and neutral humanitarian action. This basic principle has demonstrated its value over a period of nearly 150 years in innumerable situations of conflict and internal violence. It is indeed indispensable to gain acceptance of all parties to a conflict and therefore have access to the people directly affected by this conflict. Today, as in the past, the ICRC operates in scores of situations of conflict where—on the basis on this principle—the ICRC is widely accepted by many different types of actors of armed violence, including numerous non-State actors.

How can the ICRC address the challenge of not being accepted by some actors of armed violence? In the first place, it is essential to continue to demonstrate concretely through its protection and assistance programs throughout the world that the ICRC remains true to its basic principles. Its operational strategy of remaining on the ground, close to the people affected by conflicts, of being sensitive to their need for dignity and respect is equally important.

However, the security of the staff is a *sine qua non* condition to be able to implement meaningful programs. Deliberate attacks represent a type of risk that cannot be accepted. ICRC's security concept is traditionally a context-based approach that gives the delegations the main responsibility—within a clear policy framework—to manage the security of its staff and activities on the basis of national and local parameters. This is still necessary but presently no longer sufficient as regional and global threats also have to be included in the analysis. The difficulty of communicating with the groups responsible for deliberate attacks is an additional challenge that needs to be addressed.

This determination to maintain independent humanitarian action in all conflict situations entails the refusal of military protection for the implementation of the ICRC's activities in the field. Acting otherwise would unequivocally place the institution and its staff in the camp of those providing this protection, destroy its credibility as a neutral and independent institution, and thus jeopardize its activities in many other contexts, including those in which military protection would in any case not be available.

There are however situations in which—mainly for security reasons—independent humanitarian actors do not have access to the persons affected by conflicts and in need of life-saving assistance and protection. The only alternative may then well be the provision of assistance by the military themselves.

This is the place to recall that independent and neutral humanitarian action is not the only possible type of assistance in situations of conflict. There is general agreement that humanitarian assistance must be impartial. It need not necessarily be independent and neutral. Assistance can be undertaken by governmental institutions or by NGOs acting on their behalf, by intergovernmental organizations, or by NGOs that do not hesitate to take sides in a conflict. The caveat is however that it should not be implemented in a way that could jeopardize independent humanitarian action by creating confusion or uncertainty as to the nature and objectives of this type of humanitarian action. This is essential because in many contexts independent humanitarian action is the only one acceptable to all parties to a conflict and consequently the best way to reach all persons in need of protection and assistance.

Reducing the risk of confusion requires in the first place that all humanitarian organizations claiming independence as a fundamental guiding principle refrain from participating—even occasionally—in assistance programs conducted or protected by the military. Everything must be undertaken to avoid the blurring of the distinction between military and humanitarian action. If a military deployment is presented as being "mainly humanitarian," this is not the way it will be perceived by the groups who oppose the military presence, nor for that matter, by some sections of the population. The risk is high that humanitarian actions pursued by independent agencies will be perceived as part of the military efforts of a party to the conflict.

We live in a globalized world with instant global communication; the blurring of the line between military and humanitarian action in one place can affect the perception of independent humanitarian action elsewhere, including contexts where there is no military presence to carry out assistance activities and where the ICRC will be expected to assume fully its responsibility.

It could certainly be helpful to introduce a change in semantics by avoiding labeling as "humanitarian" or "mainly humanitarian" those multipurpose operations that, beside providing assistance to the population, pursue other objectives such as controlling a territory and gathering intelligence. Using different concepts for activities that are conceptually different would definitely be an important contribution by States to the promotion and protection of independent humanitarian action.[18]

Pleading for a strengthening of independent humanitarian action may seem an obsolete or unrealistic answer to a new situation. It is however appropriate to recall here—particularly to States—that the ICRC has been given a mandate to protect and assist people affected by armed conflict and that it has to fulfill that mandate in all conflict situations around the world. Experience shows that in order to be able to fulfill this mandate—wherever and whenever ICRC action is required—the institution cannot take sides or be perceived as taking sides. Neutrality and independence continue to be necessary in order to have access to all people affected by conflict or internal violence.

INTERNATIONAL HUMANITARIAN LAW AND
THE GLOBAL STRUGGLE AGAINST TERRORISM

The September 11 attacks and the response to those attacks were followed by a wide debate—with very concrete consequences—on possible legal actions in such a situation and to questions as to whether existing law was adequate to deal with it. As President Bush spoke of a global "war on terror," the question arose as to whether it was a war in the legal sense or if the word "war" had been used in a metaphorical sense as in "war on drugs" or even "war on poverty." Moreover, some lawyers, journalists, and officials questioned the adequacy of IHL in contemporary conflicts and in particular in the fight against terrorism.

When the coalition led by the US launched its campaign against the Taliban regime in Afghanistan, it was clear to all parties concerned that this particular campaign was an international armed conflict—a war in the legal sense of the term—in which the 1949 Geneva Conventions were applicable. But the fight against terrorism also includes all sorts of activities (police and judicial cooperation, financial investigations, extradition, criminal sanctions, diplomatic and economic pressure, etc) that do not involve the use of armed force and thus do not amount to an armed conflict.

International humanitarian law as it stands today does take into account the phenomenon of terrorism. Acts of terrorism are clearly prohibited by IHL[19] as well as "acts or threats of violence the primary purpose of which is to spread terror among the civilian population."[20] The protection offered by the Geneva Conventions to persons detained in the context of a conflict does not prevent perpetrators of violations of IHL to be prosecuted. International Humanitarian Law is not an obstacle to justice. On the contrary, the State parties to the Conventions are required to prosecute them. The recently created International Criminal Court is also an expression of the international community's will to prosecute such criminals.

Based on a long history of experience, IHL is designed to balance the competing considerations of humanity and military necessity. In other words, IHL reconciles the legitimate security interests of States with those of the international community at large, as well as the fundamental civil rights and judicial guarantees that any human being should enjoy. All persons arrested and detained in the context of an armed conflict enjoy the protection offered by IHL. They should be treated humanely and benefit from judicial guarantees. After all, the basic principle of the rule of law is that no institution, no individual be above the law and that no person should be treated or considered as being beyond the reach of the law.

When the fight against terrorism does not take place in the context of an armed conflict, domestic and international criminal and human rights law provide an adequate legal framework to deal with the perpetrators of acts of terrorism.

It is necessary to fight terrorism, but it would be self-defeating for this fight to lead to lower international standards of protection of the individual. The overriding moral and legal challenge facing the international community, including the ICRC, is to find ways of dealing with this form of violence while preserving existing international standards of protection of human dignity and life.

An intensive debate on these issues took place in December 2003, involving government experts and scholars. At the 28th International Red Cross and Red Crescent Conference, the participants came to the conclusion that "the existing provisions of international humanitarian law (formed) an adequate basis to meet the challenges raised by modern armed conflicts."[21]

To reaffirm the relevance of IHL today does not mean, however, that this body of law is perfect and that, like others, it cannot be changed or improved. Indeed, and this is a priority, much more work must be done to identify and promote more effective means—new or existing ones—of ensuring better compliance with the rules of IHL. It also seems necessary that new rules will have to be created, for instance, to strengthen the protection of persons affected by non-international armed conflicts. However, what is of paramount importance is that any developments of the law preserve—and better still—improve the standards of protection. But new legal norms without a strong political commitment to implement them are, if not useless, at least insufficient. Thus, beside the continuation of legal research there is a need for fostering the conviction that humanitarian law, and international law in general, are important and necessary instruments to preserve a worldwide civil society able to uphold the essential values of humanity and constructive communication and cooperation between people and nations.

THE ROLE OF STATES

The two issues raised in this article, namely maintaining a space for independent humanitarian action and reaffirming the adequacy of IHL in the context of the global fight against terrorism, are closely linked. Indeed, the goals, values, and norms of independent humanitarian action are those embodied in IHL. For the ICRC, whose responsibility is to protect and assist people affected by conflict and internal violence, promoting respect for IHL and implementing protection and assistance programs on the ground for the victims, represent the legal and operational sides of the same coin.

The ICRC can only assume this responsibility with the support of the States. In the present circumstances there are two areas in which this support can be decisive.

The first one is to achieve a clear understanding of the distinct mandate, nature and role of political and military actors on the one hand and of independent and neutral humanitarian actors of the other. Through dialogue, these actors should recognize, as a matter of principle, the necessity to maintain a space for independent humanitarian action and to avoid integrating humanitarian action as a tool for crises management. They should also recognize that, in certain circumstances—to be defined precisely—the armed forces may be called upon to provide relief to populations inaccessible to humanitarian organizations.

The second step is the implementation and appreciation of IHL by all parties. The strength and legitimacy of this body of law can only benefit from the demonstration by all States that, even in the most difficult circumstances, the norms of IHL must be respected. These norms have been designed precisely to protect individuals in the most extreme situations and take into account the legitimate security interests of governments.

Support for the States in these two areas can only assist the ICRC in its endeavors to develop a dialog with non-State actors of armed violence on the necessity to respect independent humanitarian action and basic norms of IHL.

BIBLIOGRAPHY

Børgo, Tore, ed. "Root Causes of Terrorism." Proceedings from an International Expert Meeting in Oslo, 9–11 June 2003, Norwegian Institute of International Relations (NUPI), Oslo, 2003.

Boutros-Ghali, Boutros. *An Agenda for Peace.* New York: United Nations, 1992.

Cahill, Kevin M., ed., *Tradition, Values, and Humanitarian Action.* New York: Fordham University Press, 2003.

Gasser, Hans-Peter. "Acts of Terror, Terrorism and International Humanitarian Law." *International Review of the Red Cross* 847 (September 2002).

Macrae, Joanna and Harmer, Adele. "Humanitarian Action and the 'Global War on Terror': A Review of Trends and Issues." *HPG Report* 14 (2003).

Minear, Larry. *The Humanitarian Enterprise, Dilemmas and Discoveries.* Bloomfield: Kumarian Press, 2002.

Moore, Jonathan, ed., *Hard Choices, Moral Dilemmas in Humanitarian Intervention.* Lanham: Rowan & Littlefield, 1998.

Thual, François. *Les Conflits Identitaires.* Paris: Editions Ellipses, 1995.

See also the Annex to this chapter, located in the Appendices.

Justice and the Rule of Law

There can be no peace without justice. But after the terrible wrongs that are committed during wars and conflicts, the pure pursuit of justice may itself become an obstacle to a longed for and lasting peace.

There is an evolving acceptance of the importance of truth and reconciliation commissions and the healing significance of the admission of guilt as complementary tools in post conflict resolution. In this final section Dennis McNamara, David Owen, and Richard Goldstone, all having struggled with finding the right balance in such difficult, if not impossible situations, offer their reflections on the meaning of justice and the rule of law.

A Sense of Justice

Dennis McNamara

TO ATTEMPT to assess the contribution of Sergio Vieira de Mello to the complex and difficult areas of justice and the rule of law is a daunting task. It is a challenge made even greater, as one of his close friends put it, by Sergio's basic duality: his instinctive charm and trust, looking for the best in people while pushing often pragmatic diplomacy to its limits, with quite incredible success. And at the same time his longstanding devotion to vigorous good order and discipline, epitomized professionally by his consistent advocacy for international justice, especially in the form of the International Criminal Tribunal Yugoslavia (ICTY), and later the International Criminal Court (ICC). On these issues he was a passionate advocate, perhaps because he was philosophically more comfortable with the hard logic of law, than the sometimes more woolly and ill-defined parameters of "humanitarianism."

Not uniquely, Sergio preferred the clarity of the law to the pomposity of the lawyers, as I know personally. Despite his deep intellectualism, he consistently resisted the legal "hair splitters," as he called them:

> All too often we complicate matters [to] muddy the picture and [to] remain stuck on defining rights in rarified, doctrinaire meetings, rather than simply getting on and implementing them. But I have seen enough to know that those who are denied their rights do not find the matter quite so complicated.

Or—as he said of the Timorese—they may not have been able easily to define democracy, but they certainly knew what it was not.

Basic justice, in all its many and broad aspects, and the rule of law were central themes throughout Sergio's various incarnations: the key underpinnings of what he described as "holistic democracy"—the rights content of "legitimate governance." His theme was inclusiveness, an "empowered, enabled, and protected citizenry," the essential antithesis and antidote to the tyranny either of the majority, or of any minority. But let me do what, I think, Sergio would want to have done with this discussion—bring it down to its real and practical application. How does the easy rhetoric of justice actually translate "on the ground" or "in the field," where the environment is invariably chaotic and often rife with conflict?

Let me give some random examples. By the late 1980s it was clear that the continued exodus of people from the countries of Indochina, and especially Vietnam, could not go on being treated totally as a refugee movement. With all new boat arrivals in Southeast Asia being automatically processed for resettlement as refugees in third-party countries, Sergio led the contentious UNHCR effort to put in place a Comprehensive Plan of Action (CPA) to try and resolve this massive problem humanely. The key to this was to set up formal refugee screening systems throughout the countries of Southeast Asia. These were legally based processes, formally determining those who qualified as refugees, with a right of review, and the humane return to Vietnam of those who did not qualify.

It may not seem very radical now, but in the highly charged post–Vietnam War arena the CPA was highly contentious. Crucially, Sergio kept all key governments, both regional and international, politically committed to this difficult process. It worked, despite the critics, because its solid legal basis enabled the delicate political consensus to hold. The success of the CPA brought to a humane end one of the most intense and prolonged refugee exoduses of recent times.

Three years later in Cambodia, following the Paris Peace Accords, UNTAC (United Nations Transitional Authority of Cambodia) faced an equal challenge in conducting free and fair elections in that traumatized and uprooted country within two years. Critical to this was the return of nearly 400,000 Cambodians linked to the Western-backed resistance in camps along the Thai/Cambodian border. Many commentators were convinced that their safe and orderly return was impossible. UNHCR's initial plan to return people to their original areas soon proved untenable. Sergio quickly implemented a substitute cash incentive scheme: UNTAC provided security support; UN human rights monitors followed the process; and the Cambodian refugees all came home in time to vote.

Again a controversial, sometimes criticized but ultimately effective combination of politics, diplomacy and safeguarding of basic rights were integrated to resolve a humanitarian impasse.

Sergio's sense of what justice should provide was, I believe, very deep
and sincere. We often debated, sometimes intensely (and occasionally
angrily), how to get there, but never the ultimate objective.

Trying to promote order in areas that have suffered terrible atrocities
often requires that we deal with known violators and perpetrators. Sergio
did this with calm effectiveness in Cambodia, Bosnia, Central Africa,
Afghanistan, Kosovo, and Timor. One of his journalist friends used to joke
that his autobiography should be entitled *War Criminals I Have Known!*

In doing so, he faced squarely the inherent dilemma that impartial
credibility demands: listening to all sides, however personally distasteful
that might be. But at the same time, this did not detract from his constant and unwavering support for the ICTY and later the ICC. As one
result, UNHCR become the first UN agency to testify, in closed session,
before the Tribunal in order to explain the need for protection of its staff
(and of the organization) who were witnesses to some of the atrocities
committed in the Bosnian conflict.

This commitment was to remain constant for more than a decade.
Three months after Sergio became High Commissioner for Human
Rights he said: ". . . we should never underestimate the capacity of
human beings to brutalize and dehumanize each other. But also, we
should always have confidence in the ultimate ability of the collective
human spirit to triumph over such brutality. . . . when the Rome Statute
(of the ICC) entered into force, many of us felt a wave of optimism.
Finally, a dream has come true."

Previously in East Timor, as UN Administrator for two and a half years,
Sergio had faced the complex realities of concretely promoting justice and
the rule of law probably more acutely, first hand, then ever before.

Post-conflict transitions to democracy and peace-building operations
require many varied and difficult strategies. But one thing they all need—
and often lack—is an immediate justice/rule of law "package." International tribunals can support this but can never replace it. There must be,
from the outset, (not months later) a credible capacity to provide: civilian policing (not military control); a basically functioning court system;

appropriate and adapted applicable law; and properly managed prisons. These are mundane but fundamental. We learned this in Cambodia, Haiti, El Salvador, and then—all over again—in Kosovo and East Timor. Afghanistan and Iraq have shown us painfully the price we pay—collectively—for allowing history to negatively repeat itself at our expense. Without this crucial investment in peace-building strategies, embryonic democratic processes have little chance to survive.

This justice capacity is often not available locally, at least initially, and the UN has constantly struggled, with very mixed results, to fill the void. Real expertise is needed and this can be difficult to mobilize quickly in remote and often dangerous locations. To quote again our friend Sergio, "If we are to replace the corrupt and violent, it should be with something better than the inept, however benign." This whole area is complicated, unspectacular, difficult, and sensitive but nonetheless critical. And it is where peace-building operations have often failed, or at least have not met expectations.

It is also an area where there are often frequently inherent tensions between the need for reconciliation (and truth) both politically and socially, and also for accountability for past abuses by those who have been responsible for particularly egregious crimes. In East Timor this was an acute dilemma, with the political leadership of the new country often publicly committed to the former leadership, and the UN Administration mandated by the Security Council to prosecute the main perpetrators of the most serious atrocities.

The logic of both imperatives was debated intensely in Timor as it had been elsewhere, with the UN attempting a difficult balancing act to avoid alienating proponents of either side in the process. There is no doubt that a competent international tribunal, ruled out by the Security Council in the case of East Timor, could have enormously helped this difficult undertaking.

More broadly, and on various occasions, Sergio emphasized two or three recurring themes on justice and human rights, which I think deserve special mention.

One of the most basic of these was his vision of the rule of law as the fundamental basis for his role as UN High Commissioner for Human Rights. As he told the 59th session of the Commission on Human Rights

on 17 March 2003: "The principle of the rule of law will form the cen-
terpiece of my approach as High Commissioner for Human Rights. It is
also the most solid foundation of security."

This was a theme that he was to return to constantly, including in a
persuasive article in 2003 in which he argued for a proper recognition
of and response to human rights issues as the central component in the
global response to terrorism.

As one of his colleagues has emphasized, Sergio saw human rights
particularly as a process of inclusiveness. "Ensuring both inclusively and
respect for diversity . . . We must eschew homogeneity and embrace difference" was his ambitious call. It was therefore not surprising that he
constantly reiterated the need for women to be properly and fully represented in all processes—including in peace-keeping operations and
peace-building operations. He had seen, as had many of us, that the marginalization of women and children in democratic processes was one of
the basic weaknesses of many transitions to peace. "Women are a force
for peace . . . they are the glue that binds families and they are the rec-
oncilers," he said.

The challenge of effectively applying the rhetoric of justice and the
rule of law in the complex post-conflict world—often chaotic and still conflictual—remains an agenda item that generally deserves much more
attention, both within the UN and by governments and other agencies.
I believe Sergio Vieira de Mello was among those who were firmly convinced that until this part of the equation is more adequately addressed,
our combined efforts to promote sound justice and equitable development will remain seriously hamstrung.

Justice and Reconciliation: The Contribution of War Crimes Tribunals and Truth and Reconciliation Commissions

David Owen

Justice is the outcome of individual decisions. It does not exist in the abstract; it stems from the interpretation of laws. Justice is also one of the four cardinal virtues, along with prudence, temperance, and fortitude. Virtues that cover a person's worth or merit cannot be absolute. They are of necessity qualified. Yet the quest for absolute or pure justice persists. There are qualities besides mercy which season justice and one of these is the ability to relate justice to reconciliation.

The theme—of how justice relates to reconciliation and reconciliation to justice in the pursuit of peace—was a topic on which Sergio Vieira de Mello often spoke and upon which he frequently acted. On 24 September 2002, as High Commissioner for Human Rights, he said:

> I would also like us to be equipped and ready to assist societies emerging from conflict to build democratic, representative, participatory and accountable institutions, to heal their wounds, to work on reconciliation and to ensure a credible process of accountability for the serious crimes and violations committed during conflict. I know all too well from our work in Kosovo and East Timor how onerous this task is, but I also know how vital and worthy of your support it is. Frequently, a conflict has its origins in patterns of discrimination. We need to address these basic root-causes through advancing the principle of equality. We need to strengthen our work on this bedrock of justice that is at the core of all human rights.

The start of the twenty-first century is a good time to reassess our attitudes and actions toward bringing war criminals to justice and upholding the rule of law where there has been conflict. We need to reassert that to reconcile is part of the practice of peacemaking and peacebuilding and that to devise techniques, develop mechanisms, and to help bring estranged persons or parties together is the essence of reconciliation. Upholding the rule of law by the pursuit of justice is, nevertheless, also a mechanism for reconciliation. The skill is to achieve a wise balance.

History is full of balancing acts between justice and reconciliation. The Act of Indemnity and Oblivion in the aftermath of the 1642–51 English Civil War "halted all process of revenge or retribution." Only those who actually signed Charles I's death warrant or had been involved in his execution, plus a few others, were exempted from the provision of the Act.[1] President Abraham Lincoln, on 8 December 1863, offered pardon and amnesty to all persons who took an oath of allegiance to the United States, its laws and proclamations concerning slavery, exempting only Confederate officials and high ranking officers.[2] The Nuremberg Military War Crimes Tribunal was brought to an end by a decision of the occupying powers in 1948 not to pursue further war crime investigations and trials on people in the occupied zone.

In Africa there have been very important acts of reconciliation. After the guerilla war in what was Rhodesia, Robert Mugabe, as Prime Minister, in 1980, surprised many by his readiness to reconcile. It has been a tragedy that after such an optimistic start for independence, President Mugabe's overall record will be one of destroying Zimbabwe's peace and prosperity. In Southwest Africa, the transition of Namibia under President Sam Nujoma in the 1990s was also characterized by reconciliation. In South Africa under President Mandela, it was decided that a commission should be established for Truth and Reconciliation, which provided a structured mechanism for amnesties and victim support. This has proved its worth and though there have been a number of other countries with similar successful experiences with such commissions, it is the South African experience which is likely to set the pattern for the future.

YUGOSLAVIA AND THE CREATION OF THE ICFY

The London Session which created the International Conference on the Former Yugoslavia (ICFY) on 27 August 1992 published a summary of its conclusions[3] that stated that the Co-Chairmen, Cyrus Vance and myself, had "undertaken to carry forward a study of the creation of an international criminal court." There was at the time some disagreement on this issue between countries belonging to the ICFY, and it was clear to us that if we came out against an international court being established it would not be done, since the Russian Federation would have agreed with our judgment. We discussed the issues behind this mandate frequently among our colleagues, and between ourselves as we crisscrossed the Balkans region trying to establish credibility for the ICFY with all the parties who continued fighting each other, despite numerous cease-fire agreements. The matter that concerned us as Co-Chairmen was whether instituting a legal procedure would harm or hinder the reconciliation process, which we believed was essential for any lasting peace in the region.

It soon became clear that establishing the International Criminal Court (ICC), as envisaged in the *United Nations Charter*, one which would take cases from all over the world, not just from the former Yugoslavia, was impossible to achieve.[4] There was not a sufficient consensus within the United Nations Security Council, and establishing it by treaty through the General Assembly with individual nations ratifying would have taken, even if successful, many years. Time was not on our side. The war was continuing and we hoped that the mere creation of a Yugoslav-specific tribunal might act as a deterrent to the continuation of war crimes, and that the existence of a legal process might persuade some of their leaders to belatedly stamp out such activities. The only speedy way forward, we judged, was to use the power of the United Nations (UN) Security Council under Chapter VII.

The Security Council mechanism had one important flexibility for us: the Council, having established the Tribunal, could also make political decisions as to where and when in the former Yugoslavia reconciliation would be helped if the Tribunal stopped hearing fresh cases. In this way, too, the whole process could have an end point. We felt that the promotion of justice could be balanced in this way against any benefit from stopping examining the past. The Security Council, if it judged that the time was right in any part of the former Yugoslavia, could halt the Tribunal, as a contribution to furthering reconciliation, or could continue it as an instrument for upholding justice if it felt, for example, that there had been insufficient recognition of and remorse for past crimes.

In December 1992 we wrote to the Secretary General, Boutros Boutros-Ghali, recommending that a tribunal be established. This recommendation was referred to in United Nations Resolution 808, passed on 22 February 1993 (S/25221). This followed the first ministerial level meeting of the steering committee, held in Geneva on 16 December 1992, to review the efforts of the conference since it began working on 3 September 1992. Cyrus Vance spoke for us both when he said, "that atrocities committed in the former Yugoslavia are unacceptable, and persons guilty of war crimes should be brought to justice. We therefore recommend the establishment of an international criminal court . . . ." In my remarks I suggested the court be established "through a Resolution by the Security Council. It would surely be wrong if the practitioners of ethnic cleansing are not brought to justice." The Secretary General two months later in February 1993 reported to the Security Council that we as co-chairs "repeatedly and strongly urged the members of the Security Council to establish an international criminal court to try persons accused of grave breaches of international humanitarian law in the former Yugoslavia." As a result, the tribunal was established by Security Council Resolution 827 on 25 May 1993.

Our task, as negotiators, was to build up and then retain the confidence of the parties to the conflict in order to help them negotiate in good faith. At that time there was much hatred, suspicion, and paranoia. It took over three months, for instance, to get the parties to sit down in the same room together and months more before they would even begin to negotiate among themselves without us, as negotiators, promoting ideas and concepts. The level of suspicion was high, particularly among the Serb leaders, who believed that the UN Security Council was hostile and prejudiced against them. It was essential, therefore, that as co-chairs, we drew clear lines between our role as negotiators, the role of those investigating crimes against humanity, and those who would later judge in a court of law whether or not crimes had been committed. Neither of us ever blocked in any way the investigative or the judicial process and, in fact, did all in our power to encourage and help both processes. Those who have asserted otherwise have not a shred of evidence to support their case and in most cases they were people who wanted us to abandon impartiality and become partisan. It was at the ICFY Ministerial Steering Committee in December 1992 that then U.S. Secretary of State Lawrence S. Eagleburger, U.S. who was just a few weeks away from leaving office, listed some of the war crimes that he believed had been committed. He named for the first time President Slobodan Milosevic, Dr. Radovan Karadzic, and General Ratko Mladic as people with political and command responsibility who "must eventually explain whether and how they sought to ensure, as they must under international law, that their forces complied with international law. They ought, if charged, to have the opportunity of defending themselves by demonstrating," Eagleburger said, "whether and how they took responsible action to prevent and punish the atrocities I have described which were taken by their subordinates." He went on to say, "They need, especially, to understand that a second Nuremberg awaits the practitioners of ethnic cleansing, and that the judgment and opprobrium of history awaits the people in whose name the crimes were committed."

At no time did any of the Serb leaders mentioned by Eagleburger appear to be even slightly concerned by the threat of prosecution that hung over them. Nor did they attempt, while I was the European Union (EU) negotiator, to insert amnesties for themselves or anyone else into any of the texts of the various peace agreements. They held Serb paranoid feelings about the international community and never believed any tribunal would be either fair or just. It is harder to judge whether creating the ICTY had any effect on the Croatian government, particularly its President, the late Franjo Tudjman, or on the Bosnian government, particularly its Vice-President, Ejup Ganic.

On its website, the International Criminal Tribunal for the former Yugoslavia (ICTY) uses the word reconciliation to describe its fourfold mission, which was written in harmony with the purpose of the tribunal's founding by UN Security Council Resolution 827 passed on 25 May

1993. According to its mission statement, the ICTY seeks to 1) bring to justice persons allegedly responsible for serious violations of international humanitarian law, 2) to render justice to the victims, 3) to deter further crimes, and 4) to contribute to the restoration of peace by promoting reconciliation in the former Yugoslavia. In fact the word "reconciliation" does not appear in Resolution 827. Instead it states its conviction that the Tribunal will "contribute to the restoration and maintenance of peace." Reconciliation was, however, one of the essential underlying themes behind the establishment of ICTY.

The ICTY: An Assessment

Ten years after the ICTY was established is a reasonable period to make an assessment of its record. It has successfully carried out the first two of its missions, bringing people to justice and rendering justice to victims but, for its third goal of deterring crime, it does not appear to have had much of a deterrent effect. In Bosnia two years after the inception of the ICTY, the Srebrenica massacre of 1995 occurred. In Serbia the deterioration in the situation in Kosovo continued over six more years until NATO intervened. In the Croatian region of Krajina, in the summer of 1995, the largest single episode of non-reversible ethnic cleansing occurred (since it has shown few signs of being reversed). The ICTY's fourth mission of contributing to reconciliation has, I judge, been positive in that it has forced and continues to force some of the parties to the dispute to face up to unpleasant realities and register some regret and even remorse. But it is the nature of such revelations, however shocking, that their effect fades with time. Also reconciliation is hard to achieve in less sophisticated communities where there is little awareness of the trial evidence in The Hague.

The question as to what extent genocide occurred in Bosnia-Herzegovina loomed large in the summer of 1992, when the public first became aware of the extent of the killing and again in 1995 after the Srebrenica massacre. The issue continues to be passionately debated among experts. As the ICTY has reached judgments, concerns have been expressed by human rights lawyers about the court's interpretation of genocide. In one well researched article[5] questions are raised about how few convictions have been made for genocide by the ICTY compared with what the author called the "unqualified success" of the prosecution for genocide by the International Criminal Tribunal for Rwanda which sits in Arusha in Tanzania.

Several convictions have been upheld by the Rwanda Appeals Chamber, and people are serving lengthy sentences of imprisonment for the orgy of genocidal killing in 1994. Interestingly those who used radio broadcasts to incite genocide in Rwanda have also been convicted. "In contrast," the same author writes the ICTY had, "registered only one conviction for genocide, that of General Radovan Kostic for his responsibility in the July 1995 Srebrenica massacre. "Ominously," the author writes, "the Trial Chamber seemed to conclude that the genocidal intent only emerged a few days prior to the killings, and this suggests that the Prosecutor will have difficulty establishing the existence of a more far-reaching genocidal campaign involving the highest levels of the Bosnian Serb leadership, not to mention those who ran the Federal Republic of Yugoslavia at the time. The willingness of the office of the Prosecutor to withdraw its genocide indictment of Biljana Plavsic may also," the writer claims, "be significant in this respect. Two other trials on genocide charges dealing with killings in the camps in northern Bosnia-Herzegovina at earlier stages in the war have resulted in acquittals."

Nevertheless, despite such disappointment among experts, I believe that the wider public in Europe, Canada, and the U.S. feel that justice has been meted out fairly by the ICTY. The parties to the Dayton Accords agreed that the ICTY should, in Bosnia-Herzegovina, be the gatekeeper for national prosecutions and that all future orders, warrants and indictments would have to be initially reviewed and deemed consistent with international legal standards by the Tribunal. This was because of concerns about some earlier rulings by national courts. Almost certainly, as a consequence of this decision, there have been, since Dayton, no further national trials for genocide in the former Yugoslavia.

The *Genocide Convention* of 1948 (the *Convention on the Prevention and Punishment of the Crime of Genocide*) long has been criticized by experts for the narrowness of its definition of genocide as "acts which were intended to destroy, in whole or in part, a national ethnic or racial group." Nevertheless, that wording has, in practice, in Rwanda for example, been sufficient to bring to justice the perpetrators of the world's most obvious genocide, apart from Cambodia, since the Holocaust in World War II.

The final verdict in Slobodan Milosevic's trial, where he is being charged with Genocide, in addition to Crimes against Humanity, Grave Breaches of the *Geneva Conventions* and Violations of the Laws or Customs of War, is unlikely to be reached before 2005. It is the first trial of a former Head of State in an International Court and it raises many matters of immense importance.

MILOSEVIC AT THE ICTY

On 3–4 November 2003 I gave evidence before the ICTY. Initially, I was requested to attend as a prosecution witness against Milosevic, but I felt it more appropriate for an international negotiator to come independently as a court witness. In correspondence with the chief prosecutor, published as part of my written evidence to the Court, Carla Del Ponte explained the Trial Chamber's attitude to the International Committee of the Red Cross (ICRC) not giving evidence. She saw that as a matter of customary international law where the ICRC enjoys a privilege to withhold its confidential information and that in respect of the right for non-disclosure and privilege to refuse to testify, the ICRC was a unique institution. A legal adviser of the ICRC expresses this well: "Justice cannot be administered without the cooperation of those with relevant information. Yet testimonial immunities have long been recognized in support of other values, despite the potential conflict with interests of justice."[6] I have no doubt that that is right and it is in the interest of their work that the ICRC should be able to claim immunity.

My main concern was to uphold a special position for international negotiators of the future who must be able to command the trust of the parties to any conflict, particularly one where fighting still continues during negotiations. To be involved in the prior "proofing sessions" with the office of the prosecutor would, I feared, have been construed by some Serbs as my having abandoned the impartiality of a negotiator. Yet, as I explained to the Court, no negotiator can be neutral on the question of genocide crimes against humanity or war crimes.

Everyone working in the ICFY, including the negotiators, were under no doubt that any information we came across had to be revealed to the investigators and to the ICTY, and this was scrupulously adhered to. By agreeing to call me as a Court Witness I hope the judges have established the precedent that international negotiators, though not the same as the ICRC, should nevertheless be given a somewhat different status to those called as witnesses for the Prosecution. One of the ICTY Judges–Judge Robinson–helped me when I asked for guidance on being asked a question by the Principal Trial Attorney as to whether I thought Milosevic was responsible for the Srebrenica massacre of July 1995. That tragedy occurred after I had stepped down from being Co-Chairman of ICFY and I was not sure whether I should reply. If I answered hypothetically about what I thought might have happened after I left as a negotiator, I felt I might start to abuse the impartiality that I had scrupulously tried to maintain during my period in office. Judge Robinson's view was that if my answer involved speculation then I would be wise not to speculate and so the question was not pursued.

I formed a very favorable view of the fairness of the ICTY procedures and, given that Milosevic had chosen not to defend himself, the Court was wise to take the decision to appoint three *amici curiae* to represent his interests. These appointments, in my judgment, were further justified by the concentrated and effective questions one of them put to me in the Court. It is in the interest of not only justice but also of reconciliation that the Serbs know that a case for Milosevic is being heard, as well as the case against Milosevic. Nevertheless, in the 293 trial days the prosecution had to present its case with 300 witnesses and 245 telephone intercepts, the trial did not begin Milosevic's own defense until the summer of 2004.

PROBLEMS AND COSTS FACING THE ICTY

There is a very good description of the ICTY in an essay, "War Crimes and Punishment" by Guy Lesser in the January 2004 edition of *Harpers*. As to adverse comments about the Court allowing plea bargaining for people charged with anything other than genocide, this is, to my mind, appropriate to make the functioning of the ICTY more effective and more efficient. I have, however, respect for the sentencing Judge's view that an admission of genocide requires the Judges to reflect the level of guilt in their sentences. Hence in the case of Captain Momir Nikolic, the Judges imposed a 27-year sentence rather than the 15 to 20 years recommended by the Prosecution.

One odd feature about the Court proceedings thus far is the strange absence of foreign and defense ministers of relevant countries giving evidence. The former U.S. Secretary of State, Madeleine Albright, only gave a character witness report on Biljana Plavsic, when she appeared before the Court. It is a fact that the U.S., and maybe some other countries have held out for giving evidence only *in camera*. Yet now that that procedural hurdle has, apparently, been overcome by the agreement withholding the transcript of the former Supreme Allied Commander in Europe of NATO, General Wesley Clark, for 48 hours, to allow for deletions on security grounds, maybe more political leaders will come forward to give evidence.

It is important that we hear more evidence from those politicians responsible for national intelligence information. It is very clear from a remarkably well-researched book, *Intelligence and the War in Bosnia 1992–95* by Professor Cees Wiebs, that "one can conclude that American, British, French, German, and other European services intercepted a great deal of military and communications traffic."[7] The book also claims, that in 1995 perhaps intelligence could have played an important role in preventing the Srebrenica massacre if a "secret American proposal for Dutchbat to take Comint suitcases into the enclave had been accepted."[8] Guy Lesser's description of the difficulty of analyzing such tapes shows that the Court needs to hear from Ministers what their experts believed the intercept traffic was revealing.

Successive U.S. administrations, who have financed by far the largest amounts of the budget to sustain the Court in The Hague, are still reluctant to release intelligence information over Bosnia or say categorically that they do not have any relevant intercept information for the Court. On 20 April 1999, the then British Foreign Secretary, Robin Cook, handed over British intelligence material to the ICTY concerning Kosovo. The importance of this is that under the *Genocide Convention,* governments "undertake to prevent and to punish" genocide. It is a legal

obligation, one of the few obligations imposed by international law. It is
felt by some international commentators that governments have been
reluctant to provide intelligence evidence lest it be judged in retrospect
that they deliberately failed to uphold the *Genocide Convention.* Certainly
the existence of Serbian detention camps in Bosnia-Herzegovina was
detected by satellite photography in 1992–93 and photographs have
been produced of the mass graves detected by satellite in and around
Srebrenica in 1995.

Another interesting development in the Court's procedure has been
their continuing dialogue with the Security Council. One particularly
important meeting took place on 23 July 2002 when Judge Claude Jorda,
President of the ICTY, addressed the UN Security Council. This interaction was exactly the sort of debate Cyrus Vance and I had hoped would
take place. Judge Jorda explained that his report was the product of reflec-
tion between the Prosecutor, Carla del Ponte, the Registrar, Hans
Holthuis, and himself. The report followed up a previous conversation
with the Security Council in November 2001 when he committed the
ICTY to close their investigations around 2004 and finish the first-instance
trials around 2008-. The aim is that ICTY will be wound up by 2010.

The preamble to UN Resolution 1239 of 30 November 2000 recalls
that the Judges saw their mission as trying "civilian, military and para-
military leaders . . . in preference to minor actors." Judge Jorda, reflecting the growing anxiety over the delay in bringing people to trial, said,
"At issue is the right of each accused to be tried as soon as possible and
not spend an unreasonable time in pretrial detention." Also at issue was
the reliability of testimony when some of the crimes dated back as far as
ten years. Judge Jorda went on, "More fundamentally, however, the
credibility of the Tribunal's action is at stake: if we do not act promptly,
more and more voices will be heard in favor of reconciliation for the
occasion. We all know, however, that this type of reconciliation rests on
a fragile and consequently ephemeral foundation. Only justice can guarantee a deep-rooted and lasting peace in the former Yugoslavia. Moreover, this is the meaning of the mandate you gave to us which is in
keeping with Chapter VII of the *United Nations Charter.*"

Judge Jorda's statement is a rather restrictive interpretation of the
Security Council's intentions in 1993. Additionally, the reconciliation

that has come from Truth and Reconciliation Commissions as compared to the Yugoslav and Rwanda Tribunals appears to have been far
from ephemeral and, because it involves many more cases, looks as if
it may put down far deeper roots than that which is currently being
achieved in the former Yugoslavia. Judge Jorda recommended that following the Rome Agreement of 18 February 1996 to establish procedures for the Courts of Bosnia and Herzegovina, to prosecute and try
individuals authorized by the Tribunal and, because of the lack of cooperation between the two entities, political influence on the judges and
the "monoethnic" composition of local courts in Bosnia, it was necessary to establish within the State Court of Bosnia and Herzegovina a
Chamber with special jurisdiction to try serious violations of international humanitarian law. He claimed that this was not a "mini international tribunal" but would create a three-tier judicial architecture: the
International Tribunal, a State Court Special Chamber to handle those
accused of intermediary-level war crimes referred to it by the Tribunal,
and the local courts.

The State Court of Bosnia-Herzegovina was established by a decision
of the then High Representative, Wolfgang Petritsch, on 12 November
2000, though its establishment was delayed until held by the Constitutional Court to be in accordance with the Constitution. The High Representative on 9 May 2002 appointed the first judges to be in position to
hear cases arising under the Election Law of Bosnia-Herzegovina.

It would be wise if sometime in 2004–5 the Security Council reviewed
the wisdom of creating a Special Chamber for war crimes in the State
Court in Bosnia-Herzegovina and examined an alternative strategy of
establishing a Commission for Truth and Reconciliation in Bosnia.
Endorsing a Special Chamber, with fresh legislation for issues such as
the admissibility of evidence collected by the ICTY, looks likely to continue court procedures well into the second decade of this century in
Bosnia-Herzegovina for a war that ended in 1995. There is also the possibility of a challenge as to its constitutionality before the Constitutional
Court. Unless there is a change of policy from the Security Council, legal
proceedings in relation to Kosovo could also continue for the same
length of time, though admittedly crimes there were still being committed into 1999. The Security Council needs, however, to consider whether

the time is approaching when reconciliation typified by a full statutory Commission for Truth and Reconciliation should now be given priority in Bosnia-Herzegovina rather than relying solely on war crimes prosecutions. There is already a relevant NGO and there have been talks with the ICTY about a Commission but there were anxieties in the ICTY about any Commission having the power to grant amnesty.

There must be no question that existing arrest orders from ICTY must be prosecuted, and that any system for amnesties in a Truth and Reconciliation Commission should not apply to individuals still subject to such arrest orders who have not yet been arrested. Justice would not be seen to be done if there was any amnesty for those under an arrest order, such as Dr. Karadzic and General Mladic. The Security Council would have to weigh in the balance the experience of promoting reconciliation in the former Yugoslavia in the light of the experience of reconciliations in countries that have used the Truth Commission approach. It is at least questionable whether Court procedures, grinding on well into the second decade of the twenty-first, fifteen to twenty years after the crimes were committed, could harm rather than contribute to reconciliation.

Any assessment should not be driven primarily by considerations of cost, though at well over the $100-million-a-year that the Tribunal costs for the former Yugoslavia, as well as for Rwanda, there will inevitably be a balance of judgment to be made. Some have already argued that those substantial sums of money could be better used now by promoting specific peace and reconciliation projects on the ground. Jack Straw, the British Foreign Secretary, as recently as 24 September 2003, in the Security Council meeting on Justice and the Rule of Law, said of these Tribunal costs, "We need to think about whether that has turned out to be the most efficient expenditure of money."

Interestingly, the Sierra Leone Court, located in that country, is meant to operate on a much more modest $4 million budget. The Sierre Leone Court in Freetown will judge crimes committed during that decade-long civil war. This is a new variant of an international court that aims to focus on less than 30 key decision makers, to end proceedings after only three years, while existing alongside a Truth and Reconciliation Commission. It is likely to be the closest model for a court in Iraq.

The Sierre Leone special court was created in January 2002 and started to operate in July of that year. It showed its independence by unsealing, on 4 June 2003, an indictment originally issued in March of that year, against the President of Liberia, Charles Taylor, when he went to Ghana for peace talks; an action that upset the U.S., Nigerian, and Ghanaian governments. This Court was deliberately established as a hybrid body, part international and part national, and formed as a result of negotiations between the UN and the Sierre Leone government. It is jointly administered and funded by voluntary contributions, with the U.S. as the largest donor. The Sierre Leone government appointed three judges and the UN Secretary General five judges. The Sierre Leone Court, like the Yugoslavian and Rwanda Courts, cannot impose the death penalty.[9]

TRUTH AND RECONCILIATION: SOUTH AFRICA

In 1992 when we in Europe were contemplating whether to follow up the Nuremberg military Tribunal with a Yugoslav specific war crimes Tribunal, anti-apartheid leaders in South Africa were considering, during their negotiated transition, how to deal with the appalling legacy of apartheid. Opinion was divided in South Africa; victims needed rehabilitation though many felt, like the widow of Steve Biko, that justice was best pursued through the courts. Her views at that time weighed heavily with me, and heavily influenced my views of Yugoslavia. It was Biko's death that had given Vance and I (in the Security Council in 1977, when we were both Foreign Ministers) the domestic political momentum necessary to agree to support a mandatory arms embargo on South Africa under Chapter VII of the *UN Charter*. By August 1993 the National Executive Committee of the African National Congress (ANC) in South Africa concluded that the Government needed to establish a commission to get at the truth, saying that the experiences from Chile, Argentina, and El Salvador keenly reflected the cleansing power of the truth. The situation was, therefore, very different from what we faced in the former Yugoslavia where, in 1993, we still had no peace and savage fighting was continuing in Bosnia-Herzegovina.

In South Africa, in contrast to the former Yugoslavia, there were real grounds for believing that a coalition government was possible. I was able to feel this optimism for myself when I met President F. W. de Klerk in Pretoria in early January 1990.[10] He was a very different type of man from his bullying, uncompromising, racist predecessor, P. W. Botha, with whom Vance and I had negotiated with over Namibia in 1978. President de Klerk told me in confidence that within a few weeks time he would free Nelson Mandela from prison, lift the ban on the liberation movements, and start a dialogue for a comprehensive settlement. It was never going to be an easy negotiation. Some people were shocked when Nelson Mandela demonstrated that he had not gone soft in prison by saying immediately after his release that he remained a disciplined member of the ANC. Probably the breakthrough, in the hearts and minds of most leaders who were not as enlightened as Mandela and de Klerk, came when key figures within the ANC, and the Nationalist Party, negotiated directly. Then they sensed for themselves that it could be possible for them to live together, not separated in one country.

In a powerful book, *Country of My Skull*,[11] Antjie Krog, a poet and a journalist, describes how the Chilean philosopher and activist José Zalaquett, who served on the Chilean Truth Commission, converted her to that mechanism's legitimacy by arguing that World War II military tribunals in Nuremberg and Tokyo only worked because the guilty had totally lost their political power base and their weapons, whereas in Chile, as in South Africa, the Commission was a better mechanism since the previous regime had to be part of the new government. Even so, in South Africa, powerful advocates of reconciliation had different approaches. For Archbishop Desmond Tutu reconciliation had to be the start of a transformation process. Whereas for Thabo Mbeki[12] real reconciliation could not be achieved without a thorough transformation and democratization process.

The Truth and Reconciliation Commission was established in South Africa with three Committees:

- A Human Rights Violation Committee, which examined the accounts of victims through hearings and investigations;
- An Amnesty Committee with two Commission members and three independent judges;

- A Reparation and Rehabilitation Committee to help victims and survivors.

All Committees were served by an Investigative Unit and Research Unit. The first hearings were held in April 1996. Over the following two years there were almost daily revelations widely reported. The Commission went around the country conducting hearings in cities, town halls, community centers, and churches. It received 20,000 statements from victims, 2,000 of these in public hearings and it received nearly 8,000 applications for amnesty from perpetrators. Victims questioned torturers and police interrogators and the whole experience was publicly and deeply revealing.

It was not just the upholders of apartheid whose crimes were investigated. Cases of Africans necklacing other Africans, by lighting a tire round their necks filled with petrol, were examined as was the behavior of ANC activists in their camps. P. W. Botha refused to give oral evidence and was taken to the Court in order to assert the fact that no one was beyond the reach of the Commission. Though his case was dismissed because of a legal technicality there was by then little public mood to pursue it and he was left alone, a sad, old, and tragic figure.

The whole South African experience left a deep mark on people's attitudes, which can be summed up in these words: "when the Truth Commission started last year, I realized instinctively: if you cut yourself off from this process, you will wake up in a foreign country, a country that you do not know and you will never understand."[13] What the Truth Commission established was collective responsibility, as distinct from the individual accountability that stems from the law courts.

TRUTH AND RECONCILIATION IN FORMER YUGOSLAVIA

In Bosnia-Herzegovina a Truth and Reconciliation Commission could not have been established until the war stopped in 1995. While it might have been possible in theory to have established a Commission as part of the Dayton Accords as a supplement to the ICTY, which had already been established, there was still a great gulf between the two territorial entities agreed upon at Dayton—Republika Srpska and the predominantly Muslim Croatian Federation of Bosnia-Herzegovina. However, Alex Boraine, the deputy co-person of the South African Truth Commission, in his book *A Country Unmasked*[14] describes that at a conference in Sarajevo in February 2000 he found great interest in and support for establishing a Commission. Richard Goldstone, himself a South African and the first Prosecutor of ICTY, argued at that same conference that a Commission could complement the Tribunal's work but should not grant amnesties to anyone who was subject to an arrest order. The United States and the five European countries in the Contact Group, which includes Russia, have continued to rely on the ICTY. In fairness, the situation on the ground in Bosnia remained very fragile, and it was further complicated by the build-up to NATO's military intervention on humanitarian grounds in Kosovo in 1999.

In retrospect I think the real opportunity for a Truth and Reconciliation Commission in Bosnia has only appeared in 2004–5 with a more realistic prospect emerging of limited cooperation from the Serbs and a somewhat better atmosphere between all the parties on the ground. Still, in 2003, a number of governments thought that there were too many people, felt to be guilty of war crimes, currently in positions of authority in Bosnia, particularly in Republika Srpska,. If they were not brought to trial, people feared that the already very slow transformation process would be stop or even reverse itself. This judgment was shared by the international community's High Representative in Bosnia-Herzegovina, Lord Ashdown.

The question remains, however, whether before any Special War Crime Chamber in the State Court is finally established in Bosnia-Herzegovina, to handle cases referred by the Tribunal, those very same people felt to be guilty of war crimes could not be better dealt with by way of a Truth and Reconciliation Commission? The Security Council should, with the High Representative, weigh whether a Truth and Reconciliation Commission would be a better alternative to creating a Special Chamber in the State Court. The local people in Bosnia would also need to be consulted. The local leaders would, however, need to understand that it would not be a question of whether or not *any* mechanism—either the Special Chamber or a Truth Commission—would be put in place but of *which* mechanism. That reality should concentrate minds.

The High Representative in Bosnia has the final authority regarding interpretation of the "Agreement on the Civilian Implementation of the Peace Settlement." The High Representative can impose laws in the absence of a willingness of local governing parties to adopt laws and to dismiss from office public officials.[15] In establishing the State Border Service, which the Constitutional Court ruled as compatible with the Constitution, the High Representative has imposed a very wide range of significant and important laws including license plates on vehicles and a national currency. An Independent Judicial Commission also has been established. Not withstanding all this, most independent commentators recognize that Bosnia has not yet become one country. This is despite the fact that 1 million refugees out of an original total of 2.2 million have returned and many to their own villages. It has to be recognized that those returns have in part come about because some of the local killers have been arrested and indicted by the ICTY.

Yet the present degree of reconciliation in Bosnia-Herzegovina has much further to go. The fact that Radovan Karadzic and General Mladic had still not been arrested by mid 2004 has been a serious blow. There is abundant evidence that they are being shielded by Serbs, and it is surprising that NATO special forces have not, as yet, been able to track them down. Hopefully they will be arrested soon and tried by the ICTY. Also the leaders of Republika Srpska must go much further in publicly acknowledging and apologizing for the scale of the 1995 massacre in and around Srebrenica. It is also time that the case brought by Bosnia-Herzegovina against Serbia in the International Court of Justice be reassessed with a view to it being withdrawn. All of these things could help facilitate better relations between Serbia and Bosnia.

A Truth and Reconciliation Commission for Bosnia-Herzegovina could be charged with completing all the stages of its deliberations to coincide with the winding up of the ICTY. If any people felt to be war criminals and still in positions of power in Bosnia-Herzegovina refused to apply for amnesty to a Truth Commission and did not admit to their guilt, they would, as part of that process, still be open to being charged and tried by the rather rougher justice likely to be available in the national courts of Bosnia-Herzegovina. A Truth and Reconciliation Commission is not, therefore, a soft option but a different option for

Bosnia and one which might take reconciliation deeper into the hearts and minds than creating a Special Chamber for war crimes in the State Court. The State Court has only just been tolerated by the leaders in Republika Srpska, who were tempted to challenge its legality. The addition of a Special Chamber, if it were to trigger a challenge, would be damaging certainly in the short term.

There has to come a moment fairly soon in the former Yugoslavia when the international community must accept that the choices over their future have to be determined more by those democratically elected citizens of the independent states within the former Yugoslavia and less by the international community. We cannot preach democracy and then browbeat those elected. Specifically, in Bosnia-Herzegovina, the continuation of international administration and decision-making for much longer will contribute to the weakness of its admittedly fragile democratic political institutions that have been established. In Bosnia, a Truth and Justice Commission might be accepted by the electorate, though this approach is unlikely to be agreed to in Croatia, Serbia, or Montenegro.

In Croatia, considerable resistance has been building up for some years to handing over suspected war criminals to the court in The Hague when they have been issued with arrest warrants. The government elected in 2003 comes from the Croatian Democratic Union—President Tudjman's old party. They share the previous government's extreme reluctance to send General Ante Gotovina to The Hague. Under pressure from the EU, which Croatians want to join, and from the U.S., they have sent a further batch of people who have been indicted to The Hague. It might, however, make this process more acceptable if, in 2004, the Security Council opened itself to a debate with the new government on fixing an appropriate time when no new arrest warrants would be issued in Croatia.

In Serbia, during the 2003 elections a rise in the electoral strength of the two nationalist parties led by the imprisoned Vojislav Seselj and Milosevic who are both on trial in The Hague, respectively won 82 and 21 seats out of the 250 seats. The former Prime Minister Zoran Djindjic in part paid with his life for courageously agreeing, under immense financial pressure from the EU and U.S. Secretary of State Colin Powell, to send Milosevic to The Hague. A new fragile coalition government led by Vojislav Kostunica—who took over as President from Milosevic—is being asked to send to The Hague, for alleged crimes in Kosovo, people like Streten Lukic. Lukic may have been instrumental as police chief, in achieving a peaceful transfer from Milosevic and re-asserting control in Serbia after Djindjic's assassination. Kostunica was never a Communist and was never inveigled into cooperation with Milosevic while he was President. Yet he said on 22 February 2004, "This country is not a delivery service for human merchandise to The Hague tribunal." He wants war-crime suspects to be tried in Serbian courts instead, and this may be all that will be offered to the international community. One such trial started in early 2004 for war crimes allegedly committed by Serbs in Vukovar. The Security Council must resolve the dilemma of domestic war crimes tribunals around a negotiating table, for not much more will be achieved by browbeating Serbia with economic threats. Perhaps, as in Croatia, under further U.S. financial pressure, more people will be sent to The Hague but it will not happen without a struggle. Besides, the EU's bargaining power lessens as public enthusiasm in Serbia for joining the EU decreases. It is now Macedonia that looks likely to follow Slovenia into the EU.

There are warning signs of political pressures building up again in the former Yugoslavia. The government in Serbia is also going to face great strains when, as I believe it is inevitable, the UN administration in Kosovo comes under pressure for independence. The case for early independence was persuasively argued in 2003 by Richard Holbrooke and Bernard Kouchner. They also wisely warned against the U.S. military being replaced by only EU forces. All past experience indicates that the U.S. and EU, having eventually gone into Bosnia together in 1995 with NATO troops on the ground, will stay together if more for political than military reasons. In both Bosnia and in Kosovo, troops should stay under NATO command until the task is complete. The danger otherwise is of the U.S. reverting to their 1993–94 position and giving the public appearance of favoring a Muslim majority opinion while refusing to take up responsibility on the ground for maintaining peace and security. The Security Council could help defuse some of the tension in Belgrade by opening up a dialogue with the Serbian and Montenegrin governments on fixing a date when no further arrest warrants would be issued by the ICTY in their countries. Perhaps such an agreement could be made to coincide with Kosovo independence since it will be very difficult for any government in Belgrade to agree on Kosovo's independence without at least reaching overall closure on new war crimes prosecutions. The Security Council would have to be confident, however, that neither the Serb nor Montenegrin governments were holding back or shielding, if still free, Radovan Karadzic or General Mladic.

The achievement of the ICTY in bringing former President Milosevic to trial has been a formidable one, even though the prosecution has not been able to obtain the military records they wanted from Belgrade. Also Judge Richard May, who had to step down from the Court in 2004 because of ill health, presided with impeccable fairness to Milosevic despite being sorely provoked. To a certain extent, because of the television and press coverage in Serbia and Montenegro of the trial of Milosevic, there has already been an exposure in those countries to crimes committed by their own people in the former Yugoslavia. Also there has been an apology to the Bosnians from the Serbian government. But how deeply the majority of Serbs have been affected by the The Hague court is hard to judge.

A report in December 2003 from Tim Judah, an experienced journalist, records, "In Serbia, Croatia and Bosnia, however, I met virtually no one who believed that the Tribunal was helping to reconcile people."[16] It appears from this that no one should rule out an additional mechanism of reconciliation. There needs to be no doubt, however, in any Serb's minds that Dr. Karadzic and General Mladic will not be allowed to escape justice merely by delaying their capture. Also that when captured these two men will be brought to trial under an international court in The Hague. Given the worldwide concern about the 1995 massacre in Srebrenica, any trial needs to be authoritative and that could not come from a Special Chamber in the State Court of Bosnia-Herzegovina. It is surely reasonable to hope that the American government might, at least, abstain on a Security Council Resolution put forward in the next few years that would declare that these two men would be brought to the International Criminal Court (ICC) in The Hague, if the ICTY had come up against its closure date. The ICC cannot itself try cases retrospectively. What the Security Council Resolution would be doing therefore would be using the infrastructure of an ICC Court but not its own statutes and would be vested for these two cases with all the powers, evidence, papers, and procedures of the ICTY. In the absence of such a Security Council decision on an alternative Court, rumor mongers will suggest that one of the reasons for establishing a Special Chamber in the State Court is to try Karadzic and Mladic. The U.S. government's position is that they reject the ICC because they want to exclude U.S. citizens from being judged by the ICC. A U.S. abstention would not weaken that position. It might be that the rest of the Security Council would also agree to exempting the Balkans from the ICC for a period longer than the present yearly extension.

The U.S. government's position is that they reject the ICC because they want to exclude U.S. citizens from being judged by the ICC. A U.S. abstention would not weaken that position. It might be that the rest of the Security Council would also agree to exempting the Balkans from the ICC for a period longer than the present yearly extension. In the medium term the present ICC model will have to be revised but the EU is not yet ready to recognize this. It is simply not credible for the authority of the ICC worldwide for the U.S. and China to be outside it and totally opposed to its present structure. The lines of a compromise will need to focus on some limited role for the Security Council to temper the unbridled freedom that the ICC has maintained in its present structure. This controversy reflects the old argument about the virtue of pure justice against practical reality. The ICC in final negotiations in Rome were able to escape the limitations of a Security Council veto, but the ICC will not be able to escape the reality that lies behind the demand for the power of veto. An essential part of the San Francisco compromise that laid the foundation for the UN was the *U.S.* insistence from the start that they would have to have a veto and the ICC will not have universal application without some recognition that that political reality exists just as strongly at the start of the twenty-first century. The French negotiated a special arrangement for their armed forces in relation to the ICC, which may provide something on which to build.

IRAQ–SPECIAL COURT

The U.S. led Coalition Provisional Authority in Iraq gave legislative authority for the Iraqi Governing council in December 2003 to appoint an Iraqi Special Tribunal to prosecute crimes including genocide and crimes against humanity. With Saddam Hussein under interrogation and awaiting trial, and the Coalition Provisional Authority due to be wound up in the summer of 2004 and replaced by a broader based Iraqi Government, it would be wise for the Governing Council to ask the UN Security Council to negotiate with the Iraqis to jointly create a Special Court as was done for Sierre Leone. Pending agreement the process of collecting evidence and vetting people for appointment to the Court is proceeding, with a view to a trial by the end of 2004. The Court could operate under Chapter VII of the *UN Charter* which was first applied to Iraq in 1990.

I supported the British Government, acting militarily with the U.S. Government, to help topple Saddam Hussein. And while I have always been against the death penalty in the United Kingdom I would not want the UN Security Council to force the Iraqis to rule out the death sentence. There is a tendency for EU countries in particular to believe that they have the moral right to impose their views on the death penalty on all sovereign countries in the UN. This is not a wise position. The existence or not of the death penalty should be a democratic choice made by the citizens in any country in a way allowed for in their country's constitution.

CONCLUSIONS

Everyone in the world, not least now in Iraq, has much to learn from the experience of achieving justice and reconciliation in the Balkans, East Timor, and in Southern and Central Africa. We have all made our mistakes—myself included. It takes time and patience but we have developed interesting new techniques and we are still learning invaluable lessons about how to balance justice and reconciliation.

What is needed after internal conflict, and particularly after international military intervention, is the restoration of strong, democratic governments helped by generous external economic support accompanied by a readiness of new governments to put the past behind them and institute far-reaching reforms. Yet those powerful nations who have, over the last fifteen years, made forcible humanitarian interventions must be more willing to learn to listen to the citizens of the country in which they intervene. Experience has shown that those intervening cannot just dictate solutions but must be ready to consult and adapt to different circumstances. Again we are seeing this in Iraq, with the UN involved in the dialogue with Iraqi leaders over the procedures and the timing of free elections.

We have witnessed many forms of humanitarian intervention over the past fifteen years: UN led interventions, NATO led interventions, interventions from coalitions of the willing, with or without UN support. We will probably see a similar mixture in the future. The *UN Charter* has certainly been more flexibly interpreted in recent years and it is questionable to what extent the Charter has actually been overridden. The old argument that military intervention can only take place in self-defense is leading to some tortuous self-justifications. I believe, for instance, that the *Charter* was stretched tighter in its interpretation over NATO's humanitarian intervention in Kosovo than over the US led intervention in Iraq. The *UN Charter* was, however, in both circumstances circumvented.

The *UN Charter* is unlikely to be amended to specifically state new circumstances in which a humanitarian intervention would be lawful. What we need instead is more wisdom and unity on the Security Council itself with fairer representation of countries so that the Council can more flexibly interpret the *Charter*. China and the Russian Federation will have their doubts but they are protected by their veto power. Experience shows that military interventions which ignore the Security Council or deliberately flout the *Charter* are far less likely to achieve peace and stability than interventions which stretch, but keep within, the *Charter*, and work with the Security Council to build on and develop flexible approaches. If the Security Council were to become instead wedded to a static, over-legalistic interpretation of the *Charter* it will be sidelined and unilateralism will gain at the expense of multilateralism. In the twenty-first century it is and will not be acceptable to return to a situation where the internal affairs of a member state are beyond the reach of international action.

We have, in the UN and in its specialized agencies, a viable and valuable international institution. For 40 years it survived the polarization of the Cold War between two superpowers. It lived with the reality that it was unable to intervene in the self-rule of its member states, however odious. All that changed with the fall of the Berlin Wall. Now what we have to develop within the UN are the skills to make the *Charter* work more effectively in the promotion of peace, justice and reconciliation. We have seen in 2004 that the U.S. Administration has recognized a positive role for the UN, whether in Iraq over election procedures or in Haiti over peacekeeping. The high-water mark of American unilateralism has, I suspect, passed. The U.S. must accept that the UN plays an important role in the twenty-first century, and hopefully the "indispensable nation" has seen that they cannot do everything on their own.

For the remainder of the twenty-first century it is a tragedy that Sergio Vieira de Mello's skills will not any longer be working for the UN. Let us, building on his past achievements, not least in Iraq, ensure that the memory of his work will continue to inspire us all.

Healing with a Single History

Richard J. Goldstone

Introduction

There is no democracy in which justice and the rule of law are not axiomatically assumed to be foundational principles. In 1895, Professor A. V. Dicey, the great English legal philosopher, defined the principles of the Rule of Law. One of them, he declared, was that "no man is punishable or can be made to suffer in body or goods except for a distinct breach of law."[1] Almost a century later, Professor Archibald Cox expressed the opinion that it is "the genius of American constitutionalism which supports the Rule of Law."[2]

The *South African Constitution* of 1996 was the product of the experience of other democratic constitutional states and its own painful history of oppression and discrimination. In the Preamble it is stated that:

"We the people of South Africa,
Recognize the injustices of our past;
Honour those who suffered for justice and freedom in our land;
Respect those who have worked to build and develop our country; and
Believe that South Africa belongs to all who live in it, united in our diversity.
We therefore, through our freely elected representatives, adopt this Constitution as the supreme law of the Republic so as to—
Heal the divisions of the past and establish a society based on democratic values, social justice and fundamental human rights
Lay the foundations for a democratic and open society in which government is based on the will of the people and every citizen is equally protected by law . . .

The *Constitution* goes on to make respect for human dignity, justice and the rule of law central principles. In one of the oldest as well as in one of the most recent democratic constitutions, there is the recognition of the fundamental nature of justice and the rule of law.

During South Africa's transition, there was much debate as to the appropriate manner in dealing with the sordid past of racial oppression. Nelson Mandela and the African National Congress would have wished for Nuremberg style prosecutions for the political and security force leaders. If then President F. W. de Klerk had his way, there would have been blanket amnesties for the Apartheid leaders. The compromise, and it was a political compromise, was a form of truth commission.

Soon after South Africa elected its first democratic legislature it decided to establish the Truth and Reconciliation Commission (TRC). The experience of other truth commissions played an important role in that endeavor, especially that of Chile. However, unlike its Chilean counterpart, the South African model provided for public hearings and the "naming of names." There was also no restriction on the kind of serious human rights violations that were investigated.

Over 20,000 victims gave their testimony to the TRC and so too, some 7000 perpetrators. Amnesty, both criminal and civil, was granted only to those perpetrators who made full confessions of the crimes in respect of which they sought the amnesty. The result was an outpouring of evidence of the heinous human rights violations that were perpetrated in the execution of the apartheid policy.

There has been much debate, both in South Africa and in the global community, about the successes and failures of the TRC. The extent to which individual perpetrators benefited is a complex subject about which there are many contradictory views. It is clear that some victims left the TRC angry and frustrated, while others were able, through their testimony, to begin a healing process.

Whatever the effect of the TRC on individual victims, in my opinion, there can be doubt that the general South African society has been a beneficiary of the TRC process. During the Apartheid era, the majority of white South Africans believed the denials of human rights violations that were put out by the government's security forces. It was more comfortable for those denials to be accepted by the people who felt they were benefiting from them. But for the work of the TRC, that acceptance of the truth of those denials would have continued into the post-apartheid era. The mass of evidence made public by the TRC has given South Africa a single history of the Apartheid era—and the denials have disappeared. My grandchildren and their black friends are being taught the same history of Apartheid and so too will their children.

Much of the violence in our contemporary world is the result of the partial history that groups believe. That is certainly the position in the Balkans where too many Serbs, Croats, and Bosniaks believe that they are the victims and the others are the perpetrators. It is those false denials that provide the toxic fuel that enable evil leaders of the ilk of Slobodan Milosevic to appeal to the nationalism of extreme groups and embark on programs that result in ethnic cleansing.

The cancer of such false denials has been removed in South Africa by the TRC. Not only does this militate against future racism in our country but it facilitates the acceptance by the white minority of government programs designed to benefit the majority of our people who were so grievously disadvantaged by hundreds of years of racist oppression. The fairness and morality that require such programs has become manifest. While not suggesting that there is no opposition to such programs, they attract substantially less criticism than would have been the case without the work of the TRC.

If we are ever to live in peace and harmony and prevent the cycles of bloody wars that dominated the twentieth century, the global community will also have to accept that justice and the rule of law are the values that should govern the relationship between sovereign states.

In all of his work, Sergio Vieira de Mello recognized the importance of both justice and the rule of law. It was those values that directed his work in particular when he worked with the United Nations High Commission for Refugees (UNHCR), in East Timor and during his short tenure of the office of the UN High Commission for Human Rights. He was working with his usual energy and commitment to convey to Iraqis the importance of those values at the time of his tragic death in Baghdad. In his dealings with governments and with people, equity and fairness were core values.

I propose, in this chapter, to undertake an overview of human rights today, examining the attitude of the United States (US) to international law, its behavior and that of some other countries since 11 September 2001, and the relationship between peace and justice. The last mentioned topic illustrates compromises between conflicting objectives—essentially the kind of compromise that needs to be undertaken in respect of national security and human rights.

THE DEVELOPMENT OF HUMAN RIGHTS

Between the end of World War II and 11 September 2001 there was an impressive and even awesome development of the rule of law within nations and, in some areas, in the governance of the global community. In the domestic arena, that development has been evident in the flowering of democratic forms of government in a number of regions of the world. It is foundational to the structure of the European Union (EU) and has been an explicit goal of the Organization of American States (OAU), the African Union (AU), and the Commonwealth of Nations.

Over the first half century of the life of the United Nations, a fundamental contradiction has emerged with regard to the protection of fundamental human rights. Article 2(4) of the *UN Charter* obliges all members to refrain from using force against the territorial integrity or political independence of any state. Article 2(7) prohibits the UN from intervening in matters that are essentially within the domestic jurisdiction of any state. It was the latter provision that enabled South Africa to object to attacks by Member States on the evil system of Apartheid. Despite that objection, in 1946 India requested the General Assembly to investigate the treatment of Indian nationals in South Africa. The resolution passed but with the opposition of the United States and the United Kingdom (UK).

As colonialism came to an end and it became less acceptable for democratic states to discriminate against their citizens on grounds of race or sex, so it became more acceptable for governments and international organizations to concern themselves with serious violations of human rights wherever they might occur. The provisions of Article 2(7) of the *Charter* were no longer recognized as a protection even when the UN or its members took punitive steps in an attempt to end such violations.

The recognition of universal jurisdiction for the most heinous international crimes further eroded the strict application of sovereignty.[3] Citizens of any country could be placed on trial before the courts of any other country for such international crimes even in the absence of a connection between the crime and such nation.

These developments reached their zenith when, in 1993, the Security Council established the International Criminal Tribunal for the former Yugoslavia and, in the following year, the International Criminal Tribunal for Rwanda. Then, there was the 1999 bombing of Serbia by the members of NATO in order to protect the Kosovar Albanians from ethnic cleansing. Even though Security Council authority was absent, and the intervention thus illegal, there was no condemnation of the action. Russia attempted to have the Council condemn the intervention but failed miserably. Instead, a UN administration was set up to govern that province of Serbia.

The contradiction in the UN system between respecting state sovereignty and protecting human rights is also illustrated in Security Council Resolution 1244 of 10 June 1999, which established the terms of the UN administration in Kosovo. It reaffirmed "the commitment of all Member States to the sovereignty and territorial integrity of the Federal Republic of Yugoslavia." It also reaffirmed the call in previous resolutions for "substantial autonomy and meaningful self-administration for Kosovo." It went on to decide on the deployment, under UN auspices, of an international civil presence and authorized member states to establish an international security presence in Kosovo.

This formula was bound to lead to contradictory policies. When members of the Independent International Commission on Kosovo met with the Foreign Affairs Committee of the Russian Duma, we were handed a long list of complaints against the UN administration in Kosovo. For example, there was a strong feeling that the UN replacing Yugoslavian currency with the German Mark as the currency of Kosovo was inconsistent with the recognition of the sovereignty of the Federal Republic of Yugoslavia. So, too, Russia objected to the issuing by the UN of visas to persons visiting Kosovo. When Russians visit Kosovo, they make a point of travelling there from Belgrade with appropriate travel documents issued by the Yugoslav Government.

The developments to which I have referred were unthinkable a little more than a decade ago. It was the widely accepted view that an international criminal court could only be treaty based. And, humanitarian intervention was a theory thought unlikely to be implemented in practice.

The consequences of these developments, whether within nations or in the global community, have been significant. Democratic ideals have spread around the world, and especially to states of the former Soviet Union, many of which are ever more enthusiastic to be accepted as members of the European Union.

Even less anticipated was that an International Criminal Court would be established early in the new millennium, that by the end of 2003 some ninety-three nations would have ratified its founding treaty, that eighteen judges would have been elected, and that that Court's Prosecutor would be preparing to launch his first investigation into serious war crimes allegedly committed in the Democratic Republic of the Congo.

Who would have thought a little more than a decade ago that the work of international criminal courts would have a profound effect on humanitarian law—that the somewhat irrational distinction with regard to the protection of innocent civilians caught up in international and non-international armed conflict would be reduced almost to the point of extinction? Who would have thought that an international criminal court would hold that systematic mass rape could be held to constitute genocide? And who would have anticipated that in wars fought by democracies, their military leaders would take the requirements of humanitarian law seriously?

Insufficient attention has been given to this last mentioned development. In World War II, civilians became the target of warfare. Cities on both sides were fire-bombed and the atomic bomb was dropped with the intention of devastating whole cities in Japan. In the wars in Korea and Vietnam, deaths of civilians outnumbered those of troops by about 90 percent. It was only in the post-international criminal tribunal world that the military leaders of Western nations became committed to attacking only military targets and taking all reasonable steps to protect non-belligerents. The consequence in the war over Kosovo was a relatively low number of civilian deaths—under 2,000 after 78 days of massive bombing.

Prior to the establishment of the war crimes tribunals, humanitarian law was a subject taught at some army colleges. Since 1993, when the Yugoslavia Tribunal was established, humanitarian law has become a subject of daily discussion in the media and is taught in thousands of law schools around the world.

I wish that the story ended on this high note. It does not. At the levels of both domestic law and international law, justice and the rule of law have been dealt grievous blows. How much permanent damage has been done, only time will tell. The tragedy is compounded by the fact that these blows have been dealt by the democratic nations of the world and none more so than by the United States.

THE UNITED STATES AND INTERNATIONAL LAW

The United States has been regarded and has regarded itself as the leader of the democratic world. It earned that reputation because of its concern for the human rights of all people. The annual State Department report on human rights discussed the manner in which human rights were respected or violated in just about every country of the world. The US played the leading role in the establishment of the UN war crimes tribunals and in calling the diplomatic conference that led to the treaty under which the International Criminal Court was established.

I know from my own experience that without the political and financial power of the US neither the Yugoslav nor the Rwandan tribunals would have become viable institutions. In their early years, the US bent the UN's financial rules in order to ensure that appropriate experts and resources reached The Hague, Kigali, and Arusha. When governments, such as Croatia, were tardy in cooperating with the Yugoslav Tribunal, it was US financial pressure that virtually compelled the surrender of indicted war criminals. It was the US ambassador to Cameroon who assisted me in making the crucial official contacts that, in turn, led to the surrender of leaders indicted for the 1994 genocide to the Rwandan Tribunal.

All this was to change. In recent years, the attitude of the US to the UN has been problematic. It has been tardy in paying its dues to the world body. In the 1990s this almost brought the UN to the point of insolvency.

In relation to the war against Iraq, it decided to act outside its *Charter* obligations. When it later welcomed an international effort to bring democracy to Iraq, the nations that opposed the war were none too keen to have their nationals become involved in the ongoing conflict.

The US's approach to ratifying international treaties has been patchy at best. It took forty years to ratify the Genocide Convention and is the only nation failing to ratify the Convention on the Rights of the Child. More recently, it refused to ratify a protocol to the Torture Convention, which would allow inspections of the prisons of nations suspected of violating the provisions of that Convention.

The US ambivalence to international law and international organizations became ever more exceptional. It refused to accept that any of its nationals should ever be brought before an international court, out of fear that such moves might be politically motivated and biased against the US. It demanded that the jurisdiction of the International Criminal Court should be subject to the approval of the Security Council and thus enable it, and the other four permanent members, to control where the Court could operate. When the overwhelming majority of nations assembled in Rome rejected that approach, the US demanded that jurisdiction be restricted to nationals of nations that ratified the Rome statute. That too was rejected and the US joined only six other countries who voted against the adoption of the Rome Treaty while 120 nations voted in favor of it.

The US approach to the International Criminal Court has become even more hostile under the second Bush Administration. While former President Bill Clinton signed the Rome Treaty, President George W. Bush "withdrew" that signature and has actively campaigned against the institution. The United States has threatened or cajoled a number of nations to enter into bilateral agreements undertaking not to hand its citizens to the international court. It has withdrawn military cooperation from some nations that have refused to enter into such agreements.

This recalcitrant attitude of the US has seriously retarded the building of international justice and the rule of law. If the most powerful nation in the world does not regard itself bound by those laws it *has* ratified, on what basis can it be expected that less powerful nations will remain law abiding?

The Effect of September 11

I turn to consider the effect of the events of 11 September 2001 on domestic justice and the rule of law. Again, the US is unfortunately the democracy so visibly denying civil liberties of persons under its control, whether they are citizens or non-citizens. I refer to the resort by the US to secret deportation hearings; the detention of citizens and non-citizens without trial and without access to a lawyer or to any court; the prospect of trials on capital crimes by military commissions from which there is no appeal to any civilian court; the indefinite detention of persons presumed by the Third Geneva Convention to be prisoners of war, without the benefits of those Conventions and again without access to lawyers or courts. A flicker of hope has been kindled by the US Supreme Court agreeing to hear an appeal from some of those detained in Guantanamo Bay who question the lawfulness of that detention.

Other democracies have also not fared too well. Prior to September 11, the UK enacted wide-ranging measures to counter terrorism. It did so predominantly in the face of IRA terrorist activities. After September 11, a new anti-terrorism statute was enacted. Its most controversial provision is that providing for the internment, without trial, of a "suspected international terrorist" if the Home Secretary reasonably believes that such person's presence in the UK is a risk to national security and suspects that such person is a terrorist. If the person is not a UK citizen, he or she can be detained for an unspecified period without charge or trial. There is no appeal to the ordinary courts but only to a government-appointed commission. It was this provision that led the UK Government to derogate from the human rights provisions of the European Convention on Human Rights.

These denials of justice and acts inconsistent with the rule of law are having serious consequences in other countries. If powerful nations can act in such a way, what stops weaker nations from acting in a similar fashion in their regions of the world? Of course there is a knock-on effect.

Recent Indian legislation invades the privacy of persons in material respects and allows detention of terrorist suspects without trial for periods of up to 90 days. Pending South African legislation also provided for detention without trial. The cruelty and abuses that accompanied detention without trial during the apartheid era led to protests and these contentious provisions have now been removed.

In a recent report by the Lawyers Committee for Human Rights,[4] one reads that Egypt has passed even more draconian laws allegedly to fight terrorism. Egypt's President Mubarak declared that the new US policies "proved that we were right from the beginning in using all means, including military tribunals, to combat terrorism."

The United Nations Security Council itself was tardy in making an effort to ensure that civil liberties were respected in legislation that member states were peremptorily required, by Resolution 1373, to enact. The attitude, as conveyed to me by the first chairman of the Counter-Terrorism Committee, Sir Jeremy Greenstock, was that human rights are not the concern of the Security Council.

In the same Human Rights Watch report, there is reference to an instruction given to US ambassadors. They were to report human rights violations to the State Department in preparation for the 2002 report (issued in March 2003). According to the instruction, "Actions by governments taken at the request of the United States or with the expressed support of the United States should not be included in the report."

There is no doubt that the events of September 11 created a new concept of democracy that differs from the one that Western states defended before those events took place, and especially so with respect to the freedom of the individual. There is no better illustration than the Bush Administration attempting to justify the indefinite detention of citizens and non-citizens without any court intervention. This is based primarily on the President's declaration that such persons are "unlawful combatants."

The oppressive former dictator of Liberia, Charles Taylor, before he ignominiously left his country and accepted asylum in Nigeria, used the American "unlawful combatant" formula to justify the arrest and torture of innocent journalists. In November 2001, President Robert Mugabe of Zimbabwe claimed that foreign correspondents, including American correspondents, were terrorist sympathizers for reporting on political attacks against white Zimbabweans. His spokesman insisted that it was an open secret that such correspondents were assisting terrorists and distorting the facts. He then said the following:

As for correspondents, we would like them to know that we agree with the United States President Bush that anyone who in any way finances, harbors, or defends terrorists is himself a terrorist. We too will not make any difference between terrorists and their friends and supporters. This kind of media terrorism will not be tolerated.[5]

A third illustration from the Human Rights Watch report relates to Indonesia. The government of that nation announced in May that it was intending to build a Guantanamo Bay-like island detention camp to house prisoners in its long-standing struggle against armed separatists in northern Sumatra.

I am not suggesting that these evil leaders are doing what the US is doing. What I am saying is that when the most powerful nation in the world fails to respect its own great values, other nations will become less restrained in the manner in which they treat their own people.

During 2002, I co-chaired a Task Force established by the International Bar Association to report on international terrorism and the role of lawyers in helping combat it.[6] The Task Force included members from Africa, Asia, Europe and the Americas. In our unanimous report we recognized the right, and indeed the duty, of all governments to protect their citizens. Obviously that is one of the most important obligations of government. The challenge that international terrorism presents to justice and the rule of law is to balance the means taken to combat it and the invasion of the civil liberties of citizens. There can be no warrant for the wholesale casting aside of the freedoms for which leading democracies have fought so hard and for so long.

PEACE AND JUSTICE

Soon after he assumed office as the UN High Commissioner for Human Rights, Sergio Vieira de Mello put it as follows:

[M]easures must be taken in transparency, they must be of short duration, and must respect the fundamental non-derogable rights embodied in our human rights norms. They must take place within the framework of the law. Without that, the terrorists will ultimately win and we will ultimately lose—as we would have allowed them to destroy the very foundation of our modern human civilization. I am convinced that it is possible to fight this menace at no cost to our human rights. Protecting our citizens and upholding rights are not incompatible: on the contrary, they must go firmly together lest we lose our bearing.

We are involved in a clash of values and rights that contradict one another. In order to combat international crime, policing authorities in democracies require additional, non-traditional powers. They need to be equipped to foil the plans of sophisticated criminals who do not hesitate to use modern technology and who might have access now or in the near future to weapons of mass destruction. The right balance between national security and the protection of human rights is an excruciatingly difficult one to find, but nonetheless one that can be found.

Sergio Vieira de Mello was remarkably sensitive in finding such balance in other fraught spheres. I refer to the following two illustrations from my own relationship with him. With the establishment of the war crimes tribunals, one of the debates that arose concerned the contradiction between peace and justice. Is it worth indicting national leaders for war crimes and thereby retard the peace process? This issue arose crisply with the indictment of Radovan Karadzic in 1995 and Slobodan Milosevic in 1999. The theory advanced by opponents of the tribunals was that criminal leaders were unlikely to enter into meaningful peace negotiations in the knowledge that, if successful, they would end up before a criminal court.

During July 1995, I announced that the Yugoslavia Tribunal intended in the near future to indict Karadzic and the commander of his army, General Ratko Mladic. The reason for the announcement was the imminent application for an order against the Government of Bosnia and Herzegovina requiring it to defer its investigations against Karadzic and Mladic to the Tribunal. We were entitled to defer because of the primacy conferred on the Tribunal by the Security Council. Our indictment was in the final stage of preparation and we were against the Bosnian plan to hold a trial against Karadzic *in absentia*.

Our decision to indict Karadzic and Mladic received mixed reactions. A number of political leaders as well as the then Secretary-General were critical of the decision. Others welcomed it. I recall well that on the afternoon of the announcement, Sergio Vieira de Mello, who was then the second in command at UNHCR, called to inform me that he and Dennis McNamara and other senior colleagues had purchased champagne and were drinking a toast to me in support of the decision to indict Karadzic and Mladic. This was but one illustration of the importance that Sergio placed upon justice as a tool of peace making in the Balkans.

Of course, in the result, the indictment of Karadzic was crucial in enabling the Dayton peace process to begin and succeed. The meeting at Dayton, Ohio, was held in November 1995, a scarce two months after the massacre of over 8,000 Muslim men and boys by the Bosnian Serb army at Srebrenica. If Karadzic had not been indicted he would have insisted on representing Republika Srbska at that meeting. If he had attended the meeting, the Bosnian Government would certainly have boycotted the meeting. That was made clear then and later. The result of the indictment was that Karadzic would have been arrested by the US if he had attempted to travel to Dayton. He was forced to agree to his enclave being represented by Milosevic. The Dayton Accords managed to put an end to the war and, but for the indictment of Karadzic, would otherwise have been impossible at that time.

The second issue which Sergio Vieira de Mello and I discussed at length involved Madame Sadako Ogata, who was then the UN High Commissioner for Refugees. The question was the issue of compelling employees of the High Commissioner to serve as witnesses before the war crimes tribunals. The concern we shared was the danger to all humanitarian workers if they were to be perceived by warring parties as witnesses to war crimes. Of course, this has always been of concern to the International Committee of the Red Cross (ICRC). The conflicting interests were manifest. In the end, with the assistance of the then head of UN Peacekeeping, Kofi Annan, we reached an accord. It was agreed that UNHCR workers would not be called as witnesses unless their evidence was crucial to a prosecution and there was no other means of obtaining the evidence. It was agreed that in the event of a dispute between the Prosecutor and UNHCR, the Head of UN Peacekeeping would be the sole and final arbitrator.

THE WAY FORWARD

These problems illustrate that leaders should recognize clashes of values and make every effort to find a balanced solution in the policies that are adopted. What concerns me is that in the aftermath of September 11, politicians in too many countries feel that they have to be seen to be taking steps to combat terrorism regardless of the efficacy of those measures and regardless of the invasion of fundamental rights that they might cause. A fearful electorate becomes an acquiescent electorate.

I would suggest that governments in democratic nations should be encouraged to set up their own civil liberties monitoring departments. In other words, governments should have senior officials responsible for monitoring and reporting on violations by their own legislatures and executives of fundamental human rights. This is especially appropriate where those rights are protected by their own constitutions or by international conventions to which they are bound. This kind of public oversight would unquestionably act as an effective brake on excessive and unjustified encroachments of human rights.

If democracies lose respect for justice and the rule of law it will bode ill for the future of the human race. Not only are oppressive dictators relying on the US concept of "unlawful combatants" but it has even become acceptable in some democracies to speak publicly of killing unpopular leaders of other nations or groups.

The powerful nations of our world have a responsibility to set an example for others to follow. That is the obligation that comes with leadership. This is an issue that would have been close to the heart of Sergio Vieira de Mello and it is appropriate that it should be considered in a publication intended as a tribute to his memory.

NOTES

TRAPPED WITHIN HOSTILE BORDERS:
THE PLIGHT OF INTERNALLY DISPLACED PERSONS

1. *The Guiding Principles on Internal Displacement* (New York: OCHA, 2000) defines internally displaced persons as "persons or groups of persons who have been forced or obliged to flee or to leave their homes or places of habitual residence, in particular as a result of or in order to avoid the effects of armed conflict, situations of generalized violence, violations of human rights or natural or human-made disasters, and who have not crossed an internationally recognized State border."

2. *See* Roberta Cohen and Francis Deng, *Masses in Flight: The Global Crisis of Internal Displacement* (Washington, DC: The Brookings Institution, 1998) 23–29; United Nations High Commissioner for Refugees, *The State of the World's Refugees* (UNHCR, 1998) 112–115; and World Health Organization, "Internally Displaced Persons: Health and WHO" (paper presented at the humanitarian affairs segment of the substantive session of the ECOSOC, New York, 5 April 2000, 5).

3. *See* Francis M. Deng, "Ethnic Marginalization as Statelessness: Lessons from the Great Lakes Region of Africa" in *Citizenship Today: Global Perspectives and Practices* eds. T. Aleinikoff and Douglas Klusmeyer (Washington, DC: The Carnegie Endowment for International Peace, 2001), 183–208.

4. *See* Walter Kälin, *Guiding Principles on Internal Displacement: Annotations* (Washington, DC: American Society of International Law and The Brookings Institution Project on International Displacement, 2000). *The Handbook for Applying the Guiding Principles on Internal Displacement* (Washington, DC: The Brookings Institution Project on Internal Displacement and OCHA, 1999). *Recent Commentaries about the Nature and Application of the Guiding Principles on Internal Displacement* (Washington DC: The Brookings-CUNY Project on Internal Displacement, 2002).

5. Inter-Agency Standing Committee, *Policy Paper Series,* no. 2 (New York: United Nations, 2000).

6. The relationship between the RSG and the Unit is governed by an MOU signed by the RSG and the ERC in April 2002. The MOU emphasizes "the recognition of the respective responsibilities of each body, their distinct nature and different, but complementary expertise and the need to build on the comparative advantages of each body."

The MOU maps major areas of activity for the RSG and the Unit. For the RSG, four main areas are identified: (1) development, dissemination and promotion of the *Guiding Principles* "in particular through seminars and support of local capacities," (2) assessment of international institutional arrangements, (3) undertaking country missions to evaluate conditions and "dialogue with Governments and other actors," and (4) studying the "causes and consequences of internal displacement."

For the Unit, five main areas are identified: (1) monitoring situations of internal displacement and identifying operational gaps, (2) further developing inter-agency policies and mobilizing resources, (3) providing "training, guidance and expertise" to RCs, HCs, UNCTs and humanitarian organizations on IDP issues, including the formulation of IDP strategies, (4) supporting the advocacy efforts of the ERC and other actors, in particular the RSG, and (5) promoting "functional linkages" between political, humanitarian and development actors.

The MOU suggests the following "areas and modalities of cooperation": (1) developing and designing strategies for the promotion, dissemination and application of the *Guiding Principles* and the *Handbook,* (2) coordinating field visits, (3) collaborating in the development of policy and action-oriented research, (4) collaboration in the planning of seminars, publications and other initiatives, in particular concerning the *Guiding Principles,* and (5) undertaking joint advocacy activities (statements, public awareness, etc.).

7. *See,* for example, Omprakash Mishra, ed., *Forced Migration in the South Asian Region* (Delhi, India: Center for Refugee Studies / Brookings-SAIS Project on Internal Displacement / Manak, 2004); *Guiding Principles on Internal Displacement and the Law of the South Caucasus, Georgia, Armenia and Azerbaijan* (Washington, DC: American Society of International Law (ASIL), the Organization for Security and Cooperation in

Europe, and the Georgian Young Lawyers Association (GYLA), 2003); David A. Korn, *Exodus within Borders: An Introduction to the Crisis of Internal Displacement* (Washington, DC: Brookings Institution Press, 1999); Roberta Cohen and Francis M. Deng, *Masses in Flight: The Global Crisis of Internal Displacement* (Washington, DC: Brookings Institution Press, 1998); Roberta Cohen and Francis M. Deng, eds., *The Forsaken People: Case Studies of the Internally Displaced* (Washington, DC: Brookings Institution Press, 1998); and Francis M. Deng, *Protecting the Dispossessed: A Challenge for the International Community* (Washington, DC: Brookings Institution Press, 1993).

8. Francis M. Deng and I. William Zartman, eds., *Conflict Resolution in Africa* (Washington, DC: Brookings Institution Press, 1991).

9. Francis M. Deng, Sadikiel Kimaro, Terrence Lyons, Donald Rothchild, and I. William Zartman, eds., *Sovereignty as Responsibility: Conflict Management in Africa* (Washington, DC: Brookings Institution Press, 1996).

10. Francis M. Deng and Terrence Lyons, eds., *African Reckoning: A Quest for Good* (Washington, DC: Brookings Institution Press, 1998).

11. *See* Francis M. Deng and I. William Zartman, *A Strategic Vision for Africa: The Kampala Movement* (Washington, DC: Brookings Institution Press 2002).

12. See note 8. For my various contributions to the normative theme of the responsibility of sovereignty, see the following books, chapters, and articles: Terrence Lyons and Francis M. Deng, eds., *African Reckoning: A Quest for Good Governance* (Washington, DC: Brookings Institution Press, 1998); Francis M. Deng, "Sovereignty and Humanitarian Responsibility: A Challenge for NGOs in Africa and the Sudan," in *Vigilance and Vengeance,* ed. Robert I. Rotberg (Washington, DC: Brookings Institution Press and The World Peace Foundation:, 1996); Francis M. Deng, Sadikiel Kimaro, Terrence Lyons, Donald Rothchild, and I. William Zartman, *Sovereignty as Responsibility: Conflict Management in Africa* (Washington, DC: Brookings Institution Press, 1996); Francis M. Deng, "Sovereignty and Humanitarian Responsibility: A Challenge for NGOs in Africa and the Sudan," in *Vigilance and Vengeance,* ed. Robert I. Rotberg (Washington, DC: Brookings Institution Press and The World Peace Foundation, 1996);

ibid., "Reconciling Sovereignty with Responsibility: A Basis for International Humanitarian Action," in *Africa in World Politics,* eds. John Harbeson and Donald Rothchild (Boulder, CO: Westview, 1995); ibid., "Frontiers of Sovereignty: A Framework of Protection, Assistance and Development for the Internally Displaced," *Leiden Journal of International Law* 8, no. 2 (1995).

13. *The Responsibility to Protect: Report of the International Commission on Intervention and State Sovereignty* (Ottawa: International Development Research Center, 2001).

14. Deng, see note 3.

15. Deng, "The Return of the Displaced: A Challenge to the Country and the International Community" (presented at the Conference on Inter-Sudanese Dialogue, London, July 2002).

HUMANITARIAN ACTION IN A NEW BARBARIAN AGE

1. Raymond Aron, *Thinking Politically: A Liberal in an Age of Ideology* (New Brunswick: Transaction Publishers, 1997).

HUMANITARIANISM'S AGE OF REASON

1. Arend Lijphart, *Democracy in Plural Societies* (New Haven, CT: Yale University Press, 1977); Arend Lijphart, *Democracies: Patterns of Majoritarian and Consensus Government in Twenty-One Countries (New Haven, CT:* Yale University Press, 1984).

2. Theodor Hanf, *Coexistence in Wartime Lebanon* (London: I.B. Taurus, 1993); Hanf, Weiland, and Vierlag, *South Africa: The Prospects for Peaceful Change* (London, 1981).

CREATING LOCAL-LEVEL STABILITY AND EMPOWERMENT IN CAMBODIA

1. Signatory nations, in the presence of the Secretary-General of the United Nations, included Australia, Brunei Darussalam, Cambodia, Canada, The People's Republic of China, France, India, Indonesia, Japan, Laos, Malaysia, The Philippines, Singapore, Thailand, The Union

of Soviet Socialist Republics, the United Kingdom and Northern Ireland, the United State of America, Vietnam, and Yugoslavia.

2. Judy Ledgerwood and John Vijghen, "Decision-Making in Rural Khmer Villages," in *Cambodia Emerges from the Past: Eight Essays* (Center for Southeast Asian Studies, Northern Illinois University/Southeast Asia Publications, 2002).

3. The United Nations, "Cambodia–UNTAC Background," http://www.un.org/depts/dpko/dpko/co_mission/untacbackgr2.html

4. Judy Ledgerwood, "UN Peacekeeping Missions: The Lessons from Cambodia." *Asia Pacific Issues: Analysis from the East-West Center,* March 1994, no. 11.

5. The Khmer Rouge pulled out of the agreements on the grounds that a truly neutral political environment had not been created, and that UNTAC had failed in its responsibilities to remove all former Vietnamese troops from the country.

6. "Keys of Kampuchea" (New Zealand: New House, 1995)—a judgment (of Raoul Jennar) on the Mission of UNO.

7. See note 3.

8. See note 4

9. See note 3.

10. Grant Curtis, *Cambodia Reborn? The Transition to Democracy and Development* (Washington, DC: Brookings Institution Press, and Geneva: United Nations Research Institute for Social Development, 1998).

11. See note 3.

12. Ibid.

13. Ibid.

14. Ibid.

15. Zhou Mei, *Radio UNTAC of Cambodia: Winning Ears, Hearts and Minds* (Bangkok: White Lotus Press, 1994).

16. See note 3.

17. Ibid.

18. See note 15

19. *See* http://www.moi-coci.gov.kh/info/default.htm

20. Media Consulting and Development (MC&D), "Results of Media Monitoring Activities of December 2003" The Cambodia Press Headlines. Graphs taken from Media Consulting and Development.

The Challenges of Humanitarian Diplomacy

1. Gerard Ferrie, quoted in Hugo Slim, *Marketing Humanitarian Space: Argument and Method in Humanitarian Persuasion* (Lausanne: Humanitarian Negotiators Network, Centre for Humanitarian Dialogue, 2003).

2. Slim.

3. Joanna Macrae and Nicholas Leader, *The Politics of Coherence: Humanitarianism and Foreign Policy in the Post-Cold War Era* (London: Overseas Development Institute). Humanitarian Policy Group Briefing 1, July 2000.

4. Marie-Joelle Zahar, "Proteges, Clients, Cannon Fodder: Civil-Militia Relations in Internal Conflicts," in *Civilians in War*, Simon Chesterman, ed. (Boulder: International Peace Academy, 2001).

5. Guy Lamb, "Putting Belligerents in Context: The Cases of Namibia and Angola," in *Civilians in War*, Simon Chesterman, ed. (Boulder: International Peace Academy, 2001).

6. Lincoln Chen, M.D., "Expanding Humanitarian Space: Challenge for Global Philanthropy" (paper, Humanitarian Interventions Today: New Issues, New Ideas, New Players conference sponsored by the Conrad Hilton Foundation, New York City, September 24, 2003, www.bettersaferworld.org/issues/lincoln_chen_article).

7. Jonathan Benthall, *Humanitarianism, Islam and 11 September,* Overseas Development Institute, Humanitarian Policy Briefing, no. 11, London, July 2003.

8. Joanna Macrae, Sarah Collinson, *Uncertain Power: The changing Role of Official Donors in Humanitarian Action,* Overseas Development Institute, Humanitarian Policy Group Report, no. 12, London, December 2002.

Passion and Compassion

1. Kevin Cahill, M.D., ed., *Preventive Diplomacy* (New York: [TK], 1996).

Preserving Humanitarian Space in Long-Term Conflict

1. D. Warner, "The Politics of the Political/Humanitarian Divide," 833 *International Review of the Red Cross*, no. 833 (March 31, 1999): 109–118.

2. A. Donini, "The Future of Humanitarian Action: Implications of Iraq and Other Recent Crises—Issues Note (workshop organized by The Feinstein International Famine Center and The Friedman School of Nutrition Science and Policy, Tufts University, Boston, October 9, 2003), 3.

3. See note 1.

4. Annual Report of the Secretary-General on the work of the Organization" (annual report, United Nations, New York City, 1995, http://www.un.org/docs/sg/sg-rpt/).

5. B. Mégevand Roggo, "After the Kosovo Conflict, a Genuine Humanitarian Space: A Utopian Concept or an Essential Requirement?" *International Review of the Red Cross,* no. 837 (March 31, 2000): 31–47.

6. See note 1.

7. C. Eguizabal et al., "Humanitarian Challenges in Central America: Learning the Lessons of Recent Armed Conflicts" (Occasional Paper, no. 14, Thomas J. Watson Jr. Institute for International Studies, Brown University, 1993), 17.

8. Australian Council for Overseas Aid, "Guiding Principles for Civil-Military Action" (http://www.acfoa.asn.au/emergencies/cimic_interaction. htm.).

9. International humanitarian law regulates the conduct of armed conflict between states and non-state actors. Many of its principles exist in customary international law. In conventional form, this body of law is best exemplified by the *Geneva Conventions* of 1949, the fourth of which concerns the protection of civilian persons in time of war. Examples of how the concept of humanitarian space is incorporated into the *Fourth Geneva Convention* abound, and include *inter alia:* the designation of civilians as "protected persons" (Article 4); the establishment of "hospital and safety zones" (Article 14) as well as "neutral zones" (Article 15); the protection of the "wounded and sick, as well as the infirm, and expectant mothers" (Article 15); the protection of "hospital staff" (Article 20); protection of medical convoys (Articles 21–22) and free passage of "medical supplies, food and clothing" (articles 23 and 55); protection of children (Articles 24 and 50); protection against "collective penalties" (art. 33); protection of real and personal property (Article 53); and protection against "willful killing," "torture or inhumane treatment," "unlawful deportation or transfer,"

"unfair trials," "taking of hostages," and "extensive destruction and appropriation of property" (Article 147).

See United Nations, *Geneva Convention for the Amelioration of the Condition of the Wounded and Sick in Armed Forces in the Field,* August 12, 1949, 6 U.S.T. 3114, 75 U.N.T.S. 31 (*entered into force* October 21, 1950); United Nations, *Geneva Convention for the Amelioration of the Condition of the Wounded, Sick and Shipwrecked Members of Armed Forces at Sea,* August 12, 1949, 6 U.S.T. 3217, 75 U.N.T.S. 85 (*entered into force* October 21, 1950); United Nations, *Geneva Convention Relative to the Treatment of Prisoners of War,* August 12, 1949, 6 U.S.T. 3316, 75 U.N.T.S. 135 (*entered into force* October 21, 1950); United Nations, *Geneva Convention Relative to the Protection of Civilian Persons in Time of War,* August 12, 1949, 6 U.S.T. 3516, 75 U.N.T.S. 287 (*entered into force* October 21, 1950). [hereinafter the *Fourth Geneva Convention.*

10. T. G. Weiss, "Principles, Politics and Humanitarian Action," *Ethics and International Affairs,* vol. 13 (December 4, 1999): 1. Humanitarianism and War Project, Tufts University, http://hwproject.tufts.edu/publications/electronic/e_ppaha.html).

11. See note 2.

12. Donini, 11.

13. Ibid.

14. Mégevand Roggo.

15. Warner.

16. For instance, in April 2003 Israeli troops forcibly took over UNRWA's Tulkarem Girls School for use over several days as a mass detention center for male residents of the Tulkarem refugee camp. Likewise, in September 2002 an armed Israeli special unit made an incursion into UNRWA's Qalqilya hospital where they threatened staff and patients at gunpoint, beat five members of the hospital staff, including a female administrator and health official who had arrived at the scene to treat the wounded, and then arrested three other UNRWA staff members. Likewise, on 23 May 2003 Palestinian militants purporting to be members of the Al Aqsa Martyrs' Brigades broke into the Balata Camp Boys School and held a memorial ceremony attended by thousands of people, where political speeches were given and weapons were fired into the air.

17. Warner.

18. Ibid.

19. Weiss, 12–13.

20. M. Anderson, "Reflecting on the Practice of Outside Assistance: Can We Know What Good We Do?" (handbook, Berghof Handbook for Conflict Transformation, Berlin, April 2001). *See also* Anderson, *Do No Harm: How Aid can Support Peace or War* (Boulder, CO: Lynne Rienner Publishers, 1999).

21. *See* Anderson, "Reflecting on the Practice of Outside Assistance."

22. Ibid.

23. Ibid.

24. Michael Meyer, "Neutrality as a Fundamental Principle of the Red Cross," *International Review of the Red Cross* no 315 (December 31, 1996): 627–630.

25. Ibid.

26. See note 20, "Reflecting on the Practice of Outside Assistance."

27. Ibid.

28. Article 103 of the *UN Charter* provides that "in the event of a conflict between the obligations under any other international agreement, the obligations of the present *Charter* shall prevail." Articles 104 and 105 of the *UN Charter* provide the general concepts of privileges and immunities of the United Nations upon which the 1946 *Convention on the Privileges and Immunities of the United Nations* is based, to which the State of Israel is a party.

29. Lincoln Chen, M.D., "Expanding Humanitarian Space: Challenge for Global Philanthropy" (paper, Humanitarian Interventions Today: New Issues, New Ideas, New Players conference sponsored by the Conrad Hilton Foundation, New York City, September 24, 2003, www.bettersaferworld.org/issues/lincoln_chen_article).

30. Ibid.

31. Mégevand Roggo.

CHALLENGES TO INDEPENDENT HUMANITARIAN
ACTION IN CONTEMPORARY CONFLICTS

1. The present article reflects the personal opinions of the author and should in no way be regarded as expressing the views of the ICRC.

2. See Appendix 1 for a description of the ICRC's range of protection and assistance activities

3. Larry Minear, *The Humanitarian Enterprise, Dilemmas and Discoveries* (Bloomfield, IL: Kumara Press, 2002), 5.

4. This is documented by the increasing number of States that become parties to the four 1949 *Geneva Conventions*, the *Conventions* two *Additional Protocols* adopted in 1977, as well as to other key instruments of international humanitarian law adopted in the latter part of the twentieth century (the 1980 *Convention on Certain Conventional Weapons and its Protocols,* the *Ottawa Convention on the Prohibition of the Use, Stockpiling, Production and Transfer of Anti-Personnel Mines* of 1997, the 1998 *Rome Statute,* establishing the International Criminal Court).

5. Article 3, common to the four 1949 *Geneva Conventions.*

6. Such as those who emerged following the end of World War II in the context of armed struggles to achieve political independence from colonial rule as well as of armed opposition to established governments in independent States. The international community took some time to acknowledge this development. The existence of these actors was recognized in the Additional Protocols I and II (of 1977) to the 1949 *Geneva Conventions.*

7. *See* Joanna Macrae and Adele Harmer, "Humanitarian action and the Global War on Terror: A Review of Trends and Issues," (HPG Report, no 14, ODI, July 2003); Paul Wilkinson, "Terrorism: the Concept," in *Traditions, Values, and Humanitarian Action,* ed. Kevin M. Cahill (New York City: Fordham University Press, 2003).

8. Attempts to establish an internationally accepted definition can be traced back to the 1937 *Convention for the Prevention and Punishment of Terrorism:* terrorism was defined as "criminal acts directed against a State or intended to create a state of terror in the minds of particular persons, or a group of persons or the general public" However, the treaty never entered into force. *See* H. P. Gasser, "Acts of Terror, Terrorism and International Humanitarian Law," *International Review of the Red Cross,* no. 847 (September 2002): 552.

9. Alyson J. K. Bales, "Trends and Challenges in International Security," in *SIPRI Yearbook 2003* (Oxford: Oxford University Press, 2003), 7.

10. Ibid., 3.

11. Tore Børgo, ed., "Root Causes of Terrorism" (proceedings, International Expert Meeting, June 9–11, 2003, Norwegian Institute of International Relations (NUPI), Oslo), 234.

12. Ervand Abrahamian, "The US Media, Huntington and September 11," *Third World Quarterly* 24, no. 3 (2003).

13. In an article on suicide attacks, Robert Pape, a political scientist from the University of Chicago notes: " . . . what nearly all suicide terrorist campaigns have in common is a specific secular and strategic goal: to compel liberal democracies to withdraw military forces from territory that the terrorists consider to be their homeland. Religion is rarely the root cause, although it is often used as a tool by terrorist organizations in recruiting and in other efforts in service of the broader strategic objective. . . . Even al Qaeda fits this pattern. Although Saudi Arabia is not under American military occupation per se, the initial major objective of Osama bin Laden was the expulsion of American troops from the Gulf." Robert Pape, *International Herald Tribune,* September 29, 2003.

14. François Thual, *Les Conflits Identitaires* (Paris: Editions Ellipses 1995).

15. *International Herald Tribune,* January 31, 2002.

16. Amartya Sen, "Global Inequality and Persistent Conflicts," (paper, Nobel Peace Prize Centennial Symposium, Oslo, December 2001).

17. Boutros Boutros-Ghali, *An Agenda for Peace* (New York: United Nations, 1992).

18. It might be interesting to note in that context that the Geneva Conventions use the word "humanitarian" in relation with the activities of specifically humanitarian organizations (e.g., *Geneva Convention IV,* art. 10) and makes a clear distinction between States and such organizations (e.g., *Geneva Convention IV,* "Article 59"). The same article uses the term "relief schemes" when referring to assistance programs in favor of the civilian population. Additional Protocol I of 1977 also uses the term "relief."

19. *Additional Protocol II to the Geneva Conventions,* art. 4, ¶2d

20. *Additional Protocol I to the Geneva Conventions* art. 51,, ¶2 and *Additional Protocol II to the Geneva Conventions,* art. 13, ¶2.

21. "Protecting Human Dignity," (declaration, 28th International Red Cross and Red Crescent Conference, Geneva, December 2003).

JUSTICE AND RECONCILIATION: THE CONTRIBUTION OF WAR CRIMES TRIBUNALS AND TRUTH AND RECONCILIATION COMMISSIONS

1. J. P. Kenyon, ed., *The Stuart Constitution 1603–1688* (Cambridge: Cambridge University Press, 1986), 336.

2. Hugh Brogan, *History of the United States of America* (London and New York: Longman, 1985), 383–84.

3. B. G. Ramcharan, ed., *The International Conference on the Former Yugoslavia Official Papers* vol 1, §8, "Violation of International Humanitarian Law" (New York: Kluwer Law International, 1997).

4. David Owen, "Reconciliation: Applying Historical Lessons to Modern Conflicts," *Fordham International Law Journal,* no 2 (December 1992): 331–34.

5. William A. Schabas, "National Courts Finally Begin to Prosecute Genocide, the 'Crime of Crimes,'" *Journal of Criminal Justice* (April 2003).

6. Gabor Rona, *The ICRC Privilege Not to Testify: Confidentiality in Action,* no. 845 (March 3, 2002): 207–9.

7. Cees Wiebes, *Lit Verlag Munster,* http://www.lit-verlag.de (2003): 274.

8. Ibid., 279

9. International Crisis Group, "The Special Court for Sierra Leone," *Africa Briefing,* Freetown/Brussels, August 4, 2003.

10. David Owen, *Time to Declare* (Michael Joseph, 1991), 423.

11. Antjie Krog, *Country of My Skull,* (Jonathan Cape, 1998), 23.

12. Reconciliation Graduation Ceremony at the University of Natal, 1996.

13. See note 11. Krog, 131.

14. Alex Boraine, *A Country Unmasked* (Oxford: Oxford University Press, 2000).

15. Richard Caplan, *A New Trusteeship. The International Administration of War-Torn Territories* (Adelphi Paper 341, Oxford University Press, 2002), 43.

16. Tim Judah, "The Fog of Justice," *New York Review of Books,* January 15, 2004, 23.

HEALING WITH A SINGLE HISTORY

1. A. V. Dicey, *Law of the Constitution* (London: Macmillan, 1895).

2. A. Cox, *The Court and the Constitution, 10 ed.* (Boston: Houghton Mifflin & Co., 1987), 202.

3. The *Geneva Conventions* of 1949, the 1973 *Convention* which declared Apartheid to be a crime against humanity, the 1984 *Torture Convention* and some sixteen United Nations' *Conventions* dealing with acts of terrorism all recognized universal jurisdiction.

4. "Assessing the New Normal" (paper, Human Rights Watch, New York, September 2003).

5. Ibid.

6. "International Terrorism: Legal Challenges and Responses" (paper, International Bar Association, Ardsley, New York, September 2003).

CONTRIBUTORS

H.E. Kofi Annan is the Secretary-General of the United Nations.

Kevin M. Cahill, M.D., is University Professor and Director of the Institute of International Humanitarian Affairs at Fordham University and President of the Center for International Health and Cooperation.

Francis Deng is Representative of the UN Secretary-General on Internally Displaced Persons and a Director of the Center for International Health and Cooperation.

Arthur Dewey is U.S. Assistant Secretary of State for Population, Refugees, and Migration and former Deputy UN High Commissioner for Refugees.

Jan Egeland is UN Under-Secretary-General for Humanitarian Affairs and Emergency Relief Coordinator.

Roland Eng is the Ambassador of Cambodia to the United States.

Jan Eliasson is the Ambassador of Sweden to the United States and a Director of the Center for International Health and Cooperation.

Jacques Forster is Vice President of the International Committee of the Red Cross.

Richard Goldstone is Retired Justice of the Constitutional Court of South Africa and Former Chief Prosecutor of the United Nations International Criminal Tribunal for the former Yugoslavia and Rwanda.

Peter Hansen is Commissioner-General of the United Nations Relief and Works Agency for Palestine Refugees (UNRWA) and a Director of the Center for International Health and Cooperation.

Irene Khan is Secretary General of Amnesty International.

Mark Malloch Brown is Administrator of the United Nations Development Program.

Dennis McNamara is Inspector-General of the UN High Commissioner for Refugees and Former Deputy Special Representative of the UN Secretary-General for East Timor.

Reverend Joseph McShane, S.J., is President of Fordham University.

Sadako Ogata is President of the Japan International Cooperation Agency and a former UN High Commissioner for Refugees.

David Owen is a former Co-Chairman of the International Conference on the Former Yugoslavia and a former British Foreign Secretary. He is a Director of the Center for International Health and Cooperation.

David Rieff is an author and journalist whose books include *Slaughterhouse: Bosnia and the Failure of the West,* and *A Bed for the Night: Humanitarianism in Crisis.* He is the co-editor, with Roy Gutman, of *Crimes of War: What the Public Should Know.*

Ghassan Salamé is former Senior Political Adviser to the Special Representative of the Secretary-General for Iraq, United Nations.

Shashi Tharoor is UN Under-Secretary-General for Communications and Public Information, and an award-winning author of eight books, including *India: From Midnight to the Millennium* and, most recently, *Nehru: The Invention of India.* These are his personal views.

Appendices

Preamble to the Charter
of the United Nations

WE THE PEOPLES OF THE UNITED NATIONS DETERMINED

- to save succeeding generations from the scourge of war, which twice in our lifetime has brought untold sorrow to mankind, and
- to reaffirm faith in fundamental human rights, in the dignity and worth of the human person, in the equal rights of men and women and of nations large and small, and
- to establish conditions under which justice and respect for the obligations arising from treaties and other sources of international law can be maintained, and
- to promote social progress and better standards of life in larger freedom,

AND FOR THESE ENDS

- to practice tolerance and live together in peace with one another as good neighbors, and
- to unite our strength to maintain international peace and security, and
- to ensure, by the acceptance of principles and the institution of methods, that armed force shall not be used, save in the common interest, and
- to employ international machinery for the promotion of the economic and social advancement of all peoples,

HAVE RESOLVED TO COMBINE OUR EFFORTS TO ACCOMPLISH THESE AIMS

Accordingly, our respective Governments, through representatives assembled in the city of San Francisco, who have exhibited their full powers found to be in good and due form, have agreed to the present *Charter of the United Nations* and do hereby establish an international organization to be known as the United Nations.

The Universal Declaration of Human Rights: A *Magna Carta* for All Humanity

Some 50 years have elapsed since the *Universal Declaration of Human Rights* was adopted by the United Nations on 10 December 1948. The *Declaration* was one of the first major achievements of the United Nations, and after 50 years remains a powerful instrument which continues to exert an enormous effect on people's lives all over the world. This was the first time in history that a document considered to have universal value was adopted by an international organization. It was also the first time that human rights and fundamental freedoms were set forth in such detail. There was broad-based international support for the *Declaration* when it was adopted. It represented "a world milestone in the long struggle for human rights," in the words of a UN General Assembly representative from France.

The adoption of theUniversal Declaration stems in large part from the strong desire for peace in the aftermath of the Second World War. Although the 58 Member States which formed the United Nations at that time varied in their ideologies, political systems and religious and cultural backgrounds and had different patterns of socio-economic development, the *Universal Declaration of Human Rights* represented a common statement of goals and aspirations—a vision of the world as the international community would want it to become.

Since 1948, the Universal Declaration has been translated into more than 200 languages and remains one of the best known and most often cited human rights documents in the world. Over the years, the Declaration has been used in the defense and advancement of people's rights. Its principles have been enshrined in and continue to inspire national legislation and the constitutions of many newly independent states. References to the Declaration have been made in charters and resolutions of regional intergovernmental organizations as well as in treaties and resolutions adopted by the United Nations system.

The year 1998 marks the fiftieth anniversary of this *"Magna Carta* for all humanity." The theme of the fiftieth anniversary—"All Human Rights for All"— highlights the universality, the indivisibility, and the interrelationship of all human rights. It reinforces the idea that human rights— civil, cultural, economic, political, and social—should be taken in their totality and not disassociated from one another.

DRAFTING AND ADOPTING THE *DECLARATION*, A LONG AND ARDUOUS TASK

When created in 1946, the United Nations Commission on Human Rights was composed of 18 Member States. During its first sessions, the main item on the agenda was the *Universal Declaration of Human Rights.* The Commission set up a drafting committee which devoted itself exclusively to preparing the draft of the *Universal Declaration of Human Rights.* The drafting committee was composed of eight persons, from Australia, Chile, China, France, Lebanon, the Union of Soviet Socialist Republics, the United Kingdom and the United States of America. The United Nations Secretariat, under the guidance of John Humphrey, drafted the outline (400 pages in length) to serve as the basic working paper of the Committee.

During the two-year drafting process of the *Universal Declaration,* the drafters maintained a common ground for discussions and a common goal: respect for fundamental rights and freedoms. Despite their conflicting views on certain questions, they agreed to include in the document the principles of non-discrimination, civil and political rights, and social and economic rights. They also agreed that the *Declaration* had to be universal.

Personally dedicated to the task of preparing this *Declaration* Mrs. Eleanor Roosevelt, who chaired the Human Rights Commission in its first years, asked, "Where, after all, do universal human rights begin? In small places, close to home – so close and so small that they cannot be seen on any maps of the world. Yet they are the world of the individual person; the neighbourhood he lives in; the school or college he attends;

the factory, farm or office where he works. Such are the places where every man, woman and child seeks equal justice, equal opportunity, equal dignity without discrimination. Unless these rights have meaning there, they have little meaning anywhere. Without concerned citizen action to uphold them close to home, we shall look in vain for progress in the larger world."

On 10 December 1948, at the Palais de Chaillot in Paris, the 58 Member States of the United Nations General Assembly adopted the Universal Declaration of Human Rights, with 48 states in favour and eight abstentions (two countries were not present at the time of the voting). General Assembly resolution 217 A (III) of 10 December 1948, which proclaimed the *Universal Declaration of Human Rights,* was adopted as follows:

In favour: Afghanistan, Argentina, Australia, Belgium, Bolivia, Brazil, Burma, Canada, Chile, China, Colombia, Costa Rica, Cuba, Denmark, the Dominican Republic, Ecuador, Egypt, El Salvador, Ethiopia, France, Greece, Guatemala, Haiti, Iceland, India, Iran, Iraq, Lebanon, Liberia, Luxembourg, Mexico, Netherlands, New Zealand, Nicaragua, Norway, Pakistan, Panama, Paraguay, Peru, Philippines, Siam (Thailand), Sweden, Syria, Turkey, United Kingdom, United States, Uruguay, Venezuela.

Abstaining: Byelorussian SSR, Czechoslovakia, Poland, Saudi Arabia, Ukrainian SSR, Union of South Africa, USSR, Yugoslavia.

The General Assembly proclaimed the *Declaration* as a "common standard of achievement for all peoples and all nations," towards which individuals and societies should "strive by progressive measures, national and international, to secure their universal and effective recognition and observance."

THE DECLARATION, A VISION OF WHAT THE WORLD SHOULD BE

Although the *Declaration,* which comprises a broad range of rights, is not a legally binding document, it has inspired more than 60 human rights instruments which together constitute an international standard of human rights. These instruments include the *International Covenant on Economic, Social and Cultural Rights* and the *International Covenant on Civil and Political Rights,* both of which are legally binding treaties. Together with the *Universal Declaration,* they constitute the International Bill of Rights.

The *Declaration* Declaration recognizes that the "inherent dignity of all members of the human family is the foundation of freedom, justice and peace in the world" and is linked to the recognition of fundamental rights towards which every human being aspires, namely the right to life, liberty and security of person; the right to an adequate standard of living; the right to seek and to enjoy in other countries asylum from persecution; the right to own property; the right to freedom of opinion and expression; the right to education, freedom of thought, conscience and religion; and the right to freedom from torture and degrading treatment, among others. These are inherent rights to be enjoyed by all human beings of the global village—men, women, and children, as well as by any group of society, disadvantaged or not—and not "gifts" to be withdrawn, withheld or granted at someone's whim or will.

Mary Robinson, who became the second United Nations High Commissioner for Human Rights in September 1997, expressed this opinion when she declared that "human rights belong to people, human rights are about people on the ground and their rights." She has stated that she would take a "bottom-up" approach in promoting human rights, an approach which reflects the first words of the *United Nations Charter,* "We the Peoples . . . ."

The rights contained in the *Declaration* and the two covenants were further elaborated in such legal documents as the *International Convention on the Elimination of All Forms of Racial Discrimination,* which declares dissemination of ideas based on racial superiority or hatred as being punishable by law; the *Convention on the Elimination of All Forms of Discrimination Against Women,* covering measures to be taken for eliminating discrimination against women in political and public life, education, employment, health, marriage and family; and the *Convention on the Rights of the Child,* which lays down guarantees in terms of the child's human rights.

INTERNATIONAL MOBILIZATION IN FAVOR OF THE *DECLARATION:* GOVERNMENT COMMITMENT

At the World Conference on Human Rights held in Vienna (Austria) in June 1993, 171 countries reiterated the universality, indivisibility, and interdependence of human rights, and reaffirmed their commitment to the *Universal Declaration of Human Rights*. They adopted the Vienna Declaration and Programme of Action, which provides the new "framework of planning, dialogue and cooperation," to enable a holistic approach to promoting human rights and involving actors at the local, national and international levels. The five-year review of the Vienna Programme of Action will also take place in 1998. This review provides a substantive dimension to the fiftieth anniversary, which many human rights activists and professionals see as a time for States to renew their commitment to the promotion and protection of human rights.

It is a time for Governments to ensure that the rights set forth in the *Declaration* are reflected in their national legislation and to move to ratify those international human rights treaties that are still pending. Governments could consider formulating and implementing a pro-active strategy in favour of the promotion of and respect for human rights. This could be translated into action by adopting national plans of action for advancing human rights and fostering human rights education. This anniversary also provides the opportunity for more countries not only to condemn blatant violations of human rights but also to take responsibility and action to break the cycle of impunity whenever human rights are violated.

PUBLIC AWARENESS CAMPAIGN

The fiftieth anniversary is a time to promote public awareness of the meaning of the *Universal Declaration* and its relevance to our daily lives. Providing information about human rights in the languages understood by peoples everywhere is one aspect of a global public awareness campaign. Falling during the Decade for Human Rights Education (1995–2004), the anniversary also provides another focus for education and action. In addition to the 200 language versions already available, a number of other local language translations are to be released for the fiftieth anniversary.

The fiftieth anniversary of the *Universal Declaration* is an opportunity for people worldwide to commemorate the adoption of this landmark document. It also represents an opportunity to mobilize all strata of society in a reinvigorated and broad-based human rights movement. The involvement of civil society and non-governmental organizations in fighting for and demanding recognition of basic rights has played a central role in the advancement and promotion of human rights around the world. National Committees have already been set up in many countries, with the aim of undertaking activities to mark the Anniversary.

Grass-roots movements to encourage entire communities to know, demand and defend their rights will send a positive and strong message: that people everywhere are adamant that human rights should be respected. At local level, concerned citizens can approach their congressional or parliamentary representatives and ask their Governments to ratify international human rights treaties if they have yet not done so.

THE UNITED NATIONS

In accordance with the recommendations made at the 1993 World Conference on Human Rights for increased coordination within the United Nations system, Kofi Annan, Secretary-General of the United Nations, stated, "I will be a champion of human rights and will ensure that human rights are fully integrated in the action of the Organization in all other domains." Human rights, indeed, cut across all the work of the United Nations, from peacekeeping, child rights, health and development to the rights of indigenous peoples to education, social development and the eradication of poverty. Consultations have already taken place among all agencies and programmes of the United Nations, leading to strategies and campaigns being devised.

CHALLENGES

Since the inception of the United Nations, the promotion and protection of human rights have been at its very core. Reference to the promotion of and respect for human rights was made in Article 1 of the *United Nations Charter* and in the establishment of a commission for the promotion of human rights, mentioned in Article 68 of the *Charter*. Over the years, the United Nations has created a wide range of mechanisms for monitoring human rights violations. Conventional mechanisms (treaty bodies) and extra-conventional mechanisms (UN special rapporteurs, representatives, experts and working groups) have been established in order to monitor compliance of States parties with the various human rights instruments and to investigate allegations of human rights abuses. In recent years, a number of field offices have been opened at the request of Governments, *inter alia*, to assist in the development of national institutions for the promotion and protection of human rights and to conduct education campaigns on human rights.

Challenges still lie ahead, despite many accomplishments in the field of human rights. Many in the international community believe that human rights, democracy and development are intertwined. Unless human rights are respected, the maintenance of international peace and security and the promotion of economic and social development cannot be achieved. The world is still plagued with incidents of ethnic hatred and acts of genocide. People are still victims of xenophobic attitudes, are subjected to discrimination because of religion or gender and suffer from exclusion. Around the world, millions of people are still denied food, shelter, access to medical care, education and work, and too many live in extreme poverty. Their inherent humanity and dignity are not recognized.

The future of human rights lies in our hands. We must all act when human rights are violated. States as well as the individual must take responsibility for the realization and effective protection of human rights.

Published by the United Nations Department of Public Information, DPI/1937/A—December 1997

Convention on the Safety of United Nations and Associated Personnel

The States Parties to this Convention,

Deeply concerned over the growing number of deaths and injuries resulting from deliberate attacks against United Nations and associated personnel,

Bearing in mind that attacks against, or other mistreatment of, personnel who act on behalf of the United Nations are unjustifiable and unacceptable, by whomsoever committed,

Recognizing that United Nations operations are conducted in the common interest of the international community and in accordance with the principles and purposes of the Charter of the United Nations,

Acknowledging the important contribution that United Nations and associated personnel make in respect of United Nations efforts in the fields of preventive diplomacy, peacemaking, peace-keeping, peace-building and humanitarian and other operations,

Conscious of the existing arrangements for ensuring the safety of United Nations and associated personnel, including the steps taken by the principal organs of the United Nations, in this regard,

Recognizing none the less that existing measures of protection for United Nations and associated personnel are inadequate,

Acknowledging that the effectiveness and safety of United Nations operations are enhanced where such operations are conducted with the consent and cooperation of the host State,

Appealing to all States in which United Nations and associated personnel are deployed and to all others on whom such personnel may rely, to provide comprehensive support aimed at facilitating the conduct and fulfilling the mandate of United Nations operations,

Convinced that there is an urgent need to adopt appropriate and effective measures for the prevention of attacks committed against United Nations and associated personnel and for the punishment of those who have committed such attacks,

Have agreed as follows:

ARTICLE 1: DEFINITIONS

For the purposes of this Convention:

(a) "United Nations personnel" means:

(i) Persons engaged or deployed by the Secretary-General of the United Nations as members of the military, police or civilian components of a United Nations operation;

(ii) Other officials and experts on mission of the United Nations or its specialized agencies or the International Atomic Energy Agency who are present in an official capacity in the area where a United Nations operation is being conducted;

(b) "Associated personnel" means:

(i) Persons assigned by a Government or an intergovernmental organization with the agreement of the competent organ of the United Nations;

(ii) Persons engaged by the Secretary-General of the United Nations or by a specialized agency or by the International Atomic Energy Agency;

(iii) Persons deployed by a humanitarian non-governmental organization or agency under an agreement with the Secretary-General of the United Nations or with a specialized agency or with the International Atomic Energy Agency, to carry out activities in support of the fulfilment of the mandate of a United Nations operation;

(c) "United Nations operation" means an operation established by the competent organ of the United Nations in accordance with the Charter of the United Nations and conducted under United Nations authority and control:

(i) Where the operation is for the purpose of maintaining or restoring international peace and security; or

(ii) Where the Security Council or the General Assembly has declared, for the purposes of this Convention, that there exists an exceptional risk to the safety of the personnel participating in the operation;

(d) "Host State" means a State in whose territory a United Nations operation is conducted;

(e) "Transit State" means a State, other than the host State, in whose territory United Nations and associated personnel or their equipment are in transit or temporarily present in connection with a United Nations operation.

ARTICLE 2: SCOPE OF APPLICATION

1. This Convention applies in respect of United Nations and associated personnel and United Nations operations, as defined in article 1.

2. This Convention shall not apply to a United Nations operation authorized by the Security Council as an enforcement action under Chapter VII of the *Charter of the United Nations* in which any of the personnel are engaged as combatants against organized armed forces and to which the law of international armed conflict applies.

ARTICLE 3: IDENTIFICATION

1. The military and police components of a United Nations operation and their vehicles, vessels and aircraft shall bear distinctive identification. Other personnel, vehicles, vessels and aircraft involved in the United Nations operation shall be appropriately identified unless otherwise decided by the Secretary-General of the United Nations.

2. All United Nations and associated personnel shall carry appropriate identification documents.

ARTICLE 4: AGREEMENTS ON THE STATUS OF THE OPERATION

The host State and the United Nations shall conclude as soon as possible an agreement on the status of the United Nations operation and all personnel engaged in the operation including, *inter alia,* provisions on privileges and immunities for military and police components of the operation.

ARTICLE 5: TRANSIT

A transit State shall facilitate the unimpeded transit of United Nations and associated personnel and their equipment to and from the host State.

ARTICLE 6: RESPECT FOR LAWS AND REGULATIONS

1. Without prejudice to such privileges and immunities as they may enjoy or to the requirements of their duties, United Nations and associated personnel shall:

(a) Respect the laws and regulations of the host State and the transit State; and

(b) Refrain from any action or activity incompatible with the impartial and international nature of their duties.

2. The Secretary-General of the United Nations shall take all appropriate measures to ensure the observance of these obligations.

ARTICLE 7: DUTY TO ENSURE THE SAFETY AND SECURITY OF

United Nations and Associated Personnel

1. United Nations and associated personnel, their equipment and premises shall not be made the object of attack or of any action that prevents them from discharging their mandate.

2. States Parties shall take all appropriate measures to ensure the safety and security of United Nations and associated personnel. In particular, States Parties shall take all appropriate steps to protect United Nations

and associated personnel who are deployed in their territory from the crimes set out in article 9.

3. States Parties shall cooperate with the United Nations and other States Parties, as appropriate, in the implementation of this Convention, particularly in any case where the host State is unable itself to take the required measures.

ARTICLE 8: DUTY TO RELEASE OR RETURN UNITED NATIONS AND ASSOCIATED PERSONNEL CAPTURED OR DETAINED

Except as otherwise provided in an applicable status-of-forces agreement, if United Nations or associated personnel are captured or detained in the course of the performance of their duties and their identification has been established, they shall not be subjected to interrogation and they shall be promptly released and returned to United Nations or other appropriate authorities. Pending their release such personnel shall be treated in accordance with universally recognized standards of human rights and the principles and spirit of the Geneva Conventions of 1949.

ARTICLE 9: CRIMES AGAINST UNITED NATIONS AND ASSOCIATED PERSONNEL

1. The intentional commission of:

(a) A murder, kidnapping or other attack upon the person or liberty of any United Nations or associated personnel;

(b) A violent attack upon the official premises, the private accommodation or the means of transportation of any United Nations or associated personnel likely to endanger his or her person or liberty;

(c) A threat to commit any such attack with the objective of compelling a physical or juridical person to do or to refrain from doing any act;

(d) An attempt to commit any such attack; and

(e) An act constituting participation as an accomplice in any such attack, or in an attempt to commit such attack, or in organizing or ordering others to commit such attack, shall be made by each State Party a crime under its national law.

2. Each State Party shall make the crimes set out in paragraph 1 punishable by appropriate penalties, which shall take into account their grave nature.

ARTICLE 10: ESTABLISHMENT OF JURISDICTION

1. Each State Party shall take such measures as may be necessary to establish its jurisdiction over the crimes set out in article 9 in the following cases:

(a) When the crime is committed in the territory of that State or on board a ship or aircraft registered in that State;

(b) When the alleged offender is a national of that State.

2. A State Party may also establish its jurisdiction over any such crime when it is committed:

(a) By a stateless person whose habitual residence is in that State; or

(b) With respect to a national of that State; or

(c) In an attempt to compel that State to do or to abstain from doing any act.

3. Any State Party which has established jurisdiction as mentioned in paragraph 2 shall notify the Secretary-General of the United Nations. If such State Party subsequently rescinds that jurisdiction, it shall notify the Secretary-General of the United Nations.

4. Each State Party shall take such measures as may be necessary to establish its jurisdiction over the crimes set out in article 9 in cases where the alleged offender is present in its territory and it does not extradite such person pursuant to article 15 to any of the States Parties which have established their jurisdiction in accordance with paragraph 1 or 2.

5. This Convention does not exclude any criminal jurisdiction exercised in accordance with national law.

ARTICLE 11: PREVENTION OF CRIMES AGAINST UNITED NATIONS AND ASSOCIATED PERSONNEL

States Parties shall cooperate in the prevention of the crimes set out in article 9, particularly by:

(a) Taking all practicable measures to prevent preparations in their respective territories for the commission of those crimes within or outside their territories; and

(b) Exchanging information in accordance with their national law and coordinating the taking of administrative and other measures as appropriate to prevent the commission of those crimes.

ARTICLE 12: COMMUNICATION OF INFORMATION

1. Under the conditions provided for in its national law, the State Party in whose territory a crime set out in article 9 has been committed shall, if it has reason to believe that an alleged offender has fled from its territory, communicate to the Secretary-General of the United Nations and, directly or through the Secretary-General, to the State or States concerned all the pertinent facts regarding the crime committed and all available information regarding the identity of the alleged offender.

2. Whenever a crime set out in article 9 has been committed, any State Party which has information concerning the victim and circumstances of the crime shall endeavour to transmit such information, under the conditions provided for in its national law, fully and promptly to the Secretary-General of the United Nations and the State or States concerned.

ARTICLE 13: MEASURES TO ENSURE PROSECUTION OR EXTRADITION

1. Where the circumstances so warrant, the State Party in whose territory the alleged offender is present shall take the appropriate measures under its national law to ensure that person's presence for the purpose of prosecution or extradition.

2. Measures taken in accordance with paragraph 1 shall be notified, in conformity with national law and without delay, to the Secretary-General

of the United Nations and, either directly or through the Secretary-General, to:

(a) The State where the crime was committed;

(b) The State or States of which the alleged offender is a national or, if such person is a stateless person, in whose territory that person has his or her habitual residence;

(c) The State or States of which the victim is a national; and

(d) Other interested States.

ARTICLE 14: PROSECUTION OF ALLEGED OFFENDERS

The State Party in whose territory the alleged offender is present shall, if it does not extradite that person, submit, without exception whatsoever and without undue delay, the case to its competent authorities for the purpose of prosecution, through proceedings in accordance with the law of that State. Those authorities shall take their decision in the same manner as in the case of an ordinary offence of a grave nature under the law of that State.

ARTICLE 15: EXTRADITION OF ALLEGED OFFENDERS

1. To the extent that the crimes set out in article 9 are not extraditable offences in any extradition treaty existing between States Parties, they shall be deemed to be included as such therein. States Parties undertake to include those crimes as extraditable offences in every extradition treaty to be concluded between them.

2. If a State Party which makes extradition conditional on the existence of a treaty receives a request for extradition from another State Party with which it has no extradition treaty, it may at its option consider this Convention as the legal basis for extradition in respect of those crimes. Extradition shall be subject to the conditions provided in the law of the requested State.

3. States Parties which do not make extradition conditional on the existence of a treaty shall recognize those crimes as extraditable offences

between themselves subject to the conditions provided in the law of the requested State.

4. Each of those crimes shall be treated, for the purposes of extradition between States Parties, as if it had been committed not only in the place in which it occurred but also in the territories of the States Parties which have established their jurisdiction in accordance with paragraph 1 or 2 of article 10.

ARTICLE 16: MUTUAL ASSISTANCE IN CRIMINAL MATTERS

1. States Parties shall afford one another the greatest measure of assistance in connection with criminal proceedings brought in respect of the crimes set out in article 9, including assistance in obtaining evidence at their disposal necessary for the proceedings. The law of the requested State shall apply in all cases.

2. The provisions of paragraph 1 shall not affect obligations concerning mutual assistance embodied in any other treaty.

ARTICLE 17: FAIR TREATMENT

1. Any person regarding whom investigations or proceedings are being carried out in connection with any of the crimes set out in article 9 shall be guaranteed fair treatment, a fair trial and full protection of his or her rights at all stages of the investigations or proceedings.

2. Any alleged offender shall be entitled:

(a) To communicate without delay with the nearest appropriate representative of the State or States of which such person is a national or which is otherwise entitled to protect that person's rights or, if such person is a stateless person, of the State which, at that person's request, is willing to protect that person's rights; and

(b) To be visited by a representative of that State or those States.

ARTICLE 18: NOTIFICATION OF OUTCOME OF PROCEEDINGS

The State Party where an alleged offender is prosecuted shall communicate the final outcome of the proceedings to the Secretary-General of the United Nations, who shall transmit the information to other States Parties.

ARTICLE 19: DISSEMINATION

The States Parties undertake to disseminate this Convention as widely as possible and, in particular, to include the study thereof, as well as relevant provisions of international humanitarian law, in their programmes of military instruction.

ARTICLE 20: SAVINGS CLAUSES

Nothing in this Convention shall affect:

(a) The applicability of international humanitarian law and universally recognized standards of human rights as contained in international instruments in relation to the protection of United Nations operations and United Nations and associated personnel or the responsibility of such personnel to respect such law and standards;

(b) The rights and obligations of States, consistent with the Charter of the United Nations, regarding the consent to entry of persons into their territories;

(c) The obligation of United Nations and associated personnel to act in accordance with the terms of the mandate of a United Nations operation;

(d) The right of States which voluntarily contribute personnel to a United Nations operation to withdraw their personnel from participation in such operation; or

(e) The entitlement to appropriate compensation payable in the event of death, disability, injury or illness attributable to peace-keeping service by persons voluntarily contributed by States to United Nations operations.

ARTICLE 21: RIGHT OF SELF-DEFENCE

Nothing in this Convention shall be construed so as to derogate from the right to act in self-defence.

ARTICLE 22: DISPUTE SETTLEMENT

1. Any dispute between two or more States Parties concerning the interpretation or application of this Convention which is not settled by negotiation shall, at the request of one of them, be submitted to arbitration. If within six months from the date of the request for arbitration the parties are unable to agree on the organization of the arbitration, any one of those parties may refer the dispute to the International Court of Justice by application in conformity with the Statute of the Court.

2. Each State Party may at the time of signature, ratification, acceptance or approval of this Convention or accession thereto declare that it does not consider itself bound by all or part of paragraph 1. The other States Parties shall not be bound by paragraph 1 or the relevant part thereof with respect to any State Party which has made such a reservation.

3. Any State Party which has made a reservation in accordance with paragraph 2 may at any time withdraw that reservation by notification to the Secretary-General of the United Nations.

ARTICLE 23: REVIEW MEETINGS

At the request of one or more States Parties, and if approved by a majority of States Parties, the Secretary-General of the United Nations shall convene a meeting of the States Parties to review the implementation of the Convention, and any problems encountered with regard to its application.

ARTICLE 24: SIGNATURE

This Convention shall be open for signature by all States, until 31 December 1995, at United Nations Headquarters in New York.

Article 25: Ratification, Acceptance or Approval

This Convention is subject to ratification, acceptance or approval. Instruments of ratification, acceptance or approval shall be deposited with the Secretary-General of the United Nations.

Article 26: Accession

This Convention shall be open for accession by any State. The instruments of accession shall be deposited with the Secretary-General of the United Nations.

Article 27: Entry into Force

1. This Convention shall enter into force thirty days after twenty-two instruments of ratification, acceptance, approval or accession have been deposited with the Secretary-General of the United Nations.

2. For each State ratifying, accepting, approving or acceding to the Convention after the deposit of the twenty-second instrument of ratification, acceptance, approval or accession, the Convention shall enter into force on the thirtieth day after the deposit by such State of its instrument of ratification, acceptance, approval or accession.

Article 28: Denunciation

1. A State Party may denounce this Convention by written notification to the Secretary-General of the United Nations.

2. Denunciation shall take effect one year following the date on which notification is received by the Secretary-General of the United Nations.

Article 29: Authentic Texts

The original of this Convention, of which the Arabic, Chinese, English, French, Russian and Spanish texts are equally authentic, shall be deposited with the Secretary-General of the United Nations, who shall send certified copies thereof to all States.

DONE at New York this ninth day of December one thousand nine hundred and ninety-four.

LIST OF PERSONS WHO DIED AS A RESULT OF THE BOMBING OF THE UN HEADQUARTERS IN BAGHDAD, IRAQ, ON 19 AUGUST 2003

UN STAFF MEMBERS

Mr. Sergio Vieira de Mello, Special Representative of the Secretary-General for Iraq, United Nations High Commissioner for Human Rights

Reham Al-Farra

Raid Shaker Mustafa Al-Mahdawi

Leen Assad Al-Qadi

Ranilo Buenaventura

Richard Hooper

Reza Hosseini

Ihssan Taha Husain

Jean-Selim Kanaan

Christopher Klein-Beekman

Emaad Ahmed Salman Al-Jobory

Martha Teas

Basim Mahmood Utaiwi

Fiona Watson

Nadia Younes

NON-STAFF MEMBERS

Saad Hermiz Abona

Omar Kahtan Mohamed Al-Orfali

Gillian Clark

Arthur Helton

Manuel Martín-Oar

Khidir Saleem Sahir

Alya Ahmad Sousa

ANNEX TO JACQUES FORSTER'S "CHALLENGES TO INDEPENDENT HUMANITARIAN ACTION IN CONTEMPORARY CONFLICTS"

The International Committee of the Red Cross (ICRC) is an impartial, neutral, and independent organization whose exclusively humanitarian action is to protect the lives and dignity of victims of war and internal violence and to provide them with assistance.

The activities of the ICRC are based on the four Geneva Conventions of 1949 and their two Additional Protocols of 1977, which constitute the core of international humanitarian law (IHL).

In 2003, the ICRC maintained a permanent presence in 81 countries throughout the world. Approximately 11,000 persons make up its staff working in field delegations and in its Geneva headquarters.

ICRC's expenditure in 2003 totaled about 888 million Swiss francs. Its 2004 budget is about 894 million Swiss francs.

The main activities of the ICRC are as follows:

Protection

Visits to detainees: through its visits to persons deprived of freedom, the ICRC works to prevent or put an end to disappearances, summary executions and ill-treatment, as well as to improve conditions of detention when necessary.

Restoration of family links: the Central Tracing Agency of the ICRC works to re-establish family contact in all situations of armed conflict or internal violence through the exchange of Red Cross messages and, whenever possible, family reunifications. It puts a special accent to the clarification of the fate of missing persons and the subsequent provision of information to their families.

Respect for civilians: through its delegates in the field, the ICRC assesses the conditions of the civilian population, analyzes cases of abuses and violations of IHL and, through its dialogue with civil and military authorities at all levels, it requests preventive or corrective measures to ensure that individuals and groups who are not taking part in the hostilities are fully respected and protected in accordance with the norms of IHL.

Assistance

Economic security: ICRC seeks to ensure or restore the economic self-sufficiency of households. It is thus concerned both with the protection of the vital means of production and the provision of survival relief when essential goods can no longer be obtained through economic activities.

Water and habitat: ICRC's activities seek to ensure that victims of armed conflict have access to water for drinking and domestic use, and to protect the population from environmental hazards caused by the collapse of water and habitat systems.

Health care: through its health programmes, the ICRC ensures that victims of conflict have access to essential preventive and curative health care of a universally accepted standard. This includes: supply of essential medicines and medical equipment, war surgery, epidemiological surveillance, training of medical staff and physical rehabilitation in prosthetic/orthotic centers.

Preventive Action

Preventive action covers all steps taken to limit violence in conflict situations and to prevent, anticipate or alleviate the suffering of people affected by armed conflicts. These activities are carried out both in peacetime and in times of armed conflicts. They encompass both legal and communication activities.

The ICRC works towards the implementation of international humanitarian law through the promotion of humanitarian treaties, technical advice and support for the national implementation of these treaties, translating existing IHL texts into relevant languages. Interpretation and dissemination of IHL also represent important aspects of ICRC's work.

The development of IHL is another aspect of the ICRC legal enterprise: monitoring new developments, carrying out studies, participating to the international drafting processes relating to the protection of human life and dignity.

Communication of the rules of international humanitarian law through awareness-building, promotion of international humanitarian law through teaching and training, integration of humanitarian law into official legal, educational and operational curricula. Promotion activities are aimed at members of the armed, police and security forces as well as armed groups, leaders and opinion makers, students and other young people.

Cooperation between the National Red Cross and Red Crescent Societies

An increasing number of ICRC activities for victims of armed conflict and internal violence are implemented jointly with National Red Cross and Red Crescent Societies, wherever their network, structure and capacity permit. In situations of conflict and internal violence, the ICRC coordinates all inputs of the components of the International Red Cross and Red Crescent Movement and helps build the capacity of the concerned National Society.

Cooperation with National Societies is carried out in close consultation and coordination with the International Federation of Red Cross and Red Crescent Societies as these activities hold a long term perspective to build capacity and are part of a National Society's development process.

About The Center for International Health and Cooperation and The Institute for International Humanitarian Affairs

The Center for International Health and Cooperation (CIHC) is a public charity founded by a small group of international diplomats and physicians who believed that health and other humanitarian endeavors sometimes provide the only common ground for initiating dialogue, understanding and cooperation among people and nations shattered by war, civil conflicts and ethnic violence. The Center has sponsored symposia and published books, including *Silent Witnesses; A Framework for Survival: Health, Human Rights and Humanitarian Assistance in Conflicts and Disasters; A Directory of Somali Professionals; Clearing the Fields: Solutions to the Land Mine Crisis; Preventive Diplomacy;* the new International Humanitarian Books Series of Fordham University Press–*Basics of Humanitarian Missions; Emergency Relief Operations; Traditions, Values and Humanitarian Assistance; Technology for Humanitarian Action;* and a standard textbook, *Tropical Medicine: A Clinical Text,* that reflect this philosophy.

The Center and its Directors have been deeply involved in trying to alleviate the wounds of war in Somalia and the former Yugoslavia. A CIHC amputee center in northern Somalia was developed as a model for a simple, rapid, inexpensive program that could be replicated in other war zones. In the former Yugoslavia the CIHC was active in prisoner and hostage release, in legal assistance for human and political rights violations, and facilitated discussions between combatants.

The Center directs the International Diploma in Humanitarian Assistance (IDHA) in partnership with Fordham University in New York, the University of Geneva in Switzerland, and the Royal College of Surgeons in Ireland. It has graduated over 600 leaders in the humanitarian world from 53 nations, representing all agencies of the United Nations and most non-governmental organizations (NGOs) around the world. The CIHC also cooperates with other centers in offering specialized training courses for humanitarian negotiators and international human rights lawyers. The Center has offered staff support in recent years in crisis management in Iraq, East Timor, Aceh, Kosovo, Palestine, Albania and other trouble spots.

The Center has been afforded full consultative status at the United Nations. In the United States, it is a fully approved public charity.

The CIHC is closely linked with Fordham University's Institute of International Humanitarian Affairs (IIHA). The Directors of the CIHC serve as the Advisory Board of the Institute. The President of the CIHC is the University Professor and Director of the Institute, and CIHC Officer Larry Hollingworth is Humanitarian Programs Director for the Institute.

DIRECTORS

Kevin M. Cahill, M.D. (President)
Lord David Owen
Boutros Boutros-Ghali
Lady Helen Hamlyn
Peter Tarnoff
Jan Eliasson
Peter Hansen
Francis Deng
Joseph A. O'Hare, S.J.
Abdulrahim Abby Farah
Eoin O'Brien, M.D.
Maj. Gen. Tim Cross

INDEX